Postmodern Theatric(k)s

THEATER: Theory/Text/Performance

Enoch Brater, Series Editor

Postmodern Theatric(k)s

Monologue in Contemporary American Drama

Deborah R. Geis

Ann Arbor

THE UNIVERSITY OF MICHIGAN PRESS

First paperback edition 1995
Copyright © by the University of Michigan 1993
All rights reserved
Published in the United States of America by
The University of Michigan Press
Manufactured in the United States of America

1996 1995   4   3   2   1

Paperback ISBN 0-472-08352-X

The Library of Congress has cataloged the hardcover edition as follows:

Geis, Deborah R., 1960–
    Postmodern theatric(k)s [sic] : monologue in contemporary American
drama / Deborah R. Geis.
        p.   cm. — (Theatre—theory/text/performance)
    Includes bibliographical references and index.
    ISBN 0-472-10467-5 (alk. paper)
    1. American drama—20th century—History and criticism.
    2. Postmodernism (Literature)—United States. 3. Monologue.
    I. Title.   II. Title: Postmodern theatrics.   III. Series.
    PS352.G45   1993
    812'.04509—dc20   93-30132
                                                                CIP

A CIP catalogue record for this book is available from the British Library.

Acknowledgments

I would like to thank the Horace H. Rackham School of Graduate Studies at the University of Michigan and the PSC-CUNY Research Foundation at the City University of New York for grants that facilitated my research. Sections of the first and fourth chapters appeared in different form in "David Mamet and the Metadramatic Tradition: Seeing 'the Trick from the Back,'" in *David Mamet: A Casebook,* ed. Leslie Kane (Garland Publications, 1992), copyright © 1992 Leslie Kane; the fifth chapter is adapted from "Wordscapes of the Body: Performative Language as *Gestus* in Maria Irene Fornes's Plays," *Theatre Journal* 42 (October 1990): 291–307, copyright © 1990 Johns Hopkins University Press. Chapter 6 is adapted from "Distraught Laughter: Monologue in Ntozake Shange's Theater Pieces," in *Feminine Focus: The New Women Playwrights,* ed. Enoch Brater (Oxford University Press, 1989), copyright © 1989 Oxford University Press. I thank these publishers for granting me permission to adapt material that I had originally published with them.

It is a pleasure to thank the many people who have provided advice, intellectual support, and friendship during the writing of this book. They, along with others too numerous to list here, have made a huge difference in my scholarship and in other parts of my life, and my gratitude to them is far greater than these acknowledgments can even hope to suggest.

My first thanks go to Enoch Brater, whose encouragement, editing, and advice have been invaluable every step of the way. LeAnn Fields and Chris Milton of the University of Michigan Press have been enormously helpful and communicative, and Stephen Watt read the manuscript carefully and offered many insightful suggestions. For earlier versions of the manuscript, I also received much-appreciated readings and comments from William Alexander, Arnold Aronson, and Benedict Nightingale.

I am tremendously indebted to my colleagues and students and to the English Department staff members at Queens College, CUNY, for their conversations, guidance, and assistance. Barbara Bowen, Steven Kruger, and Ron Scapp were particularly supportive, and I also extend special thanks to Rosette

Lamont, Bette Weidman, Susan K. Harris, Anthony O'Brien, Richard Schotter, David Kleinbard, Maureen Waters, George Held, Charles Molesworth, John Reilly, Dolores G. Beckerman, Evelyn Diaz, and my students Ava Chin, Nicholas Chodoba, and Asaf Ronen.

Other individuals whose advice made a difference in the writing of this book include Robert Weisbuch, the late C. A. Patrides, Sheila Rabillard, Leslie Kane, and Julie Carroll. For their consistent enthusiasm and encouragement, I am grateful to Beth Baldwin, Regina Rousso, Tracy Cornelius, Anthony Barone, Kathleen Moore, Janet Pennisi, Lloyd Roberts, Karen Vrotsos, and David J. Weiss.

The members of my family—especially my parents, Norman and Dorothy Geis; my sisters, Nancy Bardgett and Sarah Geis; and my in-laws, Katherine Young, the late Philip Young, Stanton Garner, and Lydia M. Garner—have been sources of inspiration for their graciousness and generosity. I thank my grandmother, Shirley Geis, for first teaching me to love the theater. Finally, I owe the greatest debt in the writing of this book to my husband, Stanton B. Garner, Jr.; his tireless discussions with me, his editing, his patient supportiveness, and most of all his love have been and continue to be sources of great joy.

Contents

Introduction

"The thing I like, I mean quite immeasurably," observes one of Harold Pinter's characters, "is this kind of conversation, this class of mutual reminiscence." This character, though, is addressing an empty chair—and the name of the play is, appropriately, *Monologue.*[1] Dramatists from Sophocles to Sam Shepard have been aware of the theatrical challenges and possibilities presented by that figurative "empty chair": monologue is the quintessential instrument for demonstrating the virtuosity of both the performer and the playwright, the litmus test of an actor's or writer's ability to seize the imagination and attention of the audience. Whether a monologue consists of a sardonic lament about the unfairness of having been born a bastard, such as Edmund's in *King Lear,* or a last will and testament enumerating all of one's farm implements, such as Dodge's in *Buried Child,* its utterance constitutes a moment in which the theater must summon up all of its power to command the ear as well as the eye. In addition, by virtue of its status as performative discourse, the monologue becomes a particularly compelling means for the playwright to imprint a dramatic text with a narrative voice: one need only reflect upon the differences between a monologue by one of Samuel Beckett's characters and another by one of Ntozake Shange's to realize that this discourse encapsulates a playwright's rhythm, diction, imagery, conception of the performer, sense of temporality, awareness of relationships between subject and object, emphasis on physical or gestic language, and so forth. Of course, many of the same observations might be true for dialogue. The contention of this book, however, will be that the monologue—particularly as it has emerged in postmodern American drama—possesses narrative properties that distinguish it from dialogue in its ability to transform stage time and space into "narrative" time and space. Indeed, the very qualities that place monologue in a category that opposes dialogue—its lack of a responding "other," its refusal to relinquish the "floor," its implicit "deviance" from interpersonal discourse—are those that grant it a formidable and singular status among the various idioms of the theater.

Despite the richness of the monologue as a theatrical tradition, it has received relatively little critical attention in terms of its effect on dramatic narrative or its place in dramatic structure. Ken Frieden has written perceptively on the relationship between monologue and the workings of genius, and his study includes useful examinations of such characters as Hamlet—but it is not intended to highlight the *theatrical* status of monologic language.[2] Ruby Cohn and Andrew Kennedy have both published explorations of dramatic *dialogue,* and their remarks help to provide valuable contexts for a discussion of monologue; yet in these two studies monologue inevitably becomes the absent opposition, the implicit other to which dialogue is compared.[3] In the specific field of contemporary American drama, considerations of the role of monologue have been equally absent. Even with the increase in attention to the works of Shepard, Karen Finley, and others, the use of monologue by these artists has yet to receive sufficient consideration in terms of its place in an ongoing theatrical discourse.

To a striking and perhaps unprecedented degree, contemporary American playwrights have been inclined to draw upon the myriad dramatic and narrative opportunities to be found in monologic language. Virtually all of the established and emerging voices of the current American theater, from Arthur Miller to Spalding Gray, employ monologues as a fundamental component of their dramatic creations. This attraction to monologue may be partially a twentieth-century predilection that is not unique to the American theater: as the second chapter of this study will argue, postmodernism has theorized a fragmented and dislocated speaking subject that is more open to *replication* and dissemination— through a highly technologized culture—than it is to the dynamic of *response* inherent in dialogue. Whereas modernism highlighted the search for a responding other in the "void," thus turning toward dialogue as a means for the psychological revelation of character (as in Henrik Ibsen's plays), postmodernism refuses this completion and coherence and opts for deconstructive explorations of its own resistance to pairing and linearity. And, of course, to appropriate the monologue is to appropriate one of the basic tools for creating narrative voices in a medium that always, at some level, depends upon precarious linguistic manipulations of space and time for its very existence.

The dramatists who have come to the American stage in the past twenty-five years bring with them the postmodernist experiments of the Living Theatre, the Open Theater, and other movements that transformed our notions about the limitations of narrative and performance; they also bring the influences of American popular culture of the postmodern era—particularly film, video, and rock music—which have profoundly affected our speech idioms, our sense of pacing, and our selection of icons, even on the stage. Finally, postmodernism (particularly in its American forms) brings a new emphasis on previously marginalized voices, such as the feminist and the African-American; with these changes American dramatists have turned toward the monologue as a way of "speaking" about the attempt to enter subjectivity. One of the aims of this study, then, is to explore the ways in which several of the most striking and original of practicing American playwrights—Shepard, David Mamet, Maria Irene Fornes, Shange—and writer/performers, Gray and Finley, have taken up, through monologue, the multiplicity of aesthetic, political, and cultural concerns that characterize the postmodern American theatrical landscape. The differently focused chapters of *Postmodern Theatric(k)s* are designed to reflect this diversity of influences and the resulting range of monologic experimentation.

The first two chapters of this book provide a theoretical framework for my subsequent discussions of individual playwrights. In chapter 1, I propose an initial set of definitions for the monologue and examine both its narrative properties and its historical development (from the ancient Greeks to Shakespeare to the pivotal modernists such as Ibsen and August Strindberg). The second chapter discusses postmodernism and situates its theories in a theatrical context, emphasizing the American manifestations of postmodernist dramatic expression in the off-off-Broadway theater of the 1960s.

At the center of this study—and the subject of its longest chapter—is Sam Shepard, whose work emerged directly from the off-off-Broadway experiments in theatrical narrative. Shepard, who has shown an infatuation with the monologue form throughout his career, maintains a typically postmodern ambivalence toward popular culture and the limitations of "artistic" discourse. While many have seen Shepard as immersed in the icons of American pop culture (science fiction, westerns, television, etc.), I argue that his constant deployment of the monologic voice actually reveals an ironizing and parody of these cultural images to the extent that Shepard's later "family" plays (e.g., *Buried Child*) even parody the oedipal narrative continuum of journey and discovery as situated within the fragmented and co-opted American family.

In chapter 4 I discuss the works of David Mamet, for whom the postmodernist attraction to monologue works in a different way. Mamet populates his plays with salesmen and con artists, speakers who deploy monologic narrative as the consummate sales pitch, an assertion of territorial space through narrative. Using Jean-François Lyotard's idea that communication in a postmodern world involves a series of linguistic "tricks," or "games," I suggest that Mamet's interest in such trickery extends finally to his engagement with the "con artistry," or "fraud," of the theater or of acting itself, as embodied in such works as *Glengarry Glen Ross* and *The Shawl*.

Chapters 5 and 6 turn toward recent innovations in the monologue by feminist playwrights Maria Irene Fornes and Ntozake Shange. Monologue, I argue, is the narrative mode through which feminist dramatists "embody" the textualized voice and enter the struggle for subjectivity. Whereas Fornes plays parodically on the distinctions between "voice" and "body" as they emerge from the monologic texts of her speakers in *Mud, The Conduct of Life,* and other plays, Shange (in such pieces as *for colored girls who have considered suicide / when the rainbow is enuf*) creates a metatheatrical model of "performance," or "spectacle," to enact a movement between immersion and Brechtian alienation.

The concluding chapter of this study moves away from multi-character plays that preserve a framework of "fiction" and toward contemporary performance artists who speak exclusively through the monologic voice in a semiautobiographical mode that can be referred to as "autoperformance." Such performers as Spalding Gray frequently engage in a deliberate blurring of the lines between "character" and "actor"; Gray, for instance, sometimes concludes a monologue by recounting to the audience his activities up to and including the moment that he arrived at the theater to begin his performance. The metatheatricality of autoperformers, with their often ironic crossing of "boundaries," can be seen as parallel to the metafictional paradoxes of such postmodern novelists as John Barth, Thomas Pynchon, and Salman Rushdie. Karen Finley takes this boundary crossing to an even greater extreme, as *The Constant State of Desire* and other pieces undertake acts that challenge the boundaries of sexual and narrative discourse, ultimately calling into question the limits of theatricality itself.

Finally, a few words about the title of this study. My choice of "theatric(k)s" represents an attempt to enact the playfulness and multiplicity of meaning embodied in postmodern manipulations of language: it carries the sense of the theatrical or histrionic, but also wrapped within this word is the Lyotardian emphasis on trick, or game playing, as a postmodern mode of exchange and demonstration. And, at the risk of belaboring the pun, the *hat trick* is, in hockey, the scoring of three goals (and, in cricket, the taking of three wickets on consecutive balls). An unusual feat by a solo player in one game is thus an apt image for the performer in a play that calls for virtuoso demonstration of the monologic voice. With the postmodern emphasis on the play as spectacle, we will return again and again to this histrionic arena, this site of trickery and of breathtaking performances.

"Always Was Best at Talking to Myself": Monologue and Theatrical (Re)presentation

Think, when we talk of horses, that you see them
Printing their proud hoofs i' th' receiving earth.
—Shakespeare, Henry V (Pro. 26–27)

Defining Monologue

From a theatrical point of view, what exactly *is* a monologue? The simplest explanation is that, as the etymology of the word implies (*monologos,* or "solitary speech"), a monologue is a speech for one or a dialogue with oneself. As Ken Frieden suggests in *Genius and Monologue,* a monologue can be distinguished foremost in linguistic terms:

> Monologue is not primarily a fact of human solitude but rather a mode of linguistic individuality.... On the level of discourse, monologue is a turn away from dialogue. The language of an individual is monological to the extent that it deviates from dialogical conventions of speech.[1]

But this sense of the monologue is complicated by the presence, in the theater, of the audience. Since the status of a play presupposes that even a speech performed in the imagined solitude of a character will always include the audience as acknowledged or implicit witnesses, the inevitable status of the spectators as recipients foregrounds the "telling," or "narrating," function of the monologue.

Monologues in drama occur in a variety of forms. The monologue

7

can be a speech that a character makes to one or more other characters, particularly a speech that recounts some type of internal story, earlier event in the play (or in the hypothetical past of the character[s]), or memory. The immediate relevance of a monologue's narrative to the ongoing action of a play may not always be apparent, as in Sam Shepard's *Icarus's Mother* (1965), in which Howard provides a lengthy and seemingly unwarranted discourse on the altitude at which pilots fly.[2] A monologue can also be a formal "presentational" device for providing narration or exposition in a play, especially through a "narrator" figure who addresses the audience at structured intervals (e.g., the Chorus in ancient Greek drama or the Stage Manager in Thornton Wilder's *Our Town* [1938]). These presentational devices, as Keir Elam points out, simultaneously call attention to the "theatrical" status of the piece being performed ("since the actor is required to step out of his role and acknowledge the presence of the public") and invite the audience to step further inside the play.[3] A classic example of this device occurs in Shakespeare's *Henry V,* in which the Chorus urges us to "eche out our performance with your mind" (III.Cho.35), as we witness the stage's transformation into a battlefield.

An entire play may, of course, take the form of a monologue, as in Samuel Beckett's *A Piece of Monologue* (1979) and myriad other works. Although a monologue usually does not involve a considerable amount of exchange with (an)other character(s) as it occurs, it may also be punctuated with or interrupted by bits of dialogue, especially if the speaker is recounting a story to listeners within the play and/or if the playwright is working within a naturalistic context. At the same time the isolated monologue as a climactic moment within an otherwise dialogue-based drama can exert a tremendous amount of power precisely because it stands out from the other discursive moments in the play; Jerry's "dog story" toward the end of Edward Albee's *The Zoo Story* (1958) is an instance of this type of resonant passage.[4]

While a monologue may be introspective or may be used to address another character or to provide narrative exposition, a soliloquy is a kind of monologue that generally suggests introspection. The soliloquy is a subcategory of the monologue, although a monologue is not necessarily a soliloquy. In a soliloquy the speaker addresses him- or herself or the audience but not another character (unless, of course—as Erving Goffman reminds us in *Frame Analysis*—a character happens to overhear the soliloquizer's remarks to the audience).[5] A soliloquy usually involves the verbalization of the speaker's interior feelings or thoughts and often entails a revelation or decision that may not be ordinarily rendered in speech outside of a theatrical framework but which is enacted aloud for the benefit of the audience (e.g., Hamlet's soliloquies). Thus, even though a soliloquy may take place in a naturalistic play, it is inherently metatheatrical because it calls for the vocalization of "thoughts" for an audience. As a result, the soliloquy historically has faced charges of implausibility; William Congreve, for example, claims in his preface to *The Double Dealer* (1694) that soliloquy is only called for under certain circumstances, such as when a villain's plans need to be made known to the audience:

> In such a case therefore the audience must observe, whether the person upon the stage takes any notice of them at all, or no. For if he supposes anyone to be by when he talks to himself, it is monstrous and ridiculous to the last degree. Nay, not only in this case, but in any part of a play, if there is expressed any knowledge of an audience, it is insufferable. But otherwise when a man in soliloquy reasons with himself, and pros and cons, and weighs all his designs, we ought not to imagine that this man either talks to us, or to himself; he is only thinking, and thinking such matter as were inexcusable folly in him to speak. But because we are concealed spectators of the plot in agitation, and the poet finds it necessary to let us know the whole mystery of his contrivance, he is willing to inform us of this person's thoughts; and to that end is forced to make use of the expedient of speech, no other better way being yet invented for the communication of thought.[6]

Of course, Congreve's assertion that any acknowledgment of the audience's presence is "insufferable" seems overstated, not only because of our own post-Brechtian perspective but also because the soliloquy is predicated on the implicit recognition of the spectators' existence. The soliloquy, moreover, is indeed entirely "natural" insofar as the spectators understand it to be a necessary or expected device within the play, as Goffman shows:

> [In a soliloquy,] instead of musing alone or silently, the individual addresses the whole house. And through this structural conceit his thoughts are opened up to the audience. Of course, the peculiarity

about such flagrant exposure of self is balanced somewhat by the fact that those to whom the revelation is made are not themselves persons in ordinary participation status, but rather individuals restricted to the capacity of theatrical audience.[7]

On the most basic level, as Elam reminds us, the monologue causes us to focus our attention on the speaking subject and usually upon a single topic of discourse.[8] While a dialogue cannot exist without two speakers, the monologue—though it may certainly be inspired by and lead to a reaction from another speaker or speakers—is not dependent upon the presence of an onstage auditor. Finally, the monologue is recognizable because it often serves as the vehicle for some type of extraordinary discourse (especially in the case of the soliloquy, though this characteristic is also highly applicable to the "arias" in Shepard's drama or to the discourse of many performance artists). Ken Frieden makes quite a convincing case for the "uniqueness" of the monologue:

> Monologue may be understood either as a static opposition to communicative dialogue or as a dynamic swerve away from prior conventions of discourse. In the first case, monologue is the factual solitude of speech that is not addressed to another. More significantly, monologue signals the active break from norms of ordinary language and is thus allied with innovation, deviant discourse, and creativity. Monologues often strive to evade norms, although pure monologue, in the sense of a linguistic mode that has entirely freed itself from otherness, is an impossibility.[9]

Monologue and Narrativity

Perhaps the most striking quality of the monologue is its ability to affect the narrative of a play. One major "narrative power" of the monologue is its capacity for manipulating time, or our sense of time, in the drama that unfolds before us. As Susanne Langer reminds us in *Feeling and Form,* theater takes place in a kind of "perpetual present" consistently energized by a sense of the as yet unrevealed; even the past and future can ultimately only be evoked through the "present" of the stage action in front of us.[10] But monologue allows the playwright to dislocate, fragment, and otherwise transform this perpetual present into other temporal modes. The speaker of the monologue has the ability to compress time by narrating a series of events, to suspend time entirely by offering words that do not affect the time elapsed in the play,[11] to move either forward or backward in time (and sometimes to move the ensuing narrative with him or her as well), and to alter time by changing our perception of the rate at which time moves during the monologue itself and/or during the onstage events that follow it. In fact, it is not unusual for all four of these effects to occur in the course of a single monologue or series of monologues, particularly when the action of the play itself is established as occurring within the speaker's head (as in Arthur Miller's *After the Fall* [1964]) or when the action is conveyed primarily through the words of a central storyteller (as in David Mamet's *Prairie du Chien* [1985]).

Monologue has the capacity to transform space as well as time in a play. Elam argues that the "theatrical text is defined and perceived above all in spatial terms,"[12] and Langer has proposed the useful idea that drama relies largely on our sense of "virtual space," the "intangible image" the viewer receives as the result of seeing the relationships suggested by the set, characters, and words of a play and the "world" these establish.[13] "Speech is like a quintessence of action," says Langer,[14] and, although the monologue may be accompanied by physical actions of the speaker and/or other characters, its dominant characteristic is still the compression of action into words, of stage space into "narrative space." This is most evident when the monologue eclipses or substitutes for a series of events in the past or present of the characters whose actions we had, up to that point, witnessed onstage as part of the narrative of the play (as in Billy's, Richie's, and Cokes's stories in David Rabe's *Streamers* [1976]). But even the "psychological" monologue calls for such a transformation of space (again, e.g., Hamlet's soliloquies).[15]

A result of the monologue's ability to affect time and space, then, is that it creates types of narrative fluidity that allow the dramatic work to transcend the physical limitations of the playing space. That is, theater has certain real-life boundaries that affect its narrative form: it is confined to a particular space, time, and number of players, so its ability to appear to extend beyond these boundaries must depend primarily upon manipulation of the spectators' imaginations (again, this recalls the Chorus's instructions in *Henry V*). This manipulation may, of course, take place through the use of lights, sound, and other techniques to transform the stage space itself. But the monologue serves as a device by which non-"theatrical" leaps through time, space, and "logic" may occur with the same fluidity onstage as in written narrative (e.g., a novel) or, particularly through the use of editing, in film. Susan Sontag has claimed that the "irreducible distinction" between film and theater lies in the idea that "theatre is confined to a logical or *continuous* use of space," while film "has access to an alogical or *discontinuous* use of space."[16] Sontag's distinction may be accurate in a literal sense, but perhaps less of an "irreducibility" exists than she would contend, for the monologue allows access to what Sontag calls "alogical" or "discontinuous" space in the performed narrative.

One means by which the modern novel (e.g., William Faulkner's *As I Lay Dying* [1930], Virginia Woolf's *To the Lighthouse* [1927]) demonstrates the use of discontinuous space, as well as the breakup of linear action and time, is the stream-of-consciousness technique. Stream of consciousness represents an attempt to portray, through written language, the constantly shifting impulses and perceptions of an active thought process—including fragmented ideas, tangential connections or associations, related (or marginally related) memories, and an intricate network of emotions. When a character's and/or narrator's consciousness is presented in this "verbal equivalent" of a realm of experience that is also pre- or nonverbal, it is sometimes referred to as an "interior monologue."[17] The theatrical monologue opens up the possibility for similarly nonlinear interiority, especially in the soliloquy. If, as in Sophie Treadwell's *Machinal* (1928), a character's spoken discourse takes the form of an interior monologue, the audience is expected to understand and believe (as we have seen in the case of the soliloquy) that thoughts, hitherto guarded in silence by the character(s), may be expressed in this manner, which draws acute attention to the *theatrical* nature of the dramatic event.

In addition to providing one possible mechanism for the dramatic expression of interiority, monologue allows the playwright to create at least the impression of narrative perspective or point of view, which in a film might be portrayed with the subjective camera angle and in a novel with the guiding narratorial voice. This is not to imply that a parallel type of point of view is possible or even desirable in drama. But the monologue does permit what might more accurately be termed "hypothetical points of view" for which—as in Bernard Shaw's *Too True to Be Good* (1932)—the audience must decide how to delineate the boundaries between the speaking subject and the dramatist who speaks through that speaking subject. In other words, the speaker of the monologue tends to take on an "authorial" or "authoritative" role, especially if he or she plays the part of a narrator. Yet this very "authority" can serve as an opportunity for the playwright to manipulate the audience's judgment, especially if the dramatist chooses to offer monologues by more than one character that compete for the spectator's sense of whom to trust (as in Harold Pinter's works *Old Times* [1971] and *No Man's Land* [1974]). Tom Stoppard's *Travesties* (1974) is an example of a play in which one main character, Henry Carr, is set up as a narrator, but his monologues as well as the stage action (which is projected through Carr's faulty memory) are consistently undermined as the holes in his memory and hence in his narrative authority are revealed, particularly when Old Cecily takes issue with his imaginative constructs at the end of the play.

At the same time the speaker of a monologue *supplants* the dramatist as storyteller because it is, after all, the speaker who brings the playwright's words to life. As Elam notes:

> The actor imposes the *histrionic* subcodes regulating his performance as a whole and so his combining of messages into discourse. The actor, from this point of view, is the main agent of transcodification on stage.[18]

Unlike fiction, in which the storyteller's words go immediately to the reader, then, drama (in performance) involves a displacement of the narrator(s) from the author to the actors. It is therefore not surprising that the speaker of a monologue often seems to be serving as the playwright's narrator—and, paradoxically, to be taking on a narrative authority surpassing that which seems to inhere to the dramatist's "rights" as creator of the monologue.

At the heart of the paradoxical quality of the monologue is its simultaneous focusing and interruption of stage action; it forces the spectators to imagine things they cannot see yet is accompanied by the invisible exhortation that they "see" the speaker as a character in (or at least in the context of) the onstage action they have been witnessing up to that point. It inevitably involves, then, the *redirection* of the audience's attention. This redirection may be an acknowledged one, as in the Brechtian monologue. More often, the redirection of attention is far more subtle. In the process of *déroulement*, as the spectators gradually realize that the dialogue has transmuted into a monologue, it is as if a form of seduction has taken place: the monologue has surrounded us before we quite realize what has happened.

When a monologue seems to address the audience directly, the paradoxical position of the audience in respect to the speaker intensifies. It is possible to argue that this type of monologic utterance simultaneously includes the spectators in a more direct way than otherwise and reasserts their very powerlessness. The audience seems to be addressed, yet its members are not (except in certain forms of experimental theater) in a position to respond, for doing so would, as Goffman explains, involve breaking the "dramatic frame."[19] This indicates that the spectators have chosen to accept their role as helpless, frozen, powerless (at least in a traditional theatrical setting), yet, for the duration of the monologue addressed to them, they are given a privileged or pseudoprivileged status as the character's confidants.

Just as the playwright may choose to manipulate the apparent authority of the monologue's speaker, then, he or she may also take advantage of this curiously divided position of the spectators that ensues when a character addresses them face to face in a monologue. Peter Handke's *Offending the Audience* (1966) is an example of a piece that plays directly upon this uncomfortable position in which the audience members find themselves:

> Because we speak to you, you can become conscious of yourself. Because we speak to you, your self-awareness increases. You become aware that you are sitting. You become aware that you are sitting in a theater. . . . Try not to blink your eyelids. Try not to swallow any more. Try not to move your tongue. Try not to hear anything. Try not to smell anything. Try not to salivate. Try not to sweat. Try not to shift in your seat. Try not to breathe. Why, you are breathing. Why, you are salivating. Why, you are listening. Why, you are smelling. Why, you are swallowing. Why, you are blinking your eyelids. Why, you are belching. Why, you are sweating. Why, how terribly self-conscious you are.[20]

In Handke's play the spectators become the "actors" and are subjected to verbal assaults of this kind in the monologues of the performers (qua "spectators"), who mock and deride the actors' (audience's) feebleness and inability to "act." By emphasizing the physical qualities of the spectators' self-consciousness, the speakers draw attention to the "unnatural" relationships between observer and observed in the theatrical event. The acts of sweating, swallowing, smelling, salivating, and sitting are framed here as "dramatic" behavior in themselves, yet accompanying this is the ironic sense that the spectators in this play (i.e., the actors) have indeed rejected their traditionally passive relationship to the performers (i.e., the audience) by choosing to taunt and "offend" them.

It should be clear, then, that the monologue—even when it is not used for the purpose of straightforward narration or for the psychological or homiletic designs of the traditional soliloquy—is an essential tool for the dramatist's shaping of the audience's perception of a play and its characters. As such, we need to move away from narrow perceptions of the monologue as a poor relative of the soliloquy and to emphasize its role in the construction and enactment of theatrical narrative. If we assume that the aim of a play is, on the most basic level, to tell a story (even though that story may not necessarily involve a "plot" per se), then the monologue becomes a richly complex device for the storyteller (i.e., dramatist). Monologic language not only takes on the power to alter time and space despite the absence of a malleable printed text (as in a novel) or of editing (as in a film), but it also achieves a dramatic resonance and potential for creative manipulation all its own.

(Pre)figuring Monologue: Classic Drama and Shakespeare

The history of the monologue goes back to ancient Greek tragedy, which provides us with the earliest examples of monologic speech as well as two types of speeches that might be termed forerunners of the monologue. The "true" monologue in Greek tragedy occurs only in those plays in which a character delivers an opening discourse, either explicitly or implicitly directed toward the audience, for the purpose of exposition and commentary. One interesting example of the latter is the Nurse's speech at the outset of *Medea:* immediately after her opening lamentation/exposition ("How I wish the Argo never had reached the land / Of Colchis . . . "), the Tutor arrives onstage with Medea's children and asks, "Why are you standing all alone in front of the / Gates and moaning to yourself over your misfortune?" The Nurse responds that she has

> got into such a state of grief
> That a longing stole over me to come outside here
> And tell the earth and air of my mistress' sorrows.[21]

Euripides provides in this instance a simultaneous acknowledgment of
the audience through the expositional quality of the prologue and an
attempt to render it somewhat "naturalistic" or referential to the world
of the play by giving it the context of the Nurse's desire to speak aloud
"to the earth and air."

One traditional feature of Greek tragedy is the repeated "debate"
sequence, or agon, in which the protagonist (prompted by the Chorus)
arrives at a revelation or decision. On one level, the agon constitutes a
dialogue between the speaker and Chorus, rather than a genuine monologue. But the Chorus's ability only to react and to feel, not to act,
means that its members serve as surrogate audience members of sorts
rather than simply as characters. Since the focus is therefore upon the
protagonist's discourse, it is possible to argue that the agon prefigures
the soliloquy; Oedipus' speech after he is blinded is a powerful example.

A third type of speech in Greek tragedy arguably prefigures the
narrative or expository monologue; this occurs when a messenger or
messengerlike character delivers a report of offstage events. The Herds-
man's narrative of the rites of Dionysus performed by the women in the
forest in *The Bacchae* or the Sentry's account of the dirt scattered on
Polynice's body in *Antigone* are two cases in this category. Other examples abound, occurring partially for practical purposes (the limited
number of actors and scene changes and so forth) as well as for dramatic
ones (the increased power of that which is left to the audience's imagination). The existence of such speeches as narrative devices serves as an
early marker of the possibilities for using "narrative space" to compen-
sate for the physical limitations of the performing space.

Shakespeare, as I have already indicated, also relied on narrator
figures to bridge the play's gaps in time and space or to provide other
forms of exposition.[22] And he made multiple uses of the soliloquy, not
only for exposition but also for what Lloyd Skiffington calls "homiletic,"
or didactic, purposes.[23]

The most powerful aspect of Shakespeare's monologic language,
however, is his brilliant recourse to the "psychological" soliloquy (a
device used by slightly earlier Elizabethan dramatists such as Thomas
Kyd), particularly in such plays as *Hamlet* and *Macbeth*. Psychological
soliloquies present particular challenges to the director because they involve the suspension of time that I have noted as well as the temporary
transportation of the audience and character from staged or visible space
into the imagined, nondirectly perceivable, linguistically commanded

space of the psyche. With the Shakespearean soliloquy comes the ascendance of interiority, coupled with the singular demands that its expression places upon the visual and narrative movement of the play, for there is no conventional structural space allowed for it.

The psychological soliloquy, moreover, calls special attention to the status of the monologue as a kind of dialogue with oneself, particularly one associated with the "deviant discourse" I have mentioned. Lady Macbeth's sleepwalking speech is a vivid instance of this kind of discourse, though Hamlet's soliloquies are better examples of the connection between mad speech and creativity or self-disclosure. The speaker of the psychological soliloquy often teeters between rationality and madness; the eventual lapse into the language of soliloquy implies in itself a movement over the precipice into a frighteningly nonlinear, illogical, and monologic world. Historically, Frieden suggests, Shakespeare's creation of such worlds shows the dominance of characters' inner struggles over those created by supernatural or divine forces, though these forces continue to exert their influence (e.g., *Hamlet*, *Macbeth*):

> As the tensions between immanence and transcendence work themselves out in the dialectic of monological modes, the supposedly autonomous subject discovers its internal conflicts. To the extent that soliloquy is coupled with relationships to society and divine beings, it never entirely loses the connection with otherness and transcendent *Logos* . . . [but t]he new poetic monologue, instead of interacting with supernatural powers, turns toward contemplation on the appropriate rhetoric for imaginative expressions of the self.[24]

With Shakespeare, then, the soliloquy begins to enter the realm of "otherness" that Frieden indicates; in the process its staging and its role in the dramatic narrative become increasingly complex.

The Modern Monologue: Ibsen, Strindberg, O'Neill, Williams

A look at the early period of modern drama shows an initial rejection of the monologue in favor of supposedly more natural dialogue (particularly in Ibsen) and an eventual movement into more poetic and expressionistic modes of speech. The later works of August Strindberg, as well as the drama of Eugene O'Neill and Tennessee Williams, use monologue expressionistically, reflecting a modernist preoccupation with the isolated voice that seeks, but only occasionally achieves, an emergence into dialogue.

Ibsen's earliest plays, even before his movement from verse drama to prose drama, reveal an increasing desire on his part to achieve a form of naturalism that excluded apparently "theatrical" techniques like the soliloquy. James W. McFarlane writes in the introduction to his translation of Ibsen's plays that, after Ibsen wrote *The League of Youth* (1869), he mentioned his particular satisfaction with having written the play "without ever once having had recourse to monologues or asides."[25] And when Ibsen began to develop his brand of prose drama, beginning with *Pillars of Society* (1877), he remained true to this early conviction that monologic speech was inappropriate for a dramatic form that emphasized conversation, or what became known as the quintessentially Ibsenesque "discussion." Indeed, except for Nora's remarks to herself in the midst of her despair in three different places in act 2 of *A Doll House*—which might technically be termed soliloquies, though the passages are brief—the prose dramas of Ibsen's early to middle period (roughly 1877–90) show very little "recourse" to the monologue.

In the midst of developing his style of prose realism, however, Ibsen was actually moving toward the creation of a stage language that had the effect of poetry. Andrew Kennedy makes a convincing argument that Ibsen's shaping of a "conversational model for deeper communication" lends the conversation itself a simultaneous transparency and opacity:

> So transparent is such a conversational dialogue that the audience *seems* to recognise a replay of "the way we talk," hardly aware of the degree of "shaping." In sum, the existential and structural heightening of the duologue coincides with a certain stylistic lowering (a seeming destylisation) of the language of personal encounter. Such a conjunction, of psychological complexity and linguistic transparency, was hardly possible before Ibsen.[26]

Kennedy's observation is particularly relevant when we consider that Ibsen's later plays (*The Master Builder* [1892] through *When We Dead Awaken* [1899]) reveal an increasing dependence on language's ability to shape and sustain the drama; as Ibsen's plays become more "poetic," they rely less on physical action and more on the power of words to take over time and space. Not surprisingly, then, his characters move a bit further in the direction of monologue, even though the monologues are still woven into the type of "conversational model" that Kennedy describes.

In *John Gabriel Borkman* (1896), for instance, Borkman's dialogue with Ella veers at times into monologue. As Borkman expresses his unfulfilled longings in act 4, he seems only partially aware of Ella's presence. Ella's inability to hear the spinning of the factory gears, which Borkman senses, signals his separation from her, and his language becomes more and more histrionic as he addresses the riches that constitute part of his buried life:

> But let me whisper this to you, here in the stillness of the night. I love you: you who lie in a trance of death in the darkness and the deep. I love you! You and your life-seeking treasures and all your bright retinue of power and glory. I love you, love you, love you.[27]

This type of speech, which Kennedy rightly calls "self-obsessed,"[28] reinforces the association between monologue and deviant discourse that I have mentioned; in the creation of Borkman, Ibsen allows an inclusion of monologic speech without compromising his preference for naturalism, since Borkman is a "deviant" type of character for whom such speech might be appropriate. Ella's agitated response to it, though partially sympathetic, also emphasizes the extent to which Borkman's language belongs on the side of otherness. At the same time this kind of discourse illustrates Ibsen's ultimately modernist subsuming of action to expressive language, a choice that dominates *When We Dead Awaken*. As Richard Gilman says of the two, "almost all the crucial physical action of the plays has been completed before the stage life is set in motion."[29] Since the "motion" of the plays is dependent upon their language, it is interesting that Ibsen's shaping of language in these late dramas stretches into the poetic, fragmented, dreamlike realm that includes monologic speech and even begins to take on the visionary qualities of some of Strindberg's works.

Strindberg, after an early naturalistic phase (*Miss Julie* [1888] and other works), sought to create dramatic worlds that drew upon material from the deepest parts of the imagination and the unconscious.[30] The Strindbergian monologue, with its pathway from the unconscious mind, does not depend on previous or outward signs of dementia or "deviance" on the character's part—as in the case of John Gabriel Borkman—to transpire. Rather, as Strindberg allowed the "hidden" mind to come to the foreground as part of his theatrical form itself, the monologue and other types of non-normative language were no longer linguistic material that marked a field of otherness. In his much quoted preface to *A Dream Play* (1902), Strindberg calls for the breaking of the boundaries traditionally set by time, space, and even character: "time and space do not exist," he says, and the characters, ruled by "one consciousness" (that of the dreamer), "are split, double, redouble, evaporate, condense, scatter, and converge."[31] One might extend his metaphor of the dreamer's "single consciousness" to suggest that *A Dream Play* is therefore a monologue by the dreamer; the dialogue is actually a manifestation of that splitting, doubling, and multiplication on the part of the single consciousness.[32]

Monologue becomes a more explicit narrative device for Strindberg by the time his expressionism takes the form of the "chamber plays," such as *The Ghost Sonata* (1907). The Old Man's monologue in scene 2 of this play reifies (theatrically) the same language/silence interplay that his words themselves evoke:

> Talk about the weather, which we know; ask how we are, which we know; I prefer silence; then one hears thoughts and sees the past; silence can conceal nothing . . . which words can . . . nature itself has provided man with a sense of shame, which tries to conceal what should be concealed; still, we glide into situations without wanting to, and opportunities sometimes present themselves, when the most secret of secrets must be revealed, when the mask is torn from the deceiver, when the villain is exposed. . . . *Pause; all observe each other in silence.* How quiet it has become! *Long silence.* For example: here in this respectable house, in this beautiful home, in which beauty, culture and wealth have been united. . . . *Long silence.* All of us sitting here, we know who we are . . . don't we . . . I don't need to say. . . .[33]

This speech emphasizes the stripping away of the secrets as the result of the silence that falls between words; the Colonel has suggested that the characters converse, but the Old Man's exposition, punctuated with long silences, marks a movement from conversation to monologue. Just as the Old Man calls attention to the silence that meets his words, the monologue form itself requires that a speech is typically accompanied by silence on the part of the auditors; in this respect the speech calls attention to its status as a monologue even in the course of its utterance. It is possible to argue that this effect highlights another aspect of Strindberg's modernism, since the emphasis on silence as well as language foretokens the drama inherent in pauses, or "between the lines," of Beckett and Pinter. Moreover, the Old Man's monologue serves as an example of the increasing solipsism that, according to Kennedy, accompanies the development of expressionism in modern drama.[34] If we take Kennedy's point to be in part that modernist monologues reflect an accompanying modern sense of human isolation, the silence-filled monologue of the Old Man certainly works as a prefiguration of a character who seems (despite the presence of onstage listeners) to be "speaking into the void"—as do, later, so many of Beckett's characters.

Eugene O'Neill turns to the monologue form again and again—from Brutus's reveries in the forest in *The Emperor Jones* (1920) to the "thought-asides" of *Strange Interlude* (1928) to the confessional speeches of *Long Day's Journey into Night* (1940–41) and the frustrated anecdotes of Erie in *Hughie* (1940)—as a way of exploring the texture of a dramatic language and of showing how solitary speech reflects individuals' alienation from themselves and from one another. O'Neill's working notes for *Mourning Becomes Electra* (1931) reflect his frustration with the soliloquy form: "They [the stylized soliloquies] . . . break rhythm, clog flow of dramatic development, reveal nothing of characters' motives, secret desires or dreams, that can't be shown directly or clearly suggested in their pantomime or talk."[35] But, by the time O'Neill wrote *Strange Interlude,* he was willing to experiment with a technique that he had considered, then rejected, for *Mourning Becomes Electra:* the use of thought-asides, in which the characters express their inner thoughts aloud to the audience in the middle of their ongoing dialogues. This device was the object of a great deal of criticism.[36] Because the thoughts in this play are, like the dialogues, *performed,* the technique raises inevitable questions about the extent to which the deceptive, "masking" quality of language encourages a tendency to "perform" even in the process of the narration of an inner consciousness. In this respect the thought-asides take on some of the qualities of Hamlet's soliloquies, wherein a desire to express inner turmoil is filtered through the self-conscious pose of the performer. As Travis Bogard notes, the original production of *Strange*

Interlude had the onstage action freeze whenever a character uttered a thought-aside;[37] this nonnaturalistic technique would have called particular attention to the patently dramatic nature of the thought-asides.

At first it seems difficult to reconcile O'Neill's affection for the theatrical quality of the monologue with the sense that monologic speech expresses deeply rooted human alienation and longing, as is evident in his later plays (e.g., *Long Day's Journey into Night,* especially Mary's speeches, and *Hughie*).[38] But such a juxtaposition becomes easier to understand when we realize the extent to which O'Neill's monologue speakers resemble Hamlet in their natures, which are at once isolated and performative. Bogard expresses this combination in his introduction to O'Neill's late plays when he says that the monologues are "the voices of the questers who can only imperfectly communicate the nature of their search."[39] He adds that especially in the late plays, the monologues

> serve to reinforce the sense that the action is somehow outside of time, suspended in a void of consciousness between dreaming and waking where loneliness becomes a fluid process of pain and man cannot quite attain his only anodyne—being heard and touching another human being in the dark.[40]

The monologues in Tennessee Williams's plays are similar to those of O'Neill's in that both playwrights use them to create fictional worlds through narrative and to express interiority in ways that would not otherwise be possible on the stage. Moreover, Williams and O'Neill are both concerned with the ways monologic speech can reflect individual isolation. For Laura in *The Glass Menagerie* (1945), Alma in *Summer and Smoke* (1948), Lady in *Orpheus Descending* (1957), and Felice and Clare in *The Two-Character Play* (1975), the movement out of one's isolation means a temporary chance for dialogue, a reprieve from what Williams refers to in his preface to *Cat on a Hot Tin Roof* (1955) as our "sentence" to "solitary confinement."[41] In Williams's plays the isolated individual builds a fictional world around him- or herself; although this world needs to be supported and recognized by others, the construction of it also implies a kind of madness.

Blanche DuBois of *A Streetcar Named Desire* (1947) is probably the most prominent example of the retreat into insanity that occurs when the character's narrative is forced to become monologue rather than dialogue. If the "deviant discourse" associated with monologue is creative (and, of course, provides the creative fabric of the play itself), then Williams shows the frightening and maddening side of this discourse as his characters seek a movement *out* of monologue and out of the "solitary confinement" of their fabricated worlds. In *Suddenly Last Summer* (1958), for instance, Catherine's inability to find anyone who believes her story about the cannibalization of her cousin Sebastian leads her to replicate the insanity of which she has been accused in the first place. It is only through relating her lengthy story of the gruesome events leading to Sebastian's death that Catherine is, to some extent, released from the isolation of her terrible knowledge.

Critics have tended to place the focus on Williams's thematic use of insanity as biographically influenced (his sister Rose's lobotomy, his own breakdowns, etc.) or as an artistic structural device.[42] But perhaps they need to add a third perspective to these two views, indicating that insanity in Williams's characters stands at least partly for a world in which an attempt at dialogue does not succeed. Even more than O'Neill's monologue speakers—or those of Ibsen and Strindberg—Williams's characters depend on the presence of an *auditor* who offers at least the possibility of a transition into dialogue, into some kind of exchange with an other.

(Re)figuring Monologue: Brecht and Beckett

Bertolt Brecht and Samuel Beckett changed the ways we look at theatrical monologue to a greater degree than any other twentieth-century dramatists. Their names will appear repeatedly in this study's later discussions of postmodernist monologue, for Brecht and Beckett—in markedly different ways—provided the foundation for new approaches toward the construction of narrative and theatrical space, the actor's relationship with the audience, and so forth.

When spectators go to a theatrical performance, Brecht argues, what they are actually seeing is a battle between *theater* (i.e., the representation before their eyes, the staged "event") and *play* (i.e., the text that is being performed); he says that theater, the preferred winner in this battle, "can only emerge victorious over the play if it manages to avoid the risk of the play's transforming it completely—as at present it nearly always succeeds in doing."[43] Whereas Shaw, a similarly didactic playwright—through verbose character descriptions, prefaces, and so forth (in such works as *Man and Superman* [1903])—often calls as much

attention to textual aspects of the dramatic work as to its status as a
blueprint for performance, Brecht's ultimate emphasis is on the theatrical event as a *process*. Brecht's achievement is a dramatic style that gives
primacy to the moment of performance, primarily by the use of the
"alienation effect" (*Verfremdungseffekt*) in which the desired end is detach-
ment and, ultimately, action by the spectators rather than empathy and
complacency.

The Brechtian theory of acting insists that the actor "quote" the
character he or she plays, as opposed to "becoming" that character.
"When reading his part," Brecht writes, "the actor's attitude should be
one of a man who is astounded and contradicts." Thus, the actor "is not
Lear, Harpagon, Schweik; he shows them."[44] If the acting is a form of
quotation, the actor may go so far as to speak in the third person or the
past tense and even to recite the stage directions aloud.[45] The performance becomes a type of discussion with the audience, and so a soliloquy
does not hold the same kind of ambiguity regarding the presence of the
audience as, say, a Shakespearean soliloquy: "If the actor turns to the
audience it must be a whole-hearted turn rather than the asides and
soliloquizing technique of the old-fashioned theatre."[46] In Brechtian theater, then, the notion of the soliloquy as the expression of an interior
state, which we saw in a character like Hamlet, is changed radically. A
character may still reveal his or her "feelings" or decision-making process in a soliloquy, but such an action comes forth in terms of the *actor's
explanation* or demonstration of the feelings or process; as such, the
soliloquy loses its privileged status as an intensified, resonant moment
of insight into a character.

As the soliloquy per se vanishes from the Brechtian theater, it is
replaced by monologues that tend to serve a narrative or didactic purpose. Kristin Morrison provides an example of this phenomenon in her
discussion of the Chaplain in *Mother Courage* (1939): "[when he] develops
a narrative, an *exemplum*, to demonstrate how war is like peace, there is
no unwitting self-revelation, no hidden emotions and motives revealed . . . [rather, he] would be the first to recognize that he is a gifted
charlatan; indeed, that *is* the tradition he proudly represents."[47] Similarly, at the beginning of *The Threepenny Opera* (1928), Peachum explains to the audience that his "business is trying to arouse human
pity."[48] This is not a moment of self-recognition, nor one of satiric
accusation; the speech's function is primarily an expository one that

involves a direct communication between the actor/character and the audience.

In his notes for *The Threepenny Opera* Brecht designates three "levels" of discourse—"plain speech, heightened speech, and singing"—and indicates that the three "must always remain separate from one another."[49] The "heightened speech" to which he refers is also a particularly evocative way of setting forth monologue as a type of demystifying narrative addressed to the audience. Perhaps the most memorable examples of this are in *The Good Person of Szechwan* (1948). Shen Teh, the "good person" of the title, tends to shift from an address to another character in "plain speech" into an address to the audience in "heightened speech," such as when she says to Mrs. Shin, "Why are you so mean?" and then asks the audience,

> Isn't it exhausting
> To trample your fellows? The veins in your temples
> Are swollen with the strain of your greed.[50]

Her movement toward the audience is the kind of "whole-hearted turn" that Brecht suggests, for the "heightened" discourse of Shen Teh's monologue is designed to pull the audience out of its immersion in her character and to encourage reflection on the situation that the actor is "showing." Thus, in the same play, when Shu Fu says to the spectators, "What do you think of me, ladies and gentlemen?"[51] we know that the question is not purely a rhetorical one.

Samuel Beckett—whose works, like Brecht's, play a key role in any discussion of modern and postmodern drama—also appropriated and transformed the monologue. Monologue in Samuel Beckett's plays is central as a theatrical device to such an extent that many of his later works are strictly in monologue form. In such works as *Not I* (1972) and *A Piece of Monologue* (1979), the voice of the monologue-speaker subsumes and at times supplants what we typically expect to be the "action" onstage. That is, in Beckett's monologues the play occurs through the speaker and the theatricalization of the speaker's presence onstage (the way he or she is lit, etc.); the language of the monologue constitutes and controls the dramatic action.

The role of monologue in Beckett's earlier drama, especially *Waiting for Godot* (1953), *Endgame* (1957), *Happy Days* (1961), and *Krapp's Last*

Tape (1958), has been treated extensively by other writers (most notably, Ruby Cohn and Andrew Kennedy), and so they will not be discussed at length here.[52] Briefly, *Waiting for Godot* and *Endgame* are dialogue-based plays that transform at times into monologue, as in Lucky's speech in the former and Hamm's soliloquies in the latter: Hamm and Clov seem to view the creation of narrative as a way of filling time and space. (Hamm says, "Then babble, babble, words, like the solitary child who turns himself into children, two, three, so as to be together, and whisper together, in the dark."[53]) *Happy Days* is primarily a monologue spoken by Winnie, who is immobilized in sand and who speaks at times to herself or to the audience, but it is also a dialogue with her husband Willie, who—though he answers only in grunts and occasionally a word—seems to fulfill Winnie's desire for a listener. Winnie says:

> Oh no doubt the time will come when before I can utter a word I must make sure you heard the one that went before and then no doubt another come another time when I must learn to talk to myself a thing I could never bear to do such wilderness. (*Pause.*) Or gaze before me with compressed lips.[54]

As Cohn points out in "Outward Bound Soliloquies," "If Willie didn't exist, Winnie would have had to invent him."[55] And *Krapp's Last Tape* features two voices, in that the older Krapp listens to and responds to the taped words of the younger Krapp (i.e., the recorded voice of himself many years earlier), but the play is essentially a monologue based on the ruminations of the older Krapp alone onstage with his tape recorder.[56] Krapp, like Winnie and the other characters in these early plays, uses monologue (or more aptly, soliloquy, since the speeches are articulations of inner states) as a way of struggling against silence, isolation, and the "void."

Even though Beckett wrote *Play* (1962–63) only a year after *Happy Days,* it marks the transition into a slightly different approach to the monologue. In *Play,* as in the later *Not I,* the speakers try—like Winnie and Krapp—to assert their subjectivity as a way of warding off nothingness, but now it is as if the "void" already surrounds them. The three speakers of the interwoven monologues in *Play,* and the Mouth in *Not I,* seem to be suspended in a limbo in which they are *compelled* to speak. Whereas Hamm and Winnie have the reassurance (even if it is a partial or incomplete one) that their monologues have an audience, and hence the potential to become dialogue, the characters in *Play* and Mouth have little else but their own monologic voices.[57] The movement in these plays appears to be toward a dissociation even from the speaker's ability to identify his or her status as subject with the words, especially as the Mouth insists on using third person rather than first person.[58] One might say that this is monologue taken to its starkest, most "monologic" and isolated extreme: not only is the primary action of the play reduced to the monologue of one speaker, but that speaker's monologue is in turn reduced to a mouth, a voice, and a third-person narrative.

A Piece of Monologue is another example of Beckett's abstraction and "purification" (in the sense of a minimalist painting) of the monologue form. The play features, again, an isolated speaker who (like the Mouth in *Not I*) uses the third person. Unlike in *Not I*, though, the speaker's narrative is more overtly theatricalized, as evidenced by its resemblance to a series of "stage directions" that are enacted only in words, not physically ("Takes off milk white globe and sets it down. Match goes out. . . . Strikes a third as before and sets it to wick"),[59] but which strike a parallel at the end of the play with the staged diminishing of the light as the speaker narrates it ("Such as the light going now. Beginning to go. In the room").[60] The title of the play reinforces the sense in which the monologue, when reduced to its "starkest" form, is above all theatrical: "a piece" implies a fragment of a larger whole or a larger monologue, which would suggest that we are witness to an ongoing, possibly private act, but "a piece" also invokes a theater piece, complete in itself, presented solely for the purpose of display to an audience.

The spectators of Beckett's theater pieces, then, need to experience a certain distance from the speaker, as in Brecht's plays, in order to sense the performative impact of his or her words. Beckett imposes this distance by reducing the primary stage action to the speaker's words alone and by foregrounding the theatricality of the speaker's narrative. Unlike in Brecht, the speaker expresses an *inner* consciousness—yet this consciousness is also different from the interiority that emerges in a Shakespearean soliloquy. In the case of such a play as *Not I* or *A Piece of Monologue*, the verbalization of inner thoughts is unaccompanied by insight or change; the monologue explores the realm of private speech, but that private speech is ultimately narrated and theatricalized.

Moving in the Present Tense: Monologue and the Discourses of Postmodernism in the American Experimental Theater

> Play is the vice and joy of postmodernism;
> play is fatuousness but also fantasy.
>
> —Ihab Hassan, *Paracriticisms*

As early as 1909, Georg Lukács wrote in "The Sociology of Modern Drama" that, as stage language sought to express the inexpressible qualities of human alienation and longing, both dialogue and monologue seemed inadequate for such a task:

> In a monologue the loneliness of a specific situation is compressed and expressed together with all that must remain unsaid. . . . But . . . it cannot express the ever-shifting nuances of understanding and incomprehension.[1]

Considered in the context of more recent uses of the monologue, Lukács's words are interesting in several respects. First, the sense of monologue as a problematic mirror of human isolation points toward the modernist impulse to create monologic moments that emphasize the grasping for a dialogue that is never fully realized. Mikhail Bakhtin, in his essay on "The Problem of Speech Genres," points out that even the most monologic of utterances is dialogic at its core because "the utterance is filled with *dialogic overtones*"—i.e., its "addressivity," its "quality of being directed to someone" (even when the addressee is unknown or unspecified) is what constitutes the movement from what structuralist linguists would call *langue,* or Noam Chomsky's "competence" (the knowledge of the rules of a language), into *parole,* or Chomsky's "performance" (the deployment of language in the form of an utterance).[2] This sense of the monologic voice's unanswered or unsatisfied yearning for the implied transition into dialogue might recall Erie in O'Neill's *Hughie,* Williams's Blanche DuBois, or Winnie in Beckett's *Happy Days.* And Lukács's notion of the "compressive" quality of the monologue, which allows it to hint at the repressed or the unspeakable, brings to mind characters as diverse as Arthur Miller's Elizabeth Proctor (*The Crucible* [1953]) and Edward Albee's Martha (*Who's Afraid of Virginia Woolf?* [1962]); their monologues invite us to invent multiple subtexts for the depth of feeling that the characters themselves are unable to express.

At the same time Lukács was unable to foresee the extent to which the postmodern monologue would resist the limitations of the dialogical "framework" that he imposes and would move beyond what he calls "commentary in programmatic form"[3] by emerging in dramatic contexts that allowed it (1) to perform functions in a play that are not purely expository or "psychological"; (2) to subsume, when desired, the physical and visual action occurring onstage; and (3) to transform the consciousness that a monologue is being delivered into a metaphoric construction that shapes our overall understanding of the work. This last category implies the capability of the monologue to conflate what Bernard Beckerman would call "presentational" and "representational" space,[4] a *narrative* redefinition of monologue that Lukács could not have imagined. Furthermore, it suggests the self-reflexivity that is, as I will show, one characteristic of the postmodern re-presentation of the dramatic text/performance.

The purpose of this chapter is to examine the transformations undergone by the monologue in the movement from modernism to postmodernism, particularly as manifested in the American theater. I will begin by attempting to locate some definitions for a postmodern aesthetic and its theatrical applications; this will lead to a discussion of the connections between the American experimental theater of the early 1960s (which provided the impetus for Sam Shepard, Maria Irene Fornes, and many of the performance artists whose works will be discussed in this study) and the advent of a postmodern dramatic vision.

Locating Postmodernism

The term *postmodernism* has been used both to delineate a recurring trend within the history of cultural movements, and as a historical movement (i.e., "after-modernism") taking place in the present.[5] Fredric Jameson's view of postmodernism as a "periodizing concept" is that it "expresses the inner truth of that newly emergent social order of late capitalism."[6] Jean-François Lyotard's perspective in *The Postmodern Condition* is that the postmodern is "undoubtedly a part of the modern"; he adds that a "work can become modern only if it is first postmodern. Postmodernism thus understood is not modernism at its end but in the nascent state, and this state is constant."[7] While it is generally accepted practice, following Jameson and others, to locate postmodernism historically as emerging out of the post–World War II culture of the 1950s and continuing through the present, Lyotard's more cyclical description is also compelling. One could even argue that it is possible for a writer—Beckett, for example—to be both "modern" and "postmodern." For the purpose of this study, I have chosen to rely primarily on the "periodized," or historicized, parameters of postmodernism but to turn toward the Lyotardian viewpoint as a way of understanding the strategies of postmodernism as an artistic/intellectual movement.

As Andreas Huyssen and Jonathan Arac both explain, readers initially encountered the word *postmodernism* as early as the late 1950s (through the writing of Irving Howe and Harry Levin), as a mostly negative description of the way that the projects of modernism were no longer flourishing. It was used in a more positive, creative context by literary critics (including Leslie Fiedler and Ihab Hassan) beginning in the 1960s. We then began to hear the term applied to architecture, dance, theater, painting, and music by the early and mid-1970s in the United States; it also became a popular part of French and German critical discourse (Lyotard, Julia Kristeva, Jürgen Habermas) in the late 1970s and early 1980s.[8]

The process of describing the "aesthetic" of postmodernism is a complicated one, for postmodernism itself is to some degree resistant to the "aestheticizing" quality of modernism. In his introduction to *The Anti-Aesthetic: Essays on Postmodern Culture*, Hal Foster argues that the more appropriate term is *anti-aesthetic*, not in a nihilistic sense but as "a

critique which destructures the order of representations in order to rein-
scribe them." He adds that postmodernism urges an interrogation of the
"very notion of the aesthetic," of "the idea that aesthetic experience
exists apart, without 'purpose,' all but beyond history, or that art can
now effect a world at once (inter)subjective, concrete and universal—a
symbolic totality."[9] Keeping Foster's modification of the word *aesthetic*
in mind, then, some of the characteristics of postmodernism are as follows.

Whereas high modernism rejects popular culture and tries to stand
outside of history, postmodernism incorporates popular culture and history (consider, e.g., the paintings of Andy Warhol). Jameson emphasizes
postmodernism's "effacement of the older distinction between high and
so-called mass [i.e., popular] culture,"[10] while Huyssen goes so far as to
say that "Pop in the broadest sense was the context in which a notion of
the postmodern first took shape, and from the beginning until today, the
most significant trends within postmodernism have challenged modernism's relentless hostility to mass culture."[11] One of the many paradoxes
of postmodernism, according to Linda Hutcheon, is that it "manages to
legitimize culture (high and mass) even as it subverts it."[12] Furthermore,
postmodernism embraces technology (TV, video, computers) and ac-
knowledges art's place in a technological society. Jean Baudrillard, in
"The Ecstasy of Communication," sees this movement into a world
dominated by technology as one in which the landscape of the body is
itself rendered an image, a machine, a simulation:

> The Faustian, Promethean (perhaps Oedipal) period of production
> and consumption gives way to the "proteinic" era of networks, to
> the narcissistic and protean era of connections, contact, contiguity,
> feedback and generalized interface that goes with the universe of
> communication. With the television image—the television being the
> ultimate and perfect object for this new era—our own body and the
> whole surrounding universe become a control screen.[13]

Huyssen sees a direct parallel between early postmodernism's eagerness
to embrace technology and the "technological optimism" of the 1920s
and 1930s avant-garde (Dziga Vertov, Brecht, Walter Benjamin): he
argues that what photography and film were to the former, computer,
TV, and video technology were to the latter.[14]

As Huyssen points out, moreover, postmodernism rejects modernism's impulse to colonialize or exoticize the other (female, non-Western, etc.).[15] Rather, "margins" and "edges," the "ex-centric" (with the obvious pun, but also in the senses of both "off-center" and "de-centered") receive new attention.[16] On the stage, this "decentering" may be reified through the mise-en-scène, with its ability to create visual puns and metaphors.

This ability to generate a metadiscourse, particularly in a parodic way, is another characteristic of postmodernist expression. Postmodernism puts together what Hutcheon refers to as the forces of historical/political contextuality, and self-reflexivity (as in Woody Allen's film *Zelig* [1983] and D. M. Thomas's novel *The White Hotel* [1981]).[17] She adds that parody is a quintessentially postmodern form because it "paradoxically both incorporates and challenges that which it parodies."[18] Parody, according to Hutcheon, forces a dialectical confrontation between "the aesthetic" and "a world of significance external to itself . . . [i.e.,] the political and the historical."[19] Lyotard is also interested in postmodernism's self-reflexivity but expresses this in terms of its extension of modernism's goal of referring to the "unpresentable":

> The postmodern would be that which, in the modern, puts forward the unpresentable in presentation itself; that which denies itself the solace of good forms, the consensus of a taste which would make it possible to share collectively the nostalgia for the unattainable; that which searches for new presentations, not in order to enjoy them but in order to impart a stronger sense of the unpresentable.[20]

The postmodern impulse is to fracture, or deconstruct, the "masterpiece." This rejection of "literariness" harks back to Antonin Artaud's "No More Masterpieces" in *The Theater and Its Double*: "Masterpieces of the past are good for the past: they are not good for us."[21] Whereas Artaud claims to reject textuality outright, postmodernism calls upon a redefined textuality to deconsecrate textual "value." Art, then, is recast as the non-"artistic" (see, for example, Heiner Müller's rereading of Shakespeare in *Hamletmachine*). The "meaning" of a text consequently resides not in its predetermined representation but, rather, in its reception. Referring to the work of linguist Emile Benveniste, Hutcheon points out that the generation of meaning is a "dynamic process" that happens not simply through language itself but in its moment of entry into discourse. According to Benveniste, "It is in the instance of discourse ['language put into action'] in which 'I' designates the speaker that the speaker proclaims himself as the 'subject.' And so it is literally true that the basis of subjectivity is in the exercise of language."[22] Although Hutcheon uses Benveniste's theory to address the issue of reader response, her arguments are particularly relevant to the detextualizing impulse of postmodernist drama. In the theater this means an emphasis on the performance moment (the moment at which the audience "receives" the play; its corresponding act of "readership") over the text and on stage presence over representation (consider the deconstructive stage directions of such performance artists as Holly Hughes and Karen Finley, whose works will be discussed later in this study). This accent on the moment of enactment entails a new attention to the role of the audience's cognitive processes in shaping the theatrical event, as in the works of Richard Foreman (with his use of buzzers and gongs) or in the early work of Robert Wilson (with his use of slow motion).

Subjectivity itself also demands increased attention. While modernism proclaimed "the death of the subject," postmodernism attempts to discover new articulations of subjectivity and the means by which it is constituted and expressed.[23] The postmodern subject—that is, the split, multiple, or contradictory "I"—is thus a decentered one, and so the notion of "character" is no longer holistic. I have indicated earlier the ways in which Brecht took one step toward a deconstructive notion of character by insisting that the actor "quote" the character rather than becoming him or her. As Hutcheon shows, Brecht's epic theater and postmodernist art share a similar approach to the relation between complex subjectivity and character portrayal:

> When the contradictions [emphasized over linearity and causality] are to be found in character portrayal, we get a further contesting of the notion of the coherent unified bourgeois subject—one that is constant with that of postmodernism: "The continuity of the ego is a myth." . . . The subject is an object of inquiry—and problematization. It is not taken for granted; it is not unchanging or unchangeable. Brecht's theater and postmodernist art further contest that entire set of assumptions we have seen to derive from the humanist concept of subjectivity: originality, uniqueness, authority, universality.[24]

Brecht wrote that the epic actor "has to be able to show his character's coherence despite, or rather by means of, interruptions and jumps."[25]

Postmodernism takes Brecht's vision of the fragmented character one step further, in part through the possibilities opened up by technology (e.g., the video screens in Müller's *Hamletmachine* [1977], or in The Wooster Group's *Route 1 & 9* [1981]). Perhaps the ultimate manifestation of the decentered subject is the increasing precedence that monologue takes over dialogue in postmodern drama. Moreover, monologue does not necessarily emerge from one coherent "voice" or "self"; the mono-logic texts, rather, are similarly fragmented and given multiple voices (e.g., Laurie Anderson's performance pieces or Leeny Sack's *The Survivor and the Translator* [1980]).

Theatricalizing Postmodernism

In *Paracriticisms: Seven Speculations of the Times* Hassan sets up a dialectic of "Modernist Rubrics" and "Postmodernist Notes." Many of his descriptions under the latter category hold particular applications to the connections between the experimental theater movements of the 1960s and the growth of a postmodernist poetics. For example, the modernist rubric of "eroticism" becomes the "new sexuality (end of censorship)" under postmodernism; "antinomianism" becomes "countercultures," "Zen mysticism," and the "cult of apocalypticism"; and "experimentalism" becomes "open structures," "improvisation," "neo-surrealism," "impermanent art," "parody," "self-reflexiveness," and "intermedia."[26] It is possible to argue that Hassan's impulse to categorize is a little too linear or even structuralist—and, indeed, in the "Postface 1982" to the revised edition of his *Dismemberment of Orpheus: Toward a Postmodern Literature,* Hassan created an entirely new set of modern and postmodern paired terms.[27] His schema also fails to account for the complications of periodizing postmodernism that I mentioned in the first section of this chapter. Nevertheless, such a list is valuable because Hassan's vocabulary allows for an openness that includes *theatrical* structures and possibilities in the revisioning of art.

From the mid-1960s to the early 1970s the American theater began to develop an alternative aesthetic that coincided with the growth of Pop Art, rock music, and other innovative (and, initially, countercultural) forms of artistic expression. Huyssen argues that the time was ripe for the development of such an aesthetic in the midst of the simultaneous "apocalyptic desperate" and "visionary celebratory" strains (a dichotomy that he ascribes to Gerald Graff) of early

postmodern culture; one way that these visions manifested themselves
was as "a breakthrough toward an ultimate liberation of instinct and
consciousness, into ... the new Eden of polymorphous perversity,
Paradise Now, as the Living Theater proclaimed it on stage."[28] In
addition to Judith Malina and Julian Beck's Living Theatre, among the
most important theater groups and "theatricians" of this period were
the Open Theater (Joseph Chaikin), and the Performance Group
(Richard Schechner).

Drawing upon the (sometimes contradictory) theories of Brecht and
Artaud, and politicizing their forms of expression in response to the
world events of the period, these alternative theater practitioners were
at the forefront of a postmodern approach to acting, staging, audience,
and narrative. Many of the major playwrights who began working with
these groups (Shepard, Fornes, etc.) carried the possibilities for theatrical
innovations into their own drama as they developed their distinct dramatic voices. It is important to understand that—despite Hassan's dialectics—the experimental theater of this period did not *reject* modernism,
as the interest in Artaud and Brecht should show; rather, the impulse
toward the "rupture and discontinuity" of the 1960s, and the subsequent
interest in drawing at will from modernist and premodernist culture in
the 1970s, had a great deal in common with the corresponding impulses
of the early avant-garde movements (Dadaism, surrealism, etc.); as
Huyssen points out, the key difference is that the American countercul-
ture drew upon a specifically historical and political context for its innovations.[29]

The postmodern interest in the changing constitution, fragmentation, and multiplication of the subject inevitably affected the postmodernist theater's approach to the role of the actor, which in turn had an
impact on his or her position as a speaker of monologues. At times one
or more of the actors in the productions of the experimental theater took
on the role of "storyteller" or "ringmaster," in Brechtian fashion (e.g.,
the Open Theater's *Terminal* [1969–70]). To some extent the narrational
monologues both complement and counterpoint the "text" (which, unlike in Brecht, is not always a predetermined, written text) of the performance. Often actors would deliver monologues *within* the narrated
framework as well, but the emphasis tended to be on the collective
nature of the group rather than the "psychological" development of
individual characters. Sometimes a production such as the Performance
Group's *Dionysus in 69* (1969) had the actors switch roles from one

performance to the next so that there were constantly changing interpretations of the characters.

At the same time plays like *Dionysus in 69* emphasized what may be the most radical change in the role of the actor, namely that he or she does not simply "interpret" or "become" a character; rather, the actor *as* actor/person and the character coexist because the actor presents both simultaneously. (This concept is central to the development of performance art in the later 1970s and 1980s, in which such artists as Spalding Gray—who began his career with Schechner's Performance Group—make the merging of actor and character into the very substance of their work.) Like the Method actor, the performer draws upon inner forces to create a character—but, in a rejection of the Method and a movement closer to Brecht,[30] he or she does so without letting the audience (or the actor him- or herself) get "lost" in the character. "The study of character," says Chaikin in *The Presence of the Actor,* "is the study of 'I' in relation to forces that join us."[31] *Dionysus in 69* provides striking examples of the fluid movement between "role" and actor, though to some extent the actor as a "real person" is still playing a part; as one of the performers in the piece discovered, "No matter how you try to escape the bounds of the theatrical you find yourself inside one or another succession of symbolic acts."[32] In the Open Theater's production of *The Mutation Show* (1971), the "real" person *becomes* the symbol in a sequence called "The Human Gallery," in which the actors hold up photographs of themselves, and one of them, Ellen, narrates a series of facts about each performer ("Tina Shepard's uncle John is a federal judge").[33] In such a piece, then, the blurring of the boundaries between performer and character becomes a source of the dramatic text itself.

With its postmodern revisioning of subjectivity the American experimental theater of this period also inspired new approaches to the portrayal of characters' "inner lives," and this obviously had a significant impact upon the role of monologue. The term *inner lives* in reference to characters is somewhat misleading here, since—as we have seen—these theater groups tended not to believe in creating characters with psychological depth, preferring rather to allow the *actor* to emerge when the outer layers of the character were peeled off. The experimental theater's freedom to dispense with traditional rules of performance and narrative also meant, though, that an attempt to portray various levels of inner consciousness would not be met with the same derision that O'Neill faced with *Strange Interlude.*

Traditionally, characters who soliloquize to express their inner states are doing so because their introspection distinguishes them from the others around them; thus, Hamlet (in a conventional production) steps away from the crowd to utter his mad speeches. (One might compare this to Müller's postmodern reinterpretation of Hamlet in *Hamlet-machine,* in which the substance of the play itself is the "interior" Hamlet, including the actor's rejection of the "part" of Hamlet and including the merging of Hamlet and Ophelia.) Several postmodern productions of *Hamlet* have included multiple actors (sometimes of varied race and gender) playing Hamlet, as an indication of the fragmentation of his character suggested by Shakespeare and emphasized by the director and dramaturge. For such experimental theater groups as the Open Theater, interiority often is expressed by multiple characters to show their unity as a group and to evoke the collective unconscious, as in *Viet Rock* (1966), *Terminal* (1969–70), or *Nightwalk* (1973). In fact, C. W. E. Bigsby sees part of the American attraction to experimental theater as rooted in the chance for members "of a society which has enshrined individualism" (also a characteristic of modernist artistic expression) to experience self-discovery "through the group." Bigsby contrasts such an attitude to that of the followers of Jerzy Grotowski's Theatre Laboratory in Poland, who, as part of "a collectivist society," may have felt that "the path to the collectivity lay through the discovery of self."[34]

To some extent the expression of this "group interiority" also entailed dislocating it from the realm of the verbal; the Open Theater believed that "inner experience" could be represented through physical action and visual presentation, a concept suggested by the early modernists (e.g., the French surrealists) but unheard of in the naturalistic theater. The Open Theater's piece *The Odets Kitchen* involved taking a realistic domestic scene, in the manner of Odets (or a similar playwright), and portraying it from the "inside out" by acting out what the actors "imagined to have been going on *behind* the external behavior of the three characters, but which the naturalistic mode of presentation had not made visible."[35] This concept of presenting the "unpresentable" recalls Lyotard's discussion of postmodernism quoted earlier. Rather than simply rejecting the possibility of performing "interiority," then, the Open Theater presented a critique of the extent to which the naturalistic theater masks its expression.

Additionally, while Brecht suggested a direct relationship between the actors and the audience,[36] the experimental theater takes this idea to a greater extreme by erasing (or at least smudging) the divisions between performers and spectators. I have mentioned that postmodernist expression foregrounds the role of the reader (i.e., audience member, or "recipient") in constituting its meanings and even its structure; as Hutcheon says, "The postmodernist text's self-conscious return to performative process and to the entirety of the enunciative act demands that the reader, the *you*, not be left out, even in dealing with the question of reference."[37] Herbert Blau, similarly, underscores the "emphasis on the audience as the repository of meaning in postmodern thought."[38] This impulse to revise the traditionally passive role of the spectator has one early radical manifestation in Artaud, who wrote that, in the "theater of cruelty," "the spectator is in the center and the spectacle surrounds him."[39] Artaud's interest in placing the spectator more directly into the play's action (he wrote in the *First Manifesto* of the Theater of Cruelty that, by abolishing physical audience/actor barriers, a "direct communication will be reestablished between the spectator and the spectacle")[40] had a strong impact on the experimental theater's use of nonstages, theater in the round, "found" space, and other ways of directly involving the spectators in the performance.

In Poland Grotowski (whose Artaud-inspired teachings reached American performers through *Towards a Poor Theater* [1968] and through visits to the Open Theater and other groups) expressed the call for an even more powerful elimination of actor/audience barriers when he said, "Let the most drastic scenes happen face to face with the spectator so that he is within arm's reach of the actor, can feel his breathing and smell the perspiration."[41] Performers in *Dionysus in 69* and in the Living Theatre's *Paradise Now* (1968) made the notion of audience contact literal as they caressed the spectators; the actors in the Open Theater's *Viet Rock* also touched the audience as a "celebration of presence." Robert Pasolli suggests one rationale for this by asking, "You can disbelieve what you are told, what you are shown, but can you disbelieve being touched?"[42] The point, as Pierre Biner says in his book on the Living Theatre, is "to secure the spectator's participation and through this involvement to effect change in the world."[43]

For the Living Theatre and other groups, the resulting change was accomplished by theatrical means that in themselves called for a kind of antitheatricality (a typically postmodern paradox).[44] In the Performance Group's production of *Commune* (1970), for instance, the performers at one point called for spectators to sit in a circle onstage; they told the

audience that the play would not continue until there were enough vol-
unteers—and indeed, one night the play "halted" at this point for several
hours.[45] In ancient or Restoration comedy the deliberate acknowledgment of the audience serves to pull us more deeply into the *dramatic*
nature of the speeches we are hearing. But, in the case of a play like
Commune, the result of the audience acknowledgment is a deliberate
disruption of theatricality; the speeches lose their fictional context and
become "real," even if that reality remains essentially a performed one.
As Schechner says in *Environmental Theater,* "audience participation takes
place precisely at the point when the performance breaks down and
becomes a social event."[46] Another way to express this might be that,
while the actors become "real people," the spectators become "performers" (an event Handke attempted to theatricalize in *Offending the Audience*), both in the theatrical sense and in the sense that they act rather
than simply *react* to a performance.

I have discussed in chapter 1 the sense in which the performance of
a play takes place in an ongoing present tense; in the experimental theater
the foregrounding of dramatic "present-ness" is essential from a narrative standpoint because drama that calls for action from the spectators
must provide a continual reminder that the piece is not simply a (re)pre-
sentation but, rather, an action in the process of being created. Artaud
sees an emphasis on process over repetition as essential to the creation
of a new approach to drama because "the theater is the only place in the
world where a gesture, once made, can never be made the same way
twice."[47] As Timothy Wiles points out, the ultimate forms of performance that relied on embodiment in the present moment were Happen-
ings, which were "paradigms of nonrepeatability in theater performance,
for they had no texts, and their massive, often self-destructive spectacu-
lar effects necessitated their being done only once."[48] The antinarrative
focus on the moment of performance also stems from the Artaudian
interest in ritual (as inspired by primitive ritual and myth) and play as
replacements for the linear, monolithic narrative model. Blau suggests
that the later experimental theater of the 1970s continued its interest in
what he says was a "fascination with ritual," for, "in the anti-oedipal
bias of postmodernism, there is still the desire for the perpetual present
moment that theatre seems to remember from unremembered time—the
repetitiveness of ritual and the gratuitousness of play."[49]

In somewhat different terms Chaikin provides an eloquent argument for the "embodying" of the present:

Memory and habit move on in the present, as the present. The past cannot be controlled. It is the unchosen part of the present and is liberated only through a full assimilation of its having actually taken place. . . . Moving with the present is taking an initiative in harmony with time. Rather than retreating from the moment, it is to embody the moment.[50]

Yet the ability to "embody the moment" dramatically, to enact Artaud's premise of the unrepeatable, is itself problematized as soon as it enters theatrical discourse. In his essay on "The Theater of Cruelty and the Closure of Representation" Jacques Derrida discusses this insistence on nonrepeatability in terms of the ultimate paradox of the Artaudian vision: its denial of re-presentation is always bound up within the limits of (re)presentation. The "grammar" of the Theater of Cruelty, says Derrida,

> will always remain the inaccessible limit of a representation which is not repetition, of a *re*-presentation which is full presence, which does not carry its double within itself as its death, of a present which does not repeat itself, that is, of a present outside time, a nonpresent. The present offers itself as such, appears, presents itself, opens the stage of time or the time of the stage only by harboring its own intestine difference, and only in the interior fold of its original repetition, in representation. In dialectics.[51]

Derrida sees this dialectical quality of the present as one version of a deconstructive act, for, in the moment that the "present" offers itself to be performed onstage, it enters the very realm of re-presentation that it professes to negate or deny; therefore, "true" *presentation* is a fascinating (im)possibility of Artaud's "pure" theater.

This paradoxical quality of the theatrical present has particular relevance to the narrative functions of the postmodern monologue. As I have suggested, monologue has the ability to manipulate both perceived and actual time frames in a play. Repeatedly, in the works of the experimental theater, we encounter lengthy, "riff"-like, wandering monologues in which our sense of time's passage is suspended because the monologue does not have to fit within the traditional narrative sense that the audience "paces" the performance according to "real" time. That is, since the monologue *becomes* that ongoing present, members of the audience fall into its rhythm rather than trying to adapt it to their own. These moments of immersion in the monologue constitute, perhaps, what Chaikin refers to in the above quotation as "moving with the present." Shepard and other playwrights who were inspired by the experimental theater took advantage of this sense of a fluid present tense to create their long monologue sequences, which overtake the physical action of the play.

In his 1982 "Postface" to *The Dismemberment of Orpheus* Hassan lists "Antiform (disjunctive, open)," "Play," "Chance," "Anarchy," "Process/Performance/Happening," "Decreation/Deconstruction," and "Dispersal" among the postmodern responses to modernism's "Form," "Purpose," "Design," "Hierarchy," "Art Object / Finished Work," "Creation/Totalization," and "Centering."[52] Similarly, Lyotard writes that, in postmodernism, "the narrative function is losing its functors, its great hero, its great dangers, its great voyages, its great goal,"[53] a characteristic that Hassan describes as the movement from "Narrative / *Grande Histoire*" to "Anti-narrative / *Petite Histoire*."[54] The experimental theater's reliance on this sense of the present, as well as on visuals, audience participation, and the resulting improvisations, means that the "text" of most of its theatrical creations, as Theodore Shank reminds us, "is not an end in itself."[55] This resembles Artaud's declaration in the *First Manifesto* of the Theater of Cruelty that: "We shall not act a written play, but we shall make attempts at direct staging, around themes, facts, or known works."[56] But even the "set" monologues in such plays as Shepard's *Chicago* (1965) have this processual, antiformal quality, as the following chapter will show. Clearly, the emphasis on improvisation in groups like the Open Theater encouraged playwrights to discover a new type of fluidity, providing them with the opportunity to make unexpected transitions or to choose words for their musical qualities and not just for literal meaning and formal coherence.

The possibilities that improvisation generated were manifold, and one effect of this, and of the rejection of the *grande histoire,* was that no play was limited in the leaps through time and space its narrative could take (even as the action unfolded in a continuous present). It was not unusual for a play to evoke more than one time period or event simultaneously, as when the Performance Group's *Commune* dealt with the Manson-Tate murders and My Lai or when the Open Theater's *The Serpent* treated both the biblical creation story and the King/Kennedy assassinations. Another technique for the manipulation of time and place—as well as of character and even of theatrical style—was the "transformation," an exercise developed by the Open Theater that was originally part of the actors' training but which eventually became a major component of *Viet Rock* (1966), Jean Claude Van Itallic's *Interview* (1966), Megan Terry's *Keep Tightly Closed in a Cool Dry Place* (1965), and other plays. In a transformation the actors make changes in the circumstances of the situation they are improvising, and they must communicate the changes to one another and adapt to them without breaking the flow of the improvisation. Pasolli provides a helpful discussion of the effects that transformations have upon the actor and action:

> Transformation taps the unconscious resources of the actor, who, in jumping from one set of circumstances to another, relies on links between given and potential situations which he would not necessarily understand rationally. Thus the device mines levels of meaning in a given situation which might not be otherwise evident. . . . In transformation, the actor is not limited to changing his identity (the who). He can change the place of action (the where), the clock time or epoch (the when), or the relationship between himself and his partners as defined by what goes on between them (the what).[57]

Since the monologue itself has the power to travel through time and space, it follows that Shepard and other playwrights who were inspired by the Open Theater would be attracted to the possibilities of the "transformational monologue," in which the speech has an improvised quality and creates changes of identity, place, time, and relationship—thus reflecting the open form of the postmodern text—through narrative language. As I shall discuss at greater length in the following chapter, Shepard's early plays (e.g., *Red Cross* [1966]) suggest an appropriation of the transformation as the basis for the monologues that skim so rapidly from one terrain to the next.

At the same time it is worth pointing out that there was a certain naïveté in the 1960s experimental theater's assumption that it was possible simultaneously to structure a dramatic event by the means of theatrical forms and to create the effect of utter spontaneity. Blau even argues that in the effort to "return performance to *unmediated* experience . . . [t]here is nothing more illusory in performance than the illusion of the unmediated."[58] He sees a difference between the valuable, but somewhat idealistic, visions of this period and those of subsequent alternative theater works (which he deems "postmodern"):

> What distinguishes the performative ethos of the postmodern—in a time of recuperation from the illusions of theater-as-life—is not only redoubled awareness of what is being restored, but an exponential play around the combinatory sets of stored or past experience which is, since there is utterly no assurance of an uninterrupted present, all we can make of a dubious future.[59]

Blau's distinction between the utopianism of the early experimental theater and its later, more complicated self-referentiality (and cynicism) is a provocative one. To overemphasize the status of the former period as naive, however, is to underestimate the impact that it had in redefining previously circumscribed notions of play making and playing (a point that Blau himself had made in his earlier writing).[60] "Play," with its multiple meanings, is not only one of Hassan's characteristics of postmodernism but also figures in the Derridean sense of "free play," as enactment of the resistance to totalizing discourses.[61] In *Just Gaming* Lyotard (as interviewed by Jean-Loup Thébaud) articulates the possibilities for the "pagan" (his nonperiodizing term for postmodern)[62] turn toward game playing as a creative or inventive strategy:

> I think that pagans are artists, that is, they can move from one game to another, and in each of these games (in the optimal situation) they try to figure out new moves. And even better, they try to invent new games.
> . . . This is what paganism would be. The point is not that one keeps the games, but that, in each of the existing games, one effects new moves, one opens up the possibility of new efficacies in the games with their present rules. And, in addition, one changes the rules: one can play a given game with other rules, and when one changes the rules, one has changed the game, because a game is primarily defined by its rules.[63]

If we think of the experimental theater as a locale for the invention of new "games" and new "rules" for theatrical narrative, it is easy to see that its interest in invention, along with the playful deconstruction and reappropriation of previously established texts, traditions, and relationships (e.g., actor/audience), aptly reflects the postmodern "condition."

Chapter 3

Geography of a Storyteller: Monologue in Sam Shepard's Plays

Sam Shepard has become such a romanticized figure—an image fueled in part by his status as movie star and in part by his reclusiveness—that the Shepardian "persona" has compelled as much public scrutiny as his plays themselves. At the same time Shepard's position as a "pop" figure reflects the burgeoning culture of American pop myths and counter-myths in which he developed his craft as a playwright. When Shepard began writing plays in the early 1960s, he was part of a still growing "colony" of artists in New York City's East Village who produced, directed, designed, performed in, and enthusiastically attended each other's theatrical experiments. Emerging out of a theatrical environment in which the rules of what a playwright "could" or "could not" do onstage were made to be broken, as well as the pop culture landscape of both a Californian 1950s adolescence and a Beatnik-influenced counter culture, his works draw upon multiple influences to show the makings of what could be considered a postmodernist "voice."

Shepard's plays have gone through various "phases," from the early metadramatic experiments to the "rock" plays to the "family" dramas— and perhaps his most recent piece, *States of Shock* (1991), is the beginning of yet another period in Shepard's career. But the division of Shepard's drama into these phases does not signal a lack of continuity, nor should one necessarily make the argument that Shepard has "improved" (or diminished) in a linear fashion throughout his playwriting career. Shepard's refusal to settle for the ordinary or the "traditional" (even, as I will argue, in his so-called realistic, or family, plays), his willingness to go against theatrical convention, makes his drama consistently worth approaching. Indeed, his works from all of his stages of interest share the trademark obsession with highly charged theatrical *language,* especially in the form of what may already be known as "Shepardian" monologues.

Textualizing Theatricality, Theatricalizing Textuality: Monologue in Shepard's Early Works

> I can't get out. You can get out. You can smile and laugh and kiss and cry. I am! I am! I am! I am! I am! I am! I am! I am! I am! I am! I am! Tonight. In this desert. In this space. I am.
> —Sam Shepard, *Operation Sidewinder*

The paradox of Shepard's early pieces is that, in their eagerness to subvert and manipulate our expectations about theatricality, the works themselves are unquestionably and rivetingly "dramatic."[1] Critics have repeatedly underscored the ways that Shepard's characters, by their behavior as consummate "performers," magnify the theatrical quality of the plays.[2] The characters' ability to command spectatorial attention works primarily through their verbal operatics, their performances of what have become known as Shepard's trademark "arias," which utterly subsume all other activities onstage.[3] Years after he wrote these early pieces Shepard remarked that he may have been expecting too much of the actors (or audience?) by presenting these exhausting arias unrelieved by much physical action.[4] Yet it is in part the unwieldiness of these gigantic monologues, their apparently "undramatic" nature, that makes them so exhilarating. Due in part to the dazzling virtuosity of Shepard's language, the monologues transcend their own "untheatricality" by pulling us inside the texts that are being recited.[5]

The previous chapter discussed the postmodern emphasis on the self-referential and self-questioning text; postmodern metadrama calls continual attention to the ironies and problems of its own processes of representation, its own textuality and theatricality. Moreover (as chapter 2 noted), the American experimental theater of the 1960s—in which Shepard began to develop his voice as a playwright—was profoundly committed to redefining the boundaries of dramatic narrative and performance as well as to revising the roles of the actors and spectators. In his early works (including *The Rock Garden* [1964], *Chicago* [1965], *Icarus's Mother* [1965], *Red Cross* [1966], and *Fourteen Hundred Thousand*

[1966]), Shepard draws upon the techniques of the experimental theater (still in its early stages when he began writing) but also emerges as a distinctive voice. Sometimes ingenuously and sometimes disingenuously, he explores, stretches, and even parodies the limits of theatricality by conflating the literal and the figurative (or the "[re]presentable" and the "un[re]presentable") and by substituting his time-stopping arias for linear development through dialogue or through traditional plot (i.e., that which travels along the oedipal continuum).[6] Shepard is aware of the multiple tensions that arise as a result—between text and performance, inertia and action, spoken language and visual spectacle—such that the spectators experience these early plays as a sort of battle for various levels of their engagement. Yet Shepard also allows these dialectical qualities to form the basis of the plays, as they reveal a constant confrontation between "telling" and "enacting." Ultimately, what "drives" the postmodern impulses of these early plays is the monologic language, the compulsive and explosive theatricalization of the speaking subject.

Shepard has said that, when he was writing these early plays, he would begin with a powerful stage image, like that of a man sitting onstage in a bathtub with all of his clothes on (*Chicago*), and take it from there.[7] Indeed, the visual images in these works are striking, in part because they are minimalized so as to underscore their strangeness; at times their strangeness comes *from* their minimalization or from their seeming inappropriateness as theatrically "interesting" material. Steven Putzel and Suzanne Westfall put this in a slightly different way; they refer to Shepard's "ability to manipulate cultural and theatrical codes and to produce in the audience the impression of something at once disconcertingly familiar and inexplicably strange."[8] *Rock Garden* is a series of three tableaux: a teenage girl and boy drinking milk while an older man watches; the same boy having a conversation with his mother while she lies in bed and he rocks in a rocking chair; and the boy in conversation with the Man who has entered the room at the end of the previous scene. *Chicago* has, in addition to the aforementioned man in the bathtub, biscuits thrown onstage, a character departing with a wagon, and fishing lines cast into the audience. *Icarus's Mother* presents us with friends who have just finished a beach picnic and who describe (but do not allow us to see) various real and hypothetical events that happen when a pilot flies nearby and signals at them. *Red Cross* provides the spectacle of the all-white interior of a vacation cabin (punctuated at the end with the image

of red blood), and *Fourteen Hundred Thousand* shows characters carrying
books upstairs for a bookcase they are building.

The very absurdity of these descriptions, insofar as they will frus-
trate any reader who still wants to know what these plays are "about,"
should indicate the difficulty of "encapsulating" the works by relying
on the elements of visuals and "plot." At times, though, Shepard teases
his spectators through the *refusal* of action. As Ann Wilson says, "In
Shepard's work meaning (in the sense of action which refers to a 'reality'
beyond the play) often seems to be subverted by the theatricality of the
plays because Shepard is concerned not with producing meaning but
with the production of meaning in the theatre."[9]

In the opening segment of *Rock Garden,* for instance, no words are
spoken; after a long interval, during which the boy and girl sip their
milk and exchange glances, the girl "drops her glass and spills the
milk."[10] The audience has kept expecting "something" to happen, most
likely in the form of dialogue, but Shepard reduces the action to the
spilling of the milk (it is appropriate that *Rock Garden* appeared in Kenneth Tynan's revue *Oh! Calcutta!* [1969] with Samuel Beckett's *Breath*
[1969], a piece that pushes the limits of "minimalism" in drama even
further). This refusal of action that culminates in a final "spilling" mirrors the Boy's ejaculatory monologue that—after a long series of nonac-
tions—closes the play, as the Man falls off his chair in response. In other
words, up to this point in the play language has not been given the
opportunity to build with the intensity necessary for the linguistic "or-
gasm" of a full-fledged monologue. Only with the unmasking of the
hidden sexual content is language freed and the coup de theatre made
possible. The rhythm of the Boy's "You know?" ironically (parodically?)
echoes the Man's repeated "I guess" in his tedious speech about yard
work that had immediately preceded the Boy's outburst:

> MAN: It's always wet around the sprinkler heads so it grows all the
> time, I guess. (*A long pause.*) It's harder to mow around them,
> too, I guess. It's hard to get the lawn mower in there close, I
> guess. . . .
>
> (40)

> BOY: When I come it's like a river. It's all over the bed and sheets
> and everything. You know? . . . I mean if a girl has a really small
> vagina it's really better to go in from behind. You know? I mean

she can sit with her legs together and you can sit facing her. You
know? . . .

(43)

With the movement from the banality and repression of the Man's attempt at dialogue to the explosion of the Boy's speech, Shepard implies
that the monologic voice provides a type of climax and release that is
sexual in its power and theatrical in its effect. This closing sequence plays
at "literalizing" the idea of a theatrical "climax"—as well as, perhaps,
with the Man tumbling off of his chair, the subsequent "falling action."

Even more so than in *The Rock Garden,* Shepard insists in *Chicago*
upon this impulse to literalize the theatrical, to play parodically at the
possibility that theater has of calling attention to its own processes of
creation and production. Whereas *The Rock Garden* never fully breaks
the fourth wall (even though the Boy in the last scene, in what may be
a metadramatic reference, "delivers all his lines into the air" [40] as if he
were addressing an audience rather than the Man), *Chicago* toys with the
idea that the characters may be aware that they are in a play, even as they
interact within the dramatic framework. The piece begins and ends with
a policeman delivering three blows with his club from the back of the
house, like the *trois coups* of the French theater. At the end of the play
three characters throw their fishing lines out into the audience; as Ron
Mottram suggests, this may be a signal that the audience, too, is "hung
up," as Stu says in his monologue about the fish and the fishermen,[11] for
the audience is in the position of the fish. Then again, this may be
another literalization or theatrical pun, since the action with the fishing
poles is also a "cast of characters." And in the play's concluding moments the cast faces the audience and breathes in and out in unison as Stu
exhorts the spectators to join in: "In your mouth and out your nose.
Ladies and gentlemen, it's fantastic!"[12] The characters are "teaching" the
audience members something that they obviously already know how to
do, and yet the act of breathing (another literalization of "rising and
falling action," as in *The Rock Garden?*) has also been rendered a theatrical feat, a quintessentially dramatic transformation of the ordinary into
the extraordinary: "Month after month of breathing until you can't stop.
Once you get the taste of it. The hang of it" (59).[13]

What is essential to the overt theatricality of these early plays is, of
course, the Shepardian performer: the Boy in *The Rock Garden,* Stu in
Chicago, the five friends who enact various microdramas in *Icarus's*

Mother, and Jim (as well as Carol and the Maid) in *Red Cross.* These performers are not the holistic or coherent characters of traditional theater; rather, they enact the postmodern condition of the fragmented subject. "Character" is a series of poses or identities instead of a centered, unified construct. The performing subject is split, like the endless series of mirrors in a funhouse, into multiple fictions.[14] There is no "real" character other than what is made available to us through performance. In these plays, then, the Shepardian actor is an actor without a subtext; he or she is existence without essence, a Brechtian "quotation" of character. Toby Zinman describes the "characterless"-ness of Shepard's characters thus:

> Since they [the characters] do not have identities, they cannot free themselves from them, but must perform some action merely to become somebody. . . . [They] try out various roles and bits . . . searching for the clichés which will temporarily create identity. This necessarily places an enormous burden upon the actors playing these characters, since they must imitate characters who are characterless, who try on and discard roles faster than costumes. Since there is no center, no body to dress, these roles must be performed as if the costumes themselves came temporarily to life.[15]

If character is a construct, it is above all a linguistic one, created not out of one voice but, rather, a multiplicity of voices; Leonard Wilcox calls this "polyphonic,"[16] though it also resembles Bakhtin's dialogism.[17] In *Chicago,* the striking stage image of Stu (fully clothed) in the bathtub already establishes him as the visual focus of our attention, but it is in his "polyphonic" monologues—in which he plays various roles, such as when he impersonates a little old lady—that he establishes himself as a character who has little existence outside of his own "performances." Joy (preparing to leave town to act in a role herself) and the other characters pay little attention to Stu, and so his audience is himself (and the spectators watching the play). His opening monologue, for instance, is a solipsistic exercise in sound and rhythm that seems improvised like a guitar riff or a child's play chant: "And ya' walk through the town. With yer head on the ground. And ya' look all around through the town fer yer dog. Your dog Brown" (47).

As the play continues, Stu becomes increasingly immersed in the creation of fictional worlds through his monologues as their imaginative flights go from the fish in the water to the passengers on a train, thus transferring the action of the play into his narratives.[18] His monologue sequence has the quality of a verbal version of the Open Theater's transformation exercises as well as the rapid juxtaposition of time and space that would result from the editing of a film. The emphasis on sensory experience—the split pea soup in the fishing boats, the smell of the fat man on the train, the licking and screaming and sweating of the people on the beach, and eventually, of course, the aforementioned breathing—becomes the obsessive motif of the monologues, perhaps also standing in ironic contrast to the static position of the speaker/performer, as Michael Bloom points out.[19] Stu describes a "you" on the beach that seems to be himself, or perhaps the audience members as he takes them with him, especially because of the intense emphasis on physical sensation:

> Your back shivers a little and you get goose bumps on your legs. Your toes start to sweat. The sweat runs down between your toes and your feet swell up and stick to your socks. You can't move because your feet are stuck. . . . The sweat runs down your arms and down your legs. You're looking out and you can see the water. You can see it in the dark because it's white. Like milk. . . . (58)

It is almost as if Stu, inert in the Shepardian role of performer, enacts the competing desire for sensory stimulation available only (in this play) through language. The words with which he "washes" himself in the bathtub become a vicarious means of satisfying that starvation, yet this induces a gluttony of words, as indulging in them begets the desire for more and more. He rejects the biscuits that Joy has made and that the other characters find so delicious; like the characters in the later *Curse of the Starving Class* (1978), Stu's hunger is situated in a more abstract realm despite the humorous stage presence of "real" food:

> Biscuits were invented to trick people into believing they're really eating food! They aren't any good at all. They're just dough. A hunk of dough that goes down and makes a gooey ball in your stomach. It makes you feel full. Biscuits are shit! (49)

Even Stu's rejection of the biscuits turns into the "food" of evocative monologic language; if he is the consummate Shepardian performer, he is also consuming and being consumed by his own speech.[20] Similarly, the Boy's speech *about* sex in *The Rock Garden* seems to be a substitute for sex itself, and *Icarus's Mother* opens with the characters belching after having stuffed themselves at a picnic, but they then launch into their storytelling with a ravenousness, as if their satiation from the picnic has left them with an insatiable appetite for language.[21]

The real "events" of *Icarus's Mother* consist solely of this storytelling; the characters construct the action for the spectators by talking about it rather than participating in it physically.[22] The climactic aria of the play (which narrates, rather than allows us to see, the pivotal event of the plane crashing into the water) is Frank's; in startling detail he tells Bill and Howard about the explosion he has supposedly witnessed, with an emphasis on his idea that "You guys should have been there!"[23]

> And the windows cracking and the wings tearing off. Going through seagulls now, it's so close. Heading straight for the top of the flat blue water. Almost touching in slow motion and blowing itself up six inches above sea level to the dismay of ducks bobbing along. And lighting up the air with a gold tint and a yellow tint and smacking the water so that waves go up to five hundred feet in silver white and blue. . . . (78–79)

Frank's narration is more vivid than any stage depiction of an explosion could possibly be, and yet the accompanying sound and light effects of booming and flashing (as well as the noise of a gradually increasing crowd) seem to give his story "authenticity." Yet, despite Jill's attempt to find verification for it, even Frank's story arguably belongs in the realm of the other "fictions" of the play. The stage directions indicate that Frank remains "oblivious to everything but what he's saying" (78), as the booms, colored lightning flashes, and crowd noises increase, suggesting that his *narration* of the event is somehow different from the event itself. Or perhaps the implication is that Frank's storytelling is of paramount importance and that the booms and flashes are simply Shepard's literalized, dramatized, external manifestation of this narrative; neither possibility is confirmed (or denied) by the time that the play concludes.

At the heart of *Icarus's Mother*, then, is the circling of its storytellers around their subject, their behavior of "telling" without ever really "showing." Not once in the play (as in Beckett's *Waiting for Godot*) do we ever see its central character, the pilot; his existence depends solely on the narration.[24] If, as Michael Smith suggests in his production notes, *Icarus's Mother* is essentially a play about fear (especially fear of the bomb),[25] then the narrative structure replicates this theme. The storytelling and microdramas enacted by the characters, even the technical disquisitions, are all attempts to explain the irrational and speak the unspeakable, but the fictions that the characters create remain "open" in characteristically postmodern fashion, rather than moving toward the satisfying closure of traditional theatrical plot. The play treats the ultimate fear of what *could* happen, especially as signaled (e.g., the pilot's own "text," his reported skywriting of "$E = mc^2$") by the threat of nuclear holocaust. The immersion in fiction and storytelling—and, ultimately, in acting things out, in theater—becomes a way of playing with/dramatizing this fear without having to enact the "real thing."

In *Red Cross* Carol's monologue about her fear/fantasy of her head bursting open becomes, like Stu's monologues in *Chicago,* increasingly sensational, as she describes what will happen as her head rolls down the hill and "become[s] a huge snowball and roll[s] into the city and kill[s] a million people."[26] Unexpectedly, though, Shepard indicates in the stage directions that, while Carol is performing the monologue, she should act it out "as though she were skiing on a mountain slope" (124). This physicalization of her speech has an interesting dual effect. On the one hand, the spectator dislocates her a bit more from the scene of the cabin because she seems to be "traveling"—through both narration and gesture—into another "setting." There is, on the other hand, a Brechtian distancing involved: Carol's physical enactment of the skiing in the setting of the cabin calls all the more attention to the fact that she is *not* actually on a skiing trip but, rather, is performing a monologue about a skiing trip. Our sense that we are witnessing a kind of performance is heightened by our awareness of the incongruity of her action with the scenic context. By showing us these polarities of narration and physical enactment, Shepard engages in the attempt to determine the point of *theatrical* intersection between the literal and the figurative, the presentable and the unpresentable.

Jacques Levy, who directed the original production of *Red Cross* at the Judson Poets' Theater, writes that he encouraged the actors to "follow to the limits the specific intention of a moment in the play"; he compares this to a black-and-white movie that occasionally bursts into color.[27] We can see this in the play's central sequence, the encounter

between Jim and the Maid. For most of the scene Jim overwhelms the
Maid with a barrage of verbosity, as he tries to give her a swimming
lesson (on the bed). As Ren Frutkin says, Jim's instructive narrative is
"really a lesson in talking about swimming, a lesson in imagination."[28]
But the Maid shows Jim that, while she may not be able to follow his
swimming instructions very well, she can outdo him at his own game
as a storyteller:

> You move through the water like you were born in that very same
> place and never even knew what land was like. You dive and float
> and sometimes rest on the bank and maybe chew on some water-
> cress. And the family in town forgets where you went and the
> swimming coach forgets who you are and *you* forget all about
> swimming lessons and just swim without knowing how and before
> you know it the winter has come and the lake has frozen and you
> sit on the bank staring at the ice . . . until you don't feel a thing.
> (136–37)

The Maid has captured Jim's narration of an actual physical activity and
has transposed it into her own imaginative discourse; she has stolen the
role of performer away from him—as Levy puts it, "she ha[s] left Jim
back in the quagmire of his own making, left him back at the launching
pad"—a transformation underscored in the production by having her
address the audience directly during this speech.[29] Jim's goal is to make
the Maid "swim"—but on a bed; the Maid's goal is to go one step further
and explore the sensation of drowning—but through words. Both of
them, then, conflate, or merge, the figurative and the literal, though it
is no surprise that, given the larger (and more "literal") *theatrical* context
of their world, what triumphs is the imagination possible through language, as embodied in the Maid's monologue. Yet the blood that suddenly runs down Jim's forehead at the end of the play gives this "victory" of figurative language a new twist, for it represents an inexplicable
visual embodiment (a literalization) of the kind of image that up to this
point had only been *imagined* (and had been foreshadowed by Carol's
description of the bleeding head in the snow). Shepard says that he sees
"[w]ords as tools of imagery in motion";[30] in effect, *Red Cross* brings
these words to life (another "literalization") by staging an image such as
that of Jim's bleeding head.

   The competing emphasis on the dramatization of textuality, sometimes taken to the point of parody, is particularly striking in Shepard's "technical" monologues. In *Icarus's Mother* Howard delivers a lengthy monologue that begins with a textbook-like description of the sensation of flying ("Jets fly at an altitude of approximately five thousand feet and move at a minimum of approximately five hundred miles an hour . . . " [68]) and becomes more visual and personal ("But even inside your closed eyes you can see the same thing as before. Miles and miles of cow pasture and city and town. Like a movie . . . " [69]). Even in *Red Cross* Jim's initial swimming instructions to the Maid resemble a text: "A paddle has a broad surface and reaches its highest point of thrust when it is perpendicular to the surface line of the water. This is the way you should use your arms . . . " (133). *Fourteen Hundred Thousand* is perhaps the most extreme version of this substitution of language for experience, as the characters resemble little more than talking "texts." The play seems to be about the struggle between content (i.e., the text of the play and its significance) and structure (i.e., its surface composition and the effects of this composition).

The characters in *Fourteen Hundred Thousand* create narrative texts yet refuse to allow a penetration into the "meanings" of their stories. Donna, for whom the other characters are helping to build an enormous bookcase, indicates that she wants the books lined up with attention to structure and shape rather than content:

> And it could be so lovely, too. So very pleasing to the eyeball. With various sizes and shapes and groups together. Without concern for what they're about or what they mean to me and who wrote them when. Just in terms of size and shape and color.[31]

Perhaps the play itself (or Shepard's early work in general) is an analogue for the way Donna intends to display her books. Rather than using the theatrical setting (the bookcase) for the purpose of coherent organization and linear narrative, the setting/bookcase becomes a frame for visual/imagistic pleasure, and for randomness, free play, openness to multiple interpretations or configurations. A reliance on texts nevertheless is present, but the relationship to the text is a (re)visionary one.

It is striking, finally, that the monologues—the embedded texts—in *Fourteen Hundred Thousand* return repeatedly to images of dehumanization and inertia. One narrative is about a cabin that somehow maintains itself without any human intervention: "There's no footprints around it

at all" (110). Another, which echoes parts of Stu's narrative in *Chicago,*
is Donna's threat to Tom about the consequences of *his* inertia:

> The bed will be your house and home and your head will be glued
> to the pillow. Your arms will be stuck to the sheet and your legs
> will be paralyzed from the hip down. You can't turn your head
> because you drool from the mouth and pus will run out your nose.
> Your eyes fill up with water and pour over onto your cheeks and
> each ear hums from hearing nothing. You lie in pools of urine and
> feces for days on end until the bed and you become one whole thing.
> One whole thing and there's no way of telling where the bed stops
> and you begin. (115)

Just as Tom, by the end of this monologue, is described as indistinguish-
able from his bed, the two choral "readings" that end the play reinforce
this objectification, the literalized reduction of individual "character" to
a textualized series of shapes and designs. This is echoed theatrically in
the presentation of these closing speeches. In the first, Mom and Pop
begin to recite a story about the snow, and the other characters join in
so that they are reciting it in unison; the text concerns the people's failure
to react as the snow falls down and gradually covers them up entirely.
The final narrative is an architect's vision of a (modernist?) linear city,
its dehumanized qualities echoing the way the figures of the first story
"stood in a line looking straight ahead" (116). This linear city is dazzling
in the stark absoluteness of its vision and in the near poetic rendering of
its recitative description:

> Cities enclosed in glass to see the sky.
> Forming one-mile squares.
> Cities in the sky to see the glass.
> Forming squares in between.
>
> (119)

In another sense, though, there is something terrifying about this vision,
for implicit in the linear city is a kind of homogeneity, a reduction of its
inhabitants to the status of the people lost in the snow in the preceding
story. The gridlike structure of the network of linear cities resembles the
design of the giant bookcase, suggesting (if the text about the city is one

of those that will be placed in the bookcase) an endless replication or reduplication of this vision, an infinite series of texts within texts.

Fourteen Hundred Thousand begins with characters whose conversations seem disordered and random, but also real; by the end of the play they have become choral figures, "agents" of the (play's) text whose duty it is to read and recite, not to act. In other words, the structure of the play reflects the dehumanization narrated in the texts that we hear within the play's fictional world. Shepard, then, shows us what happens when characters are stripped of their characters and are made into vehicles for texts, for stylized utterance. We might say that the same is true, to some extent, for all of these early works. The plays, as a result, pull us back and forth between our investment in "signification" and our enjoyment of their surfaces and structures. We might even say that they enact the Brechtian refusal (as appropriated by postmodernism) to "engage" the reader or spectator, preferring instead to keep him or her aware of their processes, their machinery, their status as (performative) texts.

The Prison-House of Pop Culture: Shepard's Risky Mythmaking, 1967–76

> DOCTOR: You see the territory he travels in. He's perfectly capable of living in several worlds at the same time. This is his genius.
> CODY: I was just bluffin'! Honest! I made it all up! I got no magic! I was just pretending!
> —Sam Shepard, *Geography of a Horse Dreamer*

> The cowboy dressed in fringe with buckskin gloves, silk bandana, pale clown white make up, lipstick, eyes thickly made up and a ten gallon hat, holds the reins of his horse decked out in silver studs. The cowboy squints under hot spotlights. The gaffers all giggle. The cowboy sweats but there's nowhere for the sweat to go. He sinks to his knees and screams: "Forgive me Utah! Forgive me!"
> —Sam Shepard, "Hollywood," in *Hawk Moon*

The plays that Sam Shepard wrote during the period from 1967 (the year of *Melodrama Play,* his first of the "rock plays") to 1976 (the year of *Angel City* and *Suicide in B♭*) belong to what might be termed his "pop culture" phase.[32] All, or nearly all, of the plays of this period reveal an apparent infatuation with the contemporary mythology that the

American collective unconscious has populated with images of cowboys, gangsters and detectives, movie stars and rock stars, and even creatures from outer space. I have discussed the postmodern interest in and appropriation of popular culture; postmodern artists draw at will from the images and technology of television, cinema, advertising, pop music, and so forth. But this investment in popular culture is not by any means an unquestioning one; for example, Warhol's series of Campbell Soup cans or Lichtenstein's comic strip paintings simultaneously pay homage to their sources and parody them.[33] Linda Hutcheon and others remind us that parody is integral to postmodernism; as Hutcheon says, "Parody seems to offer a perspective on the present and the past which allows an artist to speak *to* a discourse from *within* it, but without being totally recuperated by it."[34]

Much of the criticism of Shepard's plays of this period seems to be just as enamored of the icons of pop culture as Shepard's characters are—hence, the tendency to write "critiques" of these works that are in large part stylized imitations of Shepard's own language.[35] The temptation to do so can be powerful, and the results can be engrossing, but I will argue that an immersion in such readings ultimately loses track of Shepard's complicated, often ironic stance toward the characters who do his storytelling for him. At the heart of these plays is the sense that stories are performances and poses. Since pop culture appears to be an endless source of inspiration for these works, the extent to which this betrays a *nostalgia* for a kind of 1950s American pie mythology (similar to that described by the Kid in *The Unseen Hand* [1969]) has been a vexed question among Shepard critics. Too often, they have tended to see Shepard's turn toward an idealized American past as nostalgic, rather than recognizing that his interest in the past is, like that of other postmodernist artists, more critical and parodic than it is nostalgic. Lynda Hart, for instance, describes Shepard's "modernist desire to cling nostalgically to the structures of the past."[36] George Stambolian sees this a slightly different way; he insists that Shepard's *Mad Dog Blues* (1971) is an example of an immersion in popular culture that suggests nostalgia rather than parody but that such an immersion also results in a kind of (Baudrillardian?) saturation of images that leads to the envisioning of even more and more popular culture images, resulting in a kind of "disease."[37] Yet, as Hutcheon points out, postmodernism's view of the past refuses nostalgia because it is always shaped by the distance imposed upon it by the present.[38] To view Shepard's interest in popular culture as nostalgic, then, is to take his characters at face value. It is only by keeping in mind Shepard's insistence on the theatrical quality of his approach, which is accompanied by a postmodernist fragmentation of the speaking subject as it manifests itself in monologic language, that we share his overwhelmingly ironic and parodic vision of American mythology.

Shepard's earliest plays return repeatedly to the concern with their status as theatrical events performed before an audience, and this concern continues to manifest itself in the works of this "middle phase." In *Melodrama Play* (1967), for instance, when Duke finishes singing at the beginning of the play, he bows to the audience,[39] and Dana's wail to Duke, "You've thrown the letter into the audience" (119), recalls Joe's line in the earlier *4-H Club* (1965) regarding the hosing down of the apartment: "It would probably wash the stove out into the audience."[40] In the midst of his metatheatricality, though, Shepard also demonstrates an ambivalence toward the power of the theater: as the slightly later *Action* (1975) will show, he is as fascinated with the limits of what language can accomplish onstage as he is with its possibilities. Monologue, with its paradoxically "unstageable" qualities of subsuming physical action and altering both linear narrative and the perception of time, continues to be the vehicle for Shepard's explorations. The monologues in these plays are intertextual, taking on the rhythm of rock music, the spontaneity of jazz, the fluidity of film, and the craziness of science fiction. But they also return to a constant preoccupation with *performance,* including a more explicit acknowledgment of the role of the performing artist, who is often in these works a kind of surrogate *bricoleur,* mining the landscapes of pop culture and of theatricality itself, in search of the right texts.

While many of Shepard's dramas of the early 1970s (including *Cowboy Mouth* [1971], which he cowrote with Patti Smith) involve this intertextual assemblage of pop culture images in a kind of postmodernist collage, the most striking of these in terms of a fascination with pop culture's *fiction making* potential are *The Unseen Hand* (1969), *The Tooth of Crime* (1972), and *Angel City* (1976). In *The Unseen Hand* Shepard uses images culled from popular culture to enact a subversive (though, on the surface, nostalgic) network of interresponsive monologues. The various monologues spoken by Willie and by the crybaby cheerleader named the Kid reinforce the idea that throughout the play, different "fictions," or intertexts, are revealed to contain their own oppositions. One means by

which Shepard accomplishes this is to allow the clearly fictional to acknowledge its own "fabricated" status, as in Willie's hocus-pocus
speech, when he makes Cisco materialize from the dead. His words are
a series of vaguely technical terms (cf. the "technical" monologues in
Icarus's Mother and other early plays), many chosen from rock music
technology, selected for their sounds and rhythms rather than their
meanings (anticipating the stylized language of *The Tooth of Crime*):
"Hypo filament. Didactachrome! Resolve! Resolve! Resolve! Reverb!
Fuzz tone! Don't let the feedback in! Feed it back!"[41] Because Willie is
presented as a mythologized figure, painted in broad, cartoonlike
strokes, there is no need to make his hocus-pocus seem credible or even
believably mystical. The case of the Kid, though, is slightly more complicated. When he launches into his speech about the tactics of guerilla
warfare ("The guerilla band is an armed nucleus, the fighting vanguard
of the people. It draws its great force from the mass of the people
themselves," [25]) we, like Blue and the others, initially take the Kid at
his word. But it turns out that this text has no meaning for the Kid and
that he is simply reciting material he claims to have learned in school in
order to gain control over his captors. Here, then, like the history books
that Blue mentions earlier, the recitation seems confined to the level of
the purely (inter)textual, rather than attaining the status of the "enacted"
fiction.

The play's pivotal movement between different types of fictions
comes when the Kid recites his "I love Azusa" speech and Willie finally
frees himself from the power of the "unseen hand" by reciting in an
"ancient language," which is actually the Kid's speech with the words
spelled backwards. The Kid's monologue is an homage to American
boyhood, with his insistence that he loves "the county fair and peanut
butter and jelly sandwiches and the high-school band and going steady
and KFWB and white bucks . . . " (28). He creates another iconography,
another story, just as he did with the account of the guerilla warfare
tactics—only the difference this time is that the Kid believes this second
story is true and that he is providing an accurate picture of his world.
Willie's ability to free himself by literally inverting these romanticized
"American" images suggests that his liberty derives from a subversion
or inversion of this myth of an idealized American adolescence. It is
crucial to note, however, that Willie's transformation comes by *adopting*
(perhaps parodying) rather than destroying the Kid's iconography, just
as postmodernist art seeks to appropriate and rewrite the texts and myths

of the past. In fact, Shepard's stage directions indicate that, even when the Kid tries to shoot him, Willie "continues, accumulating incredible power from the language he speaks" (28).

Willie's capacity to draw strength from the simultaneous subversion/inversion of a set of icons drawn from the mythology of the American dream is not unlike the process that Shepard enacts through the appropriation and "redirection" of cultural images (e.g., the cowboy) throughout the play. Willie's speech is rendered a bit more complicated, though, by the difference between text and performance: while the reader can recognize immediately that the words are simply those of the Kid spelled backwards and recited in reverse order, the *spectator* will probably only recognize this at the end of Willie's speech, if at all. Shepard seems to be toying with the extent to which he can subordinate the play's own iconography to the larger control he holds as dramatist/ author, a recurrent postmodernist preoccupation (see, for instance, John Fowles's *The French Lieutenant's Woman*).[42] In this respect Sycamore's affirmation of his freedom at the end of the play is a paradoxical one; he says, "That's the great thing about this country, ya' know. The fact that you can make yer own moves in yer own time without some guy behind the scenes pullin' the switches on ya'" (32). This reference to the machinery of the stage, as well as the return to the monologue "frame" in which Sycamore has replaced Blue, implies that, despite his affirmation of freedom, he is controlled by the "unseen hand" of the playwright. At the same time, though, the spectators' ability to accept the multiple fictional worlds of the play depends on viewing those intertextual worlds as fluid and expansive, able to contain paradoxes.

Shepard develops an even more complex approach to the relationship between the creation of pop culture "fictions" and the role of theatrical language in *The Tooth of Crime*. More than any other Shepard play, *The Tooth of Crime* has been the focus of discussions of Shepard's (postmodernist) attraction to pop culture. This is a play *about* language, but also about the possibilities and limitations inherent in an appropriation of the language of pop culture. Since the venues of the rock star and the cowboy[43]—combined and set in a sci-fi future to form the world of *The Tooth of Crime*—are ultimately dependent upon style, Shepard uses the languages and theatric(k)s of this milieu to foreground style: the play contains everything from gangster talk to blues dialect to Crow's invented hip-speech ("Razor, Leathers. Very razor").[44]

Hoss opens the play with a Brechtian-style prologue that suggests the openly theatrical quality of the performance the audience is about to witness:[45]

> So here's another sleep-walkin' dream
> A livin' talkin' show of the way things seem. . . .
>
> (203)

Like the "Moritat of Mackie the Knife" that opens Brecht's *Threepenny Opera,* though, this prologue has a certain ominousness underneath its presentational quality; as Bruce Powe suggests, it also serves as "an admonition to the audience to watch out, to catch what happens when what 'seems to be' is pushed to extremes."[46]

Although Hoss and Crow are depicted as two warring characters, it is clear that Shepard means to illustrate that they are actually parts of the "divided self," the fractured or split subject; this is a recurrent image in such plays as *Angel City* and *Suicide in B♭.* Hoss reveals this division in his high school story about Moose; he says: "We're fightin' ourselves. Just like turnin' the blade on ourselves. Suicide, man" (224). Similarly, the "Slips Away" song contains a picture that also echoes Vince's revelations in the later *Buried Child:*

> If we could signify from far away
> Just close enough to get the touch
> You'd find your face in mine
> And all my faces tryin' to bring you back to me.
>
> (248)

The play's structure enacts this notion of split subjectivity; Hoss's frequent monologues in act 1 bring to mind the definition of monologic speech as a dialogue that one conducts with oneself, especially as his monologues move from soliloquies to a duel with a dummy that bleeds to an imaginary dialogue with his father, all of which prefigure the dialogues with Crow in the second act. Crow even physicalizes this image of the split, or divided, subject in his duel with Hoss; the referee declares a TKO in the third round after Crow describes Hoss's "fear that he's crackin' busted in two. Busted in three parts. Busted in four. Busted and dyin' and cryin' for more" (241).

Furthermore, in one of the oddest moments of the play Becky speaks a monologue in which she acts out both the male and the female roles in an attempted seduction; this is another example of the "duet for one" that (here, literally) embodies the divided subject. Becky's speech is a reminder of the extent to which subjectivity in this play is constru(ct)ed by role playing; Hoss says to her earlier, "Ya' know, you'd be O.K., Becky, if you had a self. So would I. Something to fall back on in a moment of doubt or terror or even surprise" (225). Leonard Wilcox sees a connection between this loss of a grounded subjectivity and the destabilizing of discourse in the play:

> [*The Tooth of Crime*] in fact expresses the postmodern sense that the subject is constituted in language and discourse, and as signifiers "float" the self becomes unanchored; where such slippage of signification occurs, the self, radically ungrounded, brings itself into being through words, casting out verbal filaments in an expression of desire and power to "mark" its discursive space. This is exactly what occurs in the language duel.[47]

Subjectivity is complicated, however, in a world in which Crow's "flash" (his investment in surfaces, theatricality, images) is destined to triumph over Hoss's "heart" (his emotionalism, his nostalgia for a golden age of rock'n'roll, his patriarchal role as the long-standing conqueror in the play's mysterious "game"). Crow, who inhabits the theatricalized region of style almost exclusively, tells Hoss, "The image is my survival kit" (249), and he sings, "I believe in my mask—The man I made up is me" (232). Hoss, on the other hand, seeks a "solid form," something "sure and final," and it becomes increasingly impossible for him to know "where [he] stand[s]" as he is "pulled and pushed around from one image to another" (243). The play itself replicates this dialectical struggle between flash and heart. Wilcox creates a convincing argument that Hoss represents a modernist desire for essence and identity, while Crow symbolizes the postmodern world of "immaculate surfaces" and "pop intertextuality."[48] He suggests that the play's battle between Hoss and Crow embodies Shepard's own ambivalence in the war of modernist and postmodernist aesthetics, ending in a problematized victory of postmodernist culture.

According to Wilcox, Shepard is "uneasy with the postmodern condition" because an ultimate immersion in the discourses of popular culture can also imply the dissolution of a center, an identity (as enacted through Hoss's suicide).[49] Indeed, the play's final movement into the stage directions indicating that Hoss's suicide should be enacted through "courage" rather than "jive theatrical gimmicks" (249), implies that, to a certain extent, Shepard modifies the fullness of Crow's victory. Yet it is impossible to say that in a piece as dependent upon surface, theatricality, and style as *The Tooth of Crime,* heart takes precedence. Crow's survivability is envisioned almost as a form of natural selection: Hoss tells him, "You're a master adapter. A visionary adapter" (249). Wilcox argues:

> There is a terrible inevitability in the defeat of the modernist Hoss by the postmodern Crow. . . . If Shepard's language desires to return to its origins in myth and ritual, its decentered play and pop intertextuality puts these origins into question. If his plays use popular culture as a source of constitutive myths, they do so with an awareness that these myths no longer contain plenitude. *The Tooth of Crime* is situated irretrievably in the postmodern world with its profound doubleness of exaltation and terror, where the ungrounding of the signifier both inaugurates sensual play as well as the "play" of a rhetoric of power and a language of madness.[50]

Wilcox does well to indicate Shepard's refusal in this play to "side" fully with Hoss's "modernism" or Crow's "postmodernism." Yet, in his development of this argument, Wilcox seems to view Crow's victory as a kind of victory of necessity in a world in which there is no turning back from the ascension of Crow's/postmodernism's discursive modes. To envision the play this way is, I think, to place too much weight upon Shepard's nostalgia *for* modernism as embodied in Hoss. While it is true that Shepard makes Hoss, as the protagonist, the agent for sympathy in this play, Wilcox might have done more to account for the complications of the way we are ultimately led to see Hoss's situation. Unable to maintain his position, Hoss is usurped by an antagonist who *refuses* to become a carbon copy of his predecessor, insisting instead that he will play a new game of his own: "I'm runnin' flat out to a new course" (250). But the irony of the play's final moments—as well as the reminder that Hoss and Crow may actually signify a splitting of the same subject—comes about through Crow's appropriation of the keys to Hoss's Maserati (a reminder that postmodernist discourse is "driven" by images and signals from the past?), and through the other characters' relative indifference to Hoss's demise: Becky and Cheyenne both praise Hoss for having been "a true Marker" (250), but they seem fully prepared to accept his death as an inevitability.

In *Angel City* Shepard again theatricalizes pop culture and explores it through the fragmented subject. In his preface to this piece, he writes that he has come up with a new, collage-like, or jazzlike, conception of character in this play that involves "a fractured whole with bits and pieces of character flying off the central theme," rather than a traditionally constructed unified notion of character.[51] Early on, in the discussion of the movie that Lanx and Wheeler want Rabbit to help create, Lanx insists that their film seems to be missing a meaningful character. He says, "It has to somehow transcend the very idea of 'character' as we know it today" (67)—almost the same words that Shepard uses in his preface. Obviously, there is a rather complex (and typically postmodern) game being played here, for the play replicates and parodies many of the same "Hollywood" formulas that it purports to criticize.

At the opening of the play, for instance, Rabbit wanders into the studio office and hears Lanx's narration; like the audience, he does not understand its source or context (Lanx is hidden in the swivel chair and uses a microphone) until Lanx swivels around and asks him what he thinks of it "as pure narration" (65). The moment is not unlike several moments in Beckett's *Endgame* in which Hamm follows his dramatic recitations with comments on his own performance. Lanx's question creates a kind of Brechtian rupture of the "seamless" dramatic moment. But such a rupture, we learn, is to be expected in a fictional Hollywood—and, consequently, in a play that parodies this Hollywood—where appearances are mere facades; as Lanx says to Rabbit, "That's one a' the first things you learn around here. Nothing is the way it appears to be" (70). The very nature of monologic language complicates the play's sense that "nothing is the way it appears to be," for such speeches are nearly always infused with a dual sense of confessional revelation, of a confidence to the audience, and of performing or recitation. Since reciting a monologue to the audience means taking on a stance that underscores the character's status as an actor in a play, and since this particular play calls repeated attention to the artificial nature of acting, the play is continually doubling back on itself as its insistence on the unreliability of fictionmaking renders its own narrative and structural devices elusive and problematic.

The play's concern with trancelike states—Tympani has been hired to find the percussive rhythm guaranteed to hypnotize mass audiences,

and Miss Scoons goes repeatedly into trances in which other voices seem
to speak through her—reinforces the simultaneous immersion in Holly-
wood-style "trashy" narrative and the Brechtian distancing or commen-
tary/"quotation." For instance, Miss Scoons recites her monologue
about the desire and frustration that come with an identification with the
movies in what appears to be a "hypnotic state":

> I look at the screen and I am the screen. I'm not me. I don't know
> who I am. I look at the movie and I am the movie. I am the star.
> For days I am the star and I'm not me. I'm me being the star. . . .
> (77)

Scoons speaks these lines "in a kind of flattened monotone" (77). She has
been "hypnotized" by the silver screen and all of its promises, but the
speech also suggests that her character steps outside of itself in order to
characterize this hypnosis.[52]

The speech enacts a Brechtian split subjectivity in which the subject
is embodied and disembodied at the same time. Florence Falk suggests
an interesting parallel between the "I" and the "eye" in the speech: just
as the screen is both "means and end, agent and godhead," it is also true
that "the 'I' that regards the image simultaneously is the image."[53] In
this trancelike state the subject enacts what both Deleuze and Baudrillard
describe as the schizophrenic experience of pure receptivity in which the
body acts as "a kind of body-sieve" (Deleuze) or "a switching center for
all the networks of influence" (Baudrillard).[54] Baudrillard's metaphor is
particularly apt for a play in which cinematic technology pervades and
"enters" the bodies of the characters. As the surrogate spectator, the
character risks being lost in the hypnotic world of the image; Tympani
suggests going to the movies, buying candy, and "chew[ing] ourselves
straight into oblivion" (96), while Wheeler hysterically conjures the opposite image—namely, that the movies are devouring *him:* "THEY'RE IN
MY BLOOD! . . . AND THEY CAN'T GET OUT! EVERY ONE OF THEM IS
TEARING ME APART! CHEWING AT THE WALLS! . . . TRYING TO OOZE OUT
AND TAKE ON A SHAPE THAT WE ALL CAN SEE!" (100). The movies are
a device to be consumed, but the consumer also risks being consumed
by them; this is what Baudrillard refers to as the "obscene delirium of
communication."[55]

The sequence in which Wheeler narrates an alleged segment from
his top-secret movie project, which serves as a play-within-the-play as

Miss Scoons and Lanx act out the parts of two warring generals, suggests a theatricalization of the play's dialectics. Wheeler says, "At last the generals saw their situation. They were one being with two opposing parts" (108). The two generals are like Hoss and Crow in *The Tooth of Crime*, or, in this case, like Rabbit and Wheeler, the "real" artist and the moviemaker. When Rabbit protests this idea that the two are, as Wheeler insists, "the same" (102), Wheeler responds, "I was created without my knowing. Same as you. Creation's a disease. . . . We're dying here. Right now. In front of each other" (102). This is a metatheatrical moment in the sense that Wheeler's statement about the two characters having been "created without [our] knowing" points to their status as creations of the playwright. His sense that they are "dying . . . [i]n front of each other" also echoes Herbert Blau's reminder that the fascination of theater comes from the (corpo)reality of the actor, who "can die there in front of your eyes; [who] is in fact doing so."[56]

Moreover, Shepard ends *Angel City* with Lanx and Miss Scoons enacting the parts of teenagers watching a movie in a manner that implies they could also be in a movie themselves (the final stage direction has the sax "filling in softly over the scene" [111]). The audience, then, watches Miss Scoons and Lanx watching Wheeler and Rabbit in a "movie"; Wheeler appears to be referring to both sets of spectators when he shouts: "Right now there's people watching! . . . As long as they're watching I'll be remembered!" (110). As C. W. E. Bigsby says, the "framing" of the ending turns into "an insistence that the play itself hardly differs from the movie which they have supposedly been creating," which implies that "it ends . . . in parody, in a metatheatrical gesture which decreates the text just established."[57] The moment is in this way a quintessentially postmodern one, for the pop culture milieu (the cinema) is simultaneously evoked, viewed from an ironic perspective, and deconstructed.

Angel City thus embodies the highly stylized and somewhat satiric cultural mythology of *The Unseen Hand* and *The Tooth of Crime*, but it also incorporates the more overtly phenomenological approach of the slightly earlier *Action* and the slightly later *Suicide in B♭*. More than any of the other works of this "middle" period of Shepard's playwriting, *Action* uses the metaphor of performance in an existential fashion. Its four characters—Shooter, Jeep, Lupe, and Liza—show both the possibilities and the limitations of "acting." Like Vladimir and Estragon in Beckett's *Waiting for Godot* or like Hamm and Clov in *Endgame*, the stage

space inhabited by these characters is a desolate environment that offers
no escape. Shepard had toyed earlier with the idea of a theatricalized
"imprisonment" in *Melodrama Play*. For example, at one point in that
piece Peter attempts to transcend its generic constraints by suggesting
to Drake that he improvise:

> And then you say whatever just comes into your head in that split
> second. Whatever happens to be sitting there in your memory of
> the second before and it just spiels out trippingly off the tongue. It
> just gushes out in its most accurate way. Word for word, without
> a moment's hesitation to calculate where it's going or how or why.
> It just falls out into the air and disappears as soon as it's heard.
> That's what I want to hear! That's what I want you to say to me.
> Right now, before it's too late! (141)

The ironic nature of these lines—in a manner similar to what occurs,
according to Silvio Gaggi, with Pirandello's *Tonight We Improvise*
(1930)[58]—is that they, along with what follows, are scripted; in other
words, *true* improvisation does not transpire. The characters of *Melodrama Play* are imprisoned within both their "theatrical" circumstances
and, at least ostensibly, within the genre of melodrama that the play,
however mockingly, has assigned itself.

In *Action* the characters appear to be living under primitive circumstances in an isolated cabin after some unidentified "crisis," possibly a
nuclear one.[59] The images of a postnuclear world come to us primarily
from the characters' references to the text that they have been reading
but in which they are unable to identify their place, just as they themselves (perhaps because they are only characters and therefore have no
real embodiment except in the present moment of performance) cannot
locate a "place"—a past, present, or future—for their actions. In their
(futile) efforts to find their place in their text, they ask, "Were we past
the part where the comet exploded?" (171); "Was it just after the fall of
the Great Continent?" (175); and so forth. In many ways this situation
and imagery are reminiscent of *Icarus's Mother*, again in which the characters are only able to act vicariously through a discourse that has implications beyond their comprehension. In *Action*, though, the connection
between this strangely decimated space that the characters inhabit, and
their status as actors who have no clear directions about how to act, is
rendered more explicit.[60]

As a result, the characters' search for their place in the book, along with the other physical actions they undertake in the course of the play—the turkey dinner, Lupe's gnawing on her arm, Jeep's pouring of the water over his hands, Shooter's scratching of his legs—become ways of attempting to avoid this stasis. But Shooter's story about the man who is disconnected from what his body does, like a walking corpse, is all too applicable. The characters are able to narrate their imprisonment, but they do not have the subjectivity that would allow them to transcend it. In a key monologue Shooter provides an account of where he and the others seem to stand:

> You go outside. The world is quiet. White. Everything resounding. Not a sound of a motor. Not a light. You see into the house. You see the candles. You watch the people. You can see what it's like inside. The candles draw you. You get a cold feeling being outside. Separated. You have an idea that being inside it's cosier. Friendlier. Warmth. People. Conversation. Everyone using a language. Then you go inside. It's a shock. It's not like how you expected. You lose what you had outside. You forget that there even is an outside. The inside is all you know. You hunt for a way of being with everyone. A way of finding how to behave. You find out what's expected of you. You act yourself out. (178)

Shooter's words reflect his essential disembodiment, a disembodiment shared by the other characters. He is unable to "escape" because his speech remains at the level of narration rather than enactment. As in Fredric Jameson's description of the schizophrenic's entrapment, he has lost a sense of "I" or "me" that continues through time and is instead isolated in a perpetual (theatrical) present.[61] His eventual retreat into the armchair is an effort to become merely a spectator, but once again he finds that he cannot be satisfied on the outside or on the inside; "I'm nowhere," he says (184).[62]

It is only in the final moments of the play, when Jeep begins to respond to the process of speaking a monologue about himself, that we get a glimpse of the ability of language to bestow subjectivity. Jeep tells about the terror he felt as he realized that he was a prisoner within a jail and within himself. At first the speech appears to have the same qualities as the play's other narratives—that is, it seems to be yet another "disembodied" recitation that maintains the status quo of the characters' inaction.[63] This time, however, Shepard provides a new type of stage direction for his character:

> The words animate him as though the space is the cell he's talking about but not as though he's recalling a past experience but rather that he's attempting his own escape from the space he's playing in. (190)

Again, as a character, Jeep only exists in the present moment, and so his animation does not, as Shepard specifies, stem from memory. But this is also the only point in the play during which the performer's words and his or her manipulation of the playing space merge to the extent that the experience is enacted as Jeep tries to break out of his imprisonment as a performer to become a creator. He follows, almost literally, Shooter's earlier words: he "acts himself out," meaning that he acts to "escape from the space he's playing in."

Just as Peter's exhortation to improvise fails in *Melodrama Play*, however, Jeep's effort does not prove strong enough to break through the entrapment of the theatrical frame (Shepard's text and the stage upon which it is performed), and he "just stands there" after saying, "I had no idea what the world was. I had no idea how I got there or why or who did it. I had no references for this" (19). Without "references" (*référents*), it seems, the characters do not know how to perform or behave. Shepard, then, seems to be suggesting the paradox—the Derridean *aporia*, or unpassable path[64]—that forms when language in the theatrical frame attempts to escape its own prison of "pretending," or performance, given that the confinement of the dramatic setting is unavoidable. David Savran sees this paradox as the essential problem with Shepard's work; he argues that, since the prison that Jeep creates includes everything, Shepard "fails to recognize that this impossible extension . . . confines nothing."[65] While Savran's point is a convincing one, I would argue that it is precisely Shepard's *illusion* of theatrical imprisonment that allows both an ironic rendering of theatrical inescapability and the paradoxical attempt at perpetual escape by means of the "untheatrical" narrativity of the monologues.

While *Angel City* and *Action* both end with a suggestion of Pirandellian boxes-within-boxes, of an inevitable return to theatricality as the source of both imaginative escape and imaginative entrapment, *Suicide in B♭*

picks up, in a sense, where Jeep leaves off at the end of *Action*. Jeep tries (though he is ultimately unsuccessful) to "act himself out" by using his narrative to transform the playing space. In *Suicide in B♭* Niles undergoes an "exorcism" that represents a freedom beyond that which Jeep is able to attain, and, for a time, he symbolically transcends the boundaries of his "theatrical confinement"—but the price for this apparent escape is that Niles's literal self-effacement entails a loss of his character as well.

For the first third of the play Niles, the musician-protagonist, is absent; all we see is an outline of his body on the floor as the detectives attempt to "reconstruct the imagination" of the apparent murder or suicide in which his face was blown off.[66] He has "escaped" the stage of the play itself, even though he is the figure around whom the discourse of the other characters revolves. If, as some critics have done, we view the detectives Louis and Pablo as imaginative projections of Niles's mind,[67] then we might say that Niles does indeed "appear" and "speak" onstage. But it is not necessary to accept this interpretation of the detectives' role in order to see that Niles is embodied in the play despite his physical absence, for the monologues speculating on what happened to Niles place him upon the stage through narrative. He is not acting, but he is being "acted out" (which is possibly a step beyond "acting himself out").

As a performer (musician/character), Niles has invented a number of "faces," or masks, that he shows to the world; again, he represents the postmodern split subject that appears in so many of Shepard's plays. Initially, Niles says, he allowed the voices of these masks, or identities, to talk to him, but he begins to fear that he has lost his "own" voice:

> They showed me everything I know. . . . [But now] I'm repeating them. Over and over. They talk to me all the time. (*suddenly screaming*) THERE'S VOICES COMING AT ME! (216)

The subsuming of Niles's identity to his identity as a performer places him in a position similar to that of the characters in *Angel City* and *Action*. His suicide signals a denial or obliteration of subjectivity; in an ironic reversal of Lacan's mirror stage, he literally erases his face or defaces his identity.[68] Laureen's monologue about what happens when the urge for suicide comes affirms the view that this destruction is tied up with the attempt to communicate with the other (the split subject):

You struggle to the window. You hold yourself up by both elbows and stare down at the street, looking for your life. But all you see down there is yourself looking back up at you. . . . But then you see him signaling to you from the street. He's pointing to his head, to his own head, then pointing back to you. . . . You pick up the gesture from him and start repeating it back to him. . . . He starts to nod his head and smiles as though you've finally gotten the message. But you're still not clear what he means. . . . Then you see him more clearly than before. You see for sure that he is you. . . . He yells at you so the whole street can hear him. "YOU'RE IN MY HEAD! YOU'RE ONLY IN MY HEAD!" Then he turns and walks away. . . . Then you make a clean jump all the way to the bottom. And your life goes dancing out the window. (220–21)

Her narrative reveals the moment of disembodiment or the fracturing of subjectivity that occurs when the "you" makes "a clean jump" to the bottom, but "your life goes dancing out the window," as if the two parts ("you" and "your life") undergo separate activities even in the process of self-annihilation.

Niles's presence at the scene of the crime, which he expects to manifest without being discovered, is the site of his arrest by the detectives as well as of his reentrapment within the dramatic "confines" of the play. As Louis and Pablo start to move toward him to make the arrest, he "raves" at them: "Am I inside you? . . . Or am I just like you? . . . So exactly like you that we're exactly the same. . . . Not even two things but just one. Only one. Indivisible" (229). Again, as in *The Tooth of Crime* and *Angel City,* those who are perceived first as others are revealed as parts of the same subject; here Shepard places additional emphasis on this metaphor by indicating in the stage directions that the three are to be "locked to each other" with the handcuffs (229). Niles's revelation shows, on the one hand, that he has achieved a partial reclamation of his subjectivity. But Shepard again invests this moment with irony: Niles's surrender to the detectives and possibly his final emphasis on the face that has been blown off implies that any such reclamation may have come too late, for the destruction of the face also entails the erasure of his character; his quest for escape has been so "successful," one might say, that he has paradoxically lost track of himself in the process.

In the movement from *Melodrama Play* to *Suicide in B♭,* Shepard uncovers many of the contradictions in his appropriation of the icons and images of popular culture. If his earliest works represented a tension between the theatrical and the textual, the works of this period continue to express this tension, only it is complicated by the inclusion of texts drawn from pop culture—rock'n'roll, the movies, jazz. The obvious paradox, though, is that all of these intertexts are themselves types of theater, of performance. In this sense, Shepard is a little like Willie in *The Unseen Hand:* his "deviant" speech sounds like an alien language, but it turns out to be simply a topsy-turvy version of the Kid's litany of supposed American "normalcy." Like his artist-protagonists Duke/Drake, Hoss/Crow, Rabbit/Wheeler, Shooter/Jeep, Niles/Louis/Pablo, Shepard splits his dramatic texts between a reliance on the pop culture milieu for the images of his art and a problematization or parody of the milieu that his art has created.

It is no wonder, then, that Shepard says he is fascinated by the "escapes" of Buster Keaton:

> You see him in action and you notice it's a double action with two opposites happening simultaneously. You notice the face just being a face and nothing more or less than a face and for that reason it becomes more of a face but don't worry. You notice the body performing more things than a body can perform and being sometimes more than a body and sometimes less and for that reason becoming something more than a body. You see the face not worried about the body and the body not worried about the face and then he escapes. You're trapped watching while he escapes. The thing that strikes you most is that he doesn't worry about being caught.[69]

Shepard seems troubled by the moment in which the spectator is "trapped watching while he [i.e., the performer] escapes." But it is precisely because the performer appears to be (re)acting against the boundaries established by the performance and its texts that a type of transcendent escape from the confinement of its perceptual frameworks—however ironic or problematic—occurs. One might say that Shepard attempts the same feat in the plays of this period. *Within* the dramatic text this escape is always fragmented and partial; one need only recall Jeep at the end of *Action* and his tormented attempt to act himself out. Yet, as the "double action" between performer and textual enact-

ment collides and contradicts like "two opposites happening simultaneously," we witness a deconstructive escape—not from the theatrical
(con)text but, rather, into a new realm of theatrical representation.

Burying Oedipus: Storytelling and Antinarrative in Shepard's Late Plays

> One story's as good as another. It's all in the way you tell it. That's what
> counts. That's what makes the difference.
>
> —Sam Shepard, *Seduced*

> TILDEN: You don't wanna die do you?
> DODGE: No, I don't wanna die either.
> TILDEN: Well, you gotta talk or you'll die.
> DODGE: Who told you that?
> TILDEN: That's what I know. I found that out in New Mexico. I thought
> I was dying but I just lost my voice.
>
> —Sam Shepard, *Buried Child*

Shepard's more recent plays, beginning with *Curse of the Starving Class,*
continue to reveal a passionate interest in the rewriting and rereading of
an American mythology.[70] He turns from an ironic (re)vision of American popular culture to a focus on the role of the family and the lover
within that cultural context. As in the plays of both earlier periods, his
mythology is overlaid with violence. But this is not the all-consuming
violence, Artaudian and apocalyptic, that Shepard toys with in such
earlier plays as *The Holy Ghostly* (1970), in which he specifies that at the
end, "the whole theater is consumed in flames."[71] Rather, it is the
postmodern grotesque, rooted in the corporeal (the visceral and sexual),
that simultaneously shocks its audience and creates a Brechtian alienation
effect in the comic way it is handled; one need only recall Ella's and
Weston's nonreactions to Emma being blown up in *Curse of the Starving
Class* or Mom's chillingly calm, "You're not killing him are you?"[72] as
Austin tries to strangle Lee with a telephone cord in *True West* (1980).

In recent years Shepard criticism seems to have reached a paradoxical stage. Some readers argue that the later plays (especially *A Lie of the
Mind* [1985]) reveal that Shepard has lost his original subversive touch
and has returned either to a recapitulation of tried-and-true American
dramatic formulas or to a style that is overly derivative of his own earlier
work. I hope to show, however, that these accusations fail to account

for the narrative complexities of Shepard's drama. His later work shows both a rewriting of the American family play tradition (e.g., O'Neill, Odets, Wilder, Williams, Miller) and a continued attention to postmodern re-visions of theatricality. To some critics Shepard's focus on the family play has indicated his movement into a "realistic" phase.[73] This is somewhat deceptively signaled by the works' "fuller" sets and characters and by their more elaborate plots. But Shepard actually seems to be suggesting that the domestic, realistic settings of these plays are facades for nightmarish, sometimes monstrous dramas of desire and anger; by the time we reach the booming walls of *Fool for Love* (1983) or the missing center stage of *A Lie of the Mind*, even the set is not "safely" naturalistic.

If the characters in these plays inhabit threatening domains that are perhaps all the more frightening because of their trappings of the mundane, then it is to be expected that they attempt to hold on to their ever fracturing subjectivity by talking, by deploying stories that seek to reshape and sometimes reclaim (however deceptively) their theatrical places in the world. They talk, as in *Curse of the Starving Class*, to fill up emptiness; they also talk, as in *Buried Child* (1978), in order not to have to listen. To the extent that this causes the characters in these plays to search, again and again, for "master" narratives, which are nearly always unavailable because they have been displaced or ruptured in typical postmodern fashion, and to the extent that it grants priority to the linguistic rather than the physical or visual, talking transports these so-called realistic plays into the realm of what Teresa de Lauretis and others have termed anti-oedipal narrative.[74]

Given the anti-oedipal narrative strain of these plays, their subject matter—based largely on patriarchal figures and on the son's symbolic or literal search for the missing father—creates an ironic dialectic with their narrative. The oedipal concern with unlocking a secret that lies within a family, and the theatrical unraveling (or apparent unraveling) of these secrets, would seem to put these plays in the modernist confessional mode of O'Neill's *Long Day's Journey into Night* (1940–41). But secrets in Shepard's family plays are not revealed through the confidences to the audience provided by traditional soliloquy, nor are they teased out as the climactic narrative point of a lengthy dialogue (a descendant of the revelations provided by the agon in *Oedipus Rex* and other Greek dramas), as in *Long Day's Journey*. Rather, the characters' storytelling—which moves fluidly in and out of the monologic mode—

seems to travel on the periphery of the "secret," or "buried" (i.e., absent), narratives, which, themselves, elude us continually so that their stories are never wholly revelatory even when they pretend to be leading toward expected connections or completions. This resistance to coherence, then, is set against the seemingly traditional oedipal "searches" and "discoveries" that the narratives of these works play at enacting but do not genuinely fulfill.

In *Curse of the Starving Class* Shepard establishes this dialectic by making all four of the main characters into storytellers; their narratives reveal both their individual struggles to submit to or to resist the "law of the Father,"[75] and the complicated ambivalence toward family "destiny" that Weston characterizes as a "poison"[76] and yet also as "an animal thing . . . [the way] that we were supposed to be" (186). The play's first "story," for example, is a monologue by Wesley, who narrates the experience of his father's drunken return the previous night:

> Sound of door not opening. Foot kicking door. Man's voice. Dad's voice. Dad calling Mom. No answer. Foot kicking. Foot kicking harder. Wood splitting. Man's voice. In the night. Foot kicking hard through door. One foot right through door. Bottle crashing. Glass breaking. Fist through door. Man cursing. Man going insane. Feet and hands tearing. Head smashing. Man yelling. Shoulder smashing. Whole body crashing. Woman screaming. . . . Mom screaming. . . . Mom calling cops. Dad crashing away. Back down driveway. Car door slamming. Ignition grinding. Wheels screaming. . . . Sound disappearing. No sound. No sight. Planes still hanging. Heart still pounding. No sound. Mom crying soft. Soft crying. Then no sound. . . . Then moving around through house. Then no moving. Then crying softly. Then stopping. Then, far off the freeway could be heard. (138)

Wesley's rendition of the events in this type of narrative form has a dual effect: it distances him from his father because he casts himself in a narrator's role ("Then, far off the freeway could be heard") and because he at some points substitutes *Man* for *Dad,* hence displacing the emotional content onto a character rather than a father. Yet the speech also betrays a connection between Wesley and his father; his ability to sense and articulate every sound and movement that Weston makes prefigures the way that Wesley "becomes" his father when he literally steps into his clothes toward the end of the play. The monologic voice seems to be the vehicle for both of these forces, for it expresses simultaneously the isolation and the displaced and unfulfilled desire for a narrative, or dialogic, "completion" that never comes about. Similarly, Emma seeks to create an alternative subjectivity through the Hemingwayesque adventures that she "experiences" by means of her monologues, only to face the rude return to reality: Wesley responds to one of her fantasies by saying, "If you're not doing anything, would you check the artichokes?" (162).

While all of the characters attempt to appropriate narrative space through the creation of monologic texts (including Ella, with her lengthy narratives to Emma about the dangers of menstruation), they resist relinquishing to others the liberty engendered by the solo narrative voice. A notable exception comes in the play's central story. When Weston tells his part of the story in a lengthy monologue (he saw an eagle swoop down repeatedly and take the testicles of the lambs he had been castrating from the roof where he had thrown them), he delivers the speech to the lamb in the pen onstage; in fact, he refuses to continue when Wesley, who has heard the story before and has been listening offstage, enters and asks what happens next.[77] In the last scene of the play Ella picks up on the story suddenly by looking at the lamb carcass; she says to Wesley: "Something just went right through me. Just from looking at this lamb" (199). The lamb acts as a symbolic transmitter of the narrative from one teller to the next; in this sense the lamb as "auditor" becomes a "receptacle" of the story itself, only the lamb has been slaughtered by Wesley as part of his quest to satisfy his literal and figurative hunger. Wesley's ritualistic slaughter of the lamb—he walks around naked with the blood of the lamb dripping on him—serves somehow as part of the oedipal "sacrifice" that he must make (an image of castration, perhaps, parallel to the lambs in Weston's story) in order to "identify" (with) his father.[78] That the lamb carcass generates the rest of the story Weston began, then, implies that a competing act of "transmission" has occurred on the narrative level, but not without a similar sort of "butchering" along the way.

At the same time it is worth noting that Ella and Wesley complete Weston's story through dialogue (or at least through a kind of shared monologue), the only point in the play at which a narrative is relayed in this manner. Their final image is of the eagle being torn apart in midair by the cat, with the cat afraid to let go and fall to its death; ultimately, Ella says, the two "come crashing down to the earth. Both of them come crashing down. Like one whole thing" (200). This image, which echoes the "crashing" in Wesley's opening monologue, embodies the dependent/destructive relationship among the members of the family as well as the more abstract figure of the dreamer who clings to, yet risks destruction by, his or her own dreams. If we take the "dreams" to encompass the narratives of those dreams (i.e., the play's stories), then the implications are all the more nightmarish: Shepard implies that the dreamer/narrator-of-dreams faces self-destruction by his or her discourse even as it seems to be a source of sustenance. By rescuing and completing the father's fragmented narrative, the mother and son offer the possibility that accompanying the destruction inherent in the transmission of a mythology (e.g., Oedipus), the acknowledgment of its origins and its bonds allows it to become a part of one's "blood," part of a common story, with the simultaneous result of recognition and of "poison."

It is possible to view *Buried Child* as a more cynical version of *Curse of the Starving Class,* for the family is infected with the same poison, but the possibilities offered by seeking an identification with the continuity of the generations (as Weston and Wesley do in *Curse* and as Vince does in *Buried Child*) seem to be tainted with the sense of mortality—of an always ironic oedipal inevitability—even in the apparent regeneration that accompanies the play's ending. *Curse* achieves a certain narrative liberation at the end by Ella's and Wesley's mutual re-creation of the eagle and cat story; the conclusion of *Buried Child,* however, shows a distrust of narrative or of language that contradicts the optimism of the "buried child's" resurrection from the backyard and the fertility that surrounds such a resurrection.

A literal or figurative absence marks each of the characters in the family of *Buried Child:* Dodge, who is wasting away, feels that he is "an invisible man" (68), Tilden has a quality (according to Shepard's stage directions) of being "profoundly burned out and displaced" (69), Ansel and the "other" child are dead, Vince is unrecognizable to the rest of the family and then vanishes for a good bit of the play, Bradley is an amputee who also seems to be missing any "humanity," and Halie—when she is not out with Father Dewis—speaks primarily from offstage. In a play marked by such nonpresence one might expect narrative to fill in the void. Yet the possibilities for narrative to take on any such role are consistently subsumed in this play, so that language, too, becomes part of the emptiness or ex-centricity. The characters do have a shared story—that of the baby Dodge killed—but to talk about it is taboo, and, when they do mention this repressed story, they provide conflicting and intentionally blurred accounts so that we, like Shelly, do not know which is the "full" story.

The effect, then, is that narrative in this play is constantly deferred and displaced; the present and the romanticized version of the past are less threatening to the characters than the hidden past of which the buried child is a part. It is no wonder that Dodge, when Shelly asks him about the family photographs upstairs, denies any knowledge of a connection to them: "This is it. The whole shootin' match, sittin' right in front of you" (111). He adds that he sees his lineage as a "long line of corpses! There's not a living soul behind me. . . . Who's holding me in their memory?" (112). When he recites his will, it is as if he has predicated his very existence upon the farm machinery and junk in his possession, so that they virtually constitute the bones of his body. Appropriately, the litany of items in the will is Dodge's last piece of monologue; his ability to generate language ends with the relinquishing of the linguistic "material" that represents all there is that gives any presence to this self-styled "invisible man." Or perhaps, as Johan Callens puts it, Dodge's will "is also a desperate attempt to hold on to reality by conjuring it up in words, to assert his identity by enumerating his possessions."[79] In keeping with this sense of the invisible, or the unseeable, too, Dodge's death occurs "completely unnoticed" by the others onstage (131), just as he had announced would happen only a few minutes before. His spoken will also includes a request to have his body burned after death so that "nothing remains but ash" (129)—a final displacement of the corporeal.

Vince, who returns to the household after six years' absence because he is seeking connections with the past, represents an attempt to call forth the family's "deferred," or missing, master narratives and to "reset" the oedipal narrative pattern of discovery. Any such effort, though, entails a transgression, for invoking the hidden stories would threaten the very framework of repression upon which the characters' identities have been constructed. Vince's warning to Shelly not to come outside of the living room—"This is taboo territory. No man or woman has ever crossed the line and lived to tell the tale!" (127)—may be spoken in drunken playfulness, but it also reflects the family's sense of the outside, where the buried child lies and where the secrets have been consigned, as "taboo"; indeed, no one "lived to tell the tale" because the story remains "unexcavated" and untold. Vince comes close, however, to bringing the narrative past back inside, for he attempts to forge a link between the past and the present. Echoing Tilden's earlier line when he momentarily recognizes Vince as his son ("I thought I saw a face inside his face" [100]), Vince announces that, as he was driving, he studied his face in the windshield so intensely that he felt as if he were looking at someone else's face:

> And then his face changed. His face became his father's face. Same bones. Same eyes. Same nose. Same breath. And his father's face changed to his Grandfather's face. And it went on like that. Changing. Clear on back to faces I'd never seen before but still recognized. . . . (130)

This is the play's only "revelatory" monologue, and, as such, it marks a certain uncovering of the repressed narratives of the past. Steven Putzel and Suzanne Westfall argue that "by viewing himself as an artifact, by moving from his subjective I-centered self-definition to an objective he-centered self-definition . . . [Vince] is able to see Dodge, Tilden and himself as part of a continuum."[80] At the same time, though, the liberation provided by the speech is incomplete or problematized. Strikingly, Shepard indicates in the stage directions that Vince "delivers [the] speech [facing] front" (130). Depending on the way that a director interprets this instruction, it is possible that Vince speaks his words not to the other characters but, rather, to the audience; at the very least he clearly addresses himself, in the traditional style of the soliloquy, to a far greater extent than he addresses the other characters here. The result is that Vince's words take on a metatheatrical quality, even if he does not break the fourth wall by acknowledging the audience. Vince's speech may be "sincere," then, but he is also performing.

His act of staking out and surveying "his" house after Dodge dies and wills it to him takes on a doubleness that further calls into question the "success" of Vince's monologue as an example of the recovered or newly appropriated narrative voice. One might say that Vince's air of insistent ownership in the play's final moments confirms his identification with his ancestry, but it is equally likely that he has simply taken over Dodge's role as one who clings to his possessions and rejects all else, a possibility attested to by his assuming Dodge's position on the couch when Dodge dies. Furthermore, Vince's appropriation of Dodge's place implicitly makes him the new "husband" of his own grandmother (Halie), an extension of the incestuous oedipal pattern already suggested by the implication (never fully borne out) that Vince's father, Tilden, may be the father (with Halie, *his* mother) of the buried child.[81] The play's refusal to resolve or confront these implications suggests that its narrative cannot, again, fit the traditional path of exposure, revelation, and discovery that the oedipal paradigm would seem to establish.

The play closes, moreover, not with Vince's speech but, instead, with Halie's offstage words to Dodge (not knowing he has died) about the remarkable vegetation visible outside. Her discourse provides a disturbing counterpoint to the visual action of Tilden carrying the corpse of the "buried child" onstage:

> You can't force a thing to grow. You can't interfere with it. It's all hidden. It's all unseen. You just gotta wait til it pops up out of the ground. Tiny little shoot. Tiny little white shoot. All hairy and fragile. Strong though. Strong enough to break the earth even. It's a miracle, Dodge. I've never seen a crop like this in my whole life. Maybe it's the sun. Maybe that's it. Maybe it's the sun. (132)

One of the many ironies of this moment is, of course, Halie's reference to the "sun" as the source of fertility, when it actually seems to have occurred through the nourishment of the "son" Tilden has just unearthed (who was, possibly, the child of Tilden, Halie's own son). This final narrative of Halie's is another displaced one, only here it is primarily displaced by the physical presence of the corpse in Tilden's arms. Shepard's decision to make the unearthing of the buried child into a moment that emphasizes the visual and the physical over the spoken text adds a final twist to the play's notion of the absent or displaced oedipal narrative, for the very "sign" for that narrative has lost its narrative status and become a reified, nonnarrative entity.[82] Yet this corpse, the buried child, is also the "buried" (oedipal) narrative—the missing story—which has been absent throughout the play and which manifests itself ultimately in the form of the corpse-as-text.[83] In this context the knowledge that Tilden would "make up stories" (124) to tell the child is all the more resonant, as is Dodge's reference to his ancestry as "a long line of corpses" (112)—for it is also a long line of buried stories.

If oedipal narrative is displaced, one result is that the subject as embodied in theatrical characters also faces dislocation or disembodiment. In his collaborations with Joseph Chaikin, including *Tongues* (1978) and *Savage/Love* (1981), Shepard explores this problem, which emerged more implicitly in *Curse of the Starving Class* and *Buried Child,* of the "unstable" subject seeking communication with an other (or others) who may not be able to provide an adequate response; to some degree monologue steps in where dialogue fails. *True West* posits this other as one part of the divided self, the postmodern split subject, as did such earlier plays as *The Tooth of Crime* and *Angel City*. *True West* ends with the disturbing silhouette of the two brothers, Austin and Lee, frozen in a potentially murderous confrontation.[84] *Fool for Love* extends the metaphor of the warring opposites who embody the fragmentation of the subject, only the split is now between male and female (at one point the Old Man begs Eddie to tell the "male side" of the story,[85] suggesting that the narrative itself is similarly divided).[86] As in *True West*, this conflict is not resolved on a "psychological" level; at the end of *Fool for Love* May and Eddie are filled with the same inability to be with or to be without each other, the same love/hate, as at the beginning. On the narrative level the play enacts a similar "weighing" of the split between "true" and "untrue" stories. The nature of a true story is a source of constant conflict in *True West*, as Austin and Lee argue about whether Lee's screenplay is like "real life," and Austin insists at the end of his narrative about their father throwing his new false teeth away with his chop suey: "Now's that's a true story. True to life" (42). In *Fool for Love,* though, the lines between the two different kinds of stories are blurred; as the modernist quest for "integrity" and "authenticity" (consider, e.g., Hoss's parallel quest in *The Tooth of Crime*) is replaced by the postmodernist emphasis on *narrativity* and the accompanying complications or ambiguities of representability, what matters is no longer the extent to which a narrative is authentic but, rather, the extent to which it is possible to create a story and to manufacture a subjective belief in it.

The figure of the Old Man is key to the ways that the narratives in *Fool for Love* are recounted and sustained. He serves as a commentator on the action; Shepard has him seated on "a small extended platform on the same level as the stage" and indicates that "he exists only in the minds of May and Eddie, even though they might talk to him directly and acknowledge his physical presence" (19–20).[87] As a result, the Old Man is simultaneously powerful and impotent; he is able to seize May's and Eddie's attention and to divert the audience's focus to himself, yet he is apart from the central physical action of the play (ex-centric) and is not acknowledged to be "real." Given his status as both visible and invisible, "actual" and imaginary, it is fitting that the figure of the Old Man plays a role in the validation of (and, later, in the attempt to discredit) narratives that may or may not be "merely" fictional. We first witness his enactment of such a role in his exchange with Eddie about being "married" to Barbara Mandrell (who is, significantly, not just a character but also a real person existing outside of the status of Shepard's play):[88]

> THE OLD MAN: I wanna show you somethin'. Somethin' real, okay? Somethin' actual. . . . Take a look at that picture on the wall over there. (*he points at wall stage-right. There is no picture but Eddie stares at the wall.*) Ya' see that? Take a good look at that. Ya' see it?
> EDDIE: (*staring at wall*) Yeah.
> THE OLD MAN: Ya' know who that is? . . . Barbara Mandrell . . . [W]ould you believe me if I told ya' I was married to her?
> EDDIE: (*pause*) No.
> THE OLD MAN: Well, see, now that's the difference right there. That's realism. I am actually married to Barbara Mandrell in my mind. Can you understand that?
> EDDIE: Sure.
> THE OLD MAN: Good. I'm glad we have an understanding.
>
> (27)

In a sense the Old Man's words set up a paradigm for the entire play, including his own existence as a figure within it: he suggests that the verifiability of representation comes not from visual and physical proof but, rather, from the *belief* that something is true. The Old Man himself exists because he refuses to think it possible that he does not, and so he is the nonfictive creation of May and Eddie—and, of course, of the spectators. Indeed, one might even argue that the Old Man's statement about Barbara Mandrell is a gauge for the power of narrative in Shepard's plays overall, particularly those of this late period: "realism" is not definable in terms of an empirical model; instead, that which we take to be true in these plays is a function of allowing narrative to alter and enlarge our sense of what constitutes that model in the first place.

As the "fantasist" who "dream[s] things up" (including the Old Man? [27]) Eddie claims to have come to "an understanding" about the nature of fiction. When Martin asks Eddie what he and May could do if they did not go to the movies, Eddie responds, "Well, you could uh—tell each other stories." Martin, though, as a figure who clearly lacks imagination, is baffled by this suggestion:

> MARTIN: I don't know any stories.
> EDDIE: Make 'em up.
> MARTIN: That'd be lying wouldn't it?
> EDDIE: No, no. Lying's when you believe it's true. If you already
>   know it's a lie, then it's not lying.
>
> (45)

Here Eddie has reversed the Old Man's philosophy: he says that truth comes from an admission that a story is untrue, and vice versa. Paradoxically, however, his words actually serve as an affirmation of what the Old Man has "taught" him, for the point is that there is no objective basis in reality for the "truth" of a story; rather, its status as a lie hinges on what the teller believes about the narrative.

Curiously, though, it is the Old Man who corrects and then attempts to invalidate the play's concluding story, which Eddie begins and May denies but then completes. The Old Man seems to be in possession of a narrative that is never fully articulated, except through his remarks on Eddie's and May's versions of the story; for instance, when Martin asks whether Eddie had any idea that his father was in love with two different women and had had a child by each, Eddie replies that neither he nor his mother had been aware of this. Unheard (and unseen) by Martin, the Old Man interjects, "She knew." But Eddie says to Martin, "She never knew" (48). Similarly, when May reveals the final part of the story—that Eddie's mother committed suicide when she found out about Eddie's and May's incestuous romance—the Old Man repeats adamantly that this is untrue: "Just a goddamn second here. This story doesn't hold water. . . . That's the dumbest version I ever heard in my whole life" (54). He begs Eddie to "make her see this thing in a clear light" (55), but May and Eddie are drawn together—first with their eyes, and then into an embrace. This telling of the play's final story is like that of the closing sequence in *Curse of the Starving Class,* for the two monologic narratives fuse together, like the "male" and "female" counterparts of the subject (even as, in the moments immediately afterward, the intervention of the Countess splits them apart again).[89]

Such a fusion seems to necessitate the exclusion of the Old Man, even though he is the play's "original" narrator. But the Old Man's words that close the play reverberate with the power of Eddie's and May's final story, which has enacted the Old Man's notion that the truth of a narrative is less important than its moment of narration, at the same time that it provides an ironic counterpoint to what actually happens to the two lovers:

> Ya' see that picture over there? Ya' see that? Ya' know who that is? That's the woman of my dreams. That's who that is. And she's mine. She's all mine. Forever. (57)

While May and Eddie are ultimately unable to possess each other, the Old Man is able to claim his mental marriage to Barbara Mandrell as "his" forever—in spite of or because of his romance's status as a product of the narrative imagination. It is also significant that the Old Man implicitly addresses the audience here, or at least returns to monologue and to his role as narrator (he also moves back to his platform) in this final speech, for this suggests that the play itself reaffirms its *own* status as a "story." Like the Old Man's picture, it requires the transformation of the ordinary into the extraordinary, and vice versa. The play itself, then, must grant precedence to the realm of the imaginary—that is, as Eddie tries to teach Martin, a "lie of the mind" is not necessarily a lie after all.

Much of the same interest in playing with narrative's potential to "dupe" its tellers and/or auditors permeates *A Lie of the Mind*. Throughout the first part of the play the characters—with the exception of Beth—repeatedly express skepticism about the deception inherent in acting and performance. Jake tells Frankie, for instance, that Beth must have been cheating on him as part of her immersion in the character she was portraying in a play: "This acting shit is more real than the real world to her. Can you believe that?"[90] It is striking that in a play in which the characters express a strong distrust of acting, or theatricality, the point of conflict for both Beth and Jake becomes the multiple stories, voices, and subject positions with which both of them struggle as they seek to regain their subjectivity by ending their alienation from their voices and bodies.

Jake, in a state of intense shock and guilt after he has "killed" Beth (or so he thinks), experiences a disembodiment from himself such that a monologue spoken to his reflection in the mirror ("Don't think about her feet or her calves or her knees [etc.]. . . . You'll be much better off"

[58]) becomes a kind of displaced dialogue with a second, absent body. In fact, he tells Sally that he has been "following" himself like a spy— "Like, just now I caught myself shaving. . . . I didn't know I was doing that until just now" (59). This other body is Jake's own divided self, but it is also Beth, who becomes a voice inside Jake's head (as well as a vision, such as when he seems to see her oiling her body). When he says to his sister that "there's this thing—this thing in my head . . . that the next moment . . . will blow up. Explode with a voice. A scream from a voice I don't know" (85), Beth's scream of Jake's name from the stage left "world" corroborates his description for the *audience,* as does the staging of his earlier "vision" of Beth. This underscores not only the connection between Jake and Beth but also the sense in which Jake's internal narratives are turned into dramatic creations for the audience to regard. Shepard's decision to embody on stage that which in his earlier plays would have been kept in the realm of narration may suggest, on the one hand, that these visual renderings implicate the spectators in the construction of lies of the mind: we *think* that what we see is true *because* we see it. On the other hand, such dramatizations stand in obvious counterpoint to the distrust of acting that most of the play's characters themselves manifest. Putzel indicates that "the audience must learn to cope with the 'lie of the mind' in both . . . [the] geographic sense and in the psychological sense; as in *Fool for Love* we are left with the understanding that there is no clear demarcation between 'truth' and 'lie.'"[91]

Like Jake, Beth has gone into a state—albeit an organic rather than a psychosomatic one—in which she feels separated from her body and her voice. When she first tries to walk, she seems, like Alice in Wonderland, to be looking way down at her feet, and her frequent malapropisms as she struggles to regain her speech show the splitting of her thoughts and her language. As she tries to tell Frankie: "It speaks. Speeches. Speaking. In me. Comes and goes. Again. I don't know why" (73). Beth, too, seems to have been overtaken by language and to have the impression of living apart from her own body;[92] perhaps she experiences this disembodiment as much in telepathic accord with Jake as he does with her. Having suffered brain damage, Beth, the former actress, now has virtually nothing but the possibilities offered by becoming a character and creating an inner life even though interiority—blown away by aphasia and amnesia—barely remains at all.

When she puts on her father's shirt and tries to persuade Frankie to be her "sweet man," she says: "Pretend. Because it fills me. Pretending fills. Not empty. Other. Ordinary. Is no good. Empty. Ordinary is empty" (75). While Jake seeks to end his feeling of being dispossessed by "spying" on himself and by stripping away the fictions that torture him, then, Beth tries to "fill" herself with fictions in order not to have to face the possibility that her displacement from her subjectivity will result in utter emptiness, or invisibility. Lynda Hart believes that Beth's voice in this play is marginalized, because of her brain damage, to the point that Shepard fails to include her perspective: "Beth has no objective whatsoever; she is simply an image of a destroyed woman." I would argue, however, that Beth's inability to articulate her presence through language is mitigated somewhat through both her physical presence and her "own" splintered language that she attempts to produce as she fights to speak despite her injuries. To argue, as Hart does, that Beth is "rendered inarticulate" is to diminish the power—however problematically filtered through the male gaze—that her character has both because of and despite her failed subjectivity as brought on by Jake's violence.[93]

Insofar as Jake and Beth achieve any kind of "resolution" for their displacement—however dubious or ironic such a resolution may be—they do so by a complete immersion in the realm of truth (in Jake's case) or of fiction (in Beth's case). Jake, reduced by Mike to a horse or slave and "driven" in on his hands and knees to apologize to Beth, tells her:

These things—in my head—lie to me. Everything lies. Tells me a story. Everything in me lies. But you. You stay. You are true. I know you now. You are true. I love you more than this life. You stay. You stay with him. He's my brother. (128–29)

Even Jake's diction now resembles Beth's, with the short sentences that seem to be a struggle with the tenuousness of language in order to express emotions that have a power beyond speech. But for Beth—now in the bizarre costume that she has chosen for announcing her plans to "marry" Frankie—Jake's words are not enough to pull her for more than a moment out of the withdrawal into the "pretend," which with Jake's retreat is on the verge of becoming the equivalent of her "reality."[94]

Inevitably, then, we are left with the uncomfortable task of assessing Shepard's attitude toward the fiction of the play itself: Does the ambivalence of the ending suggest that fiction making, or "pretending," is ultimately destructive? In *Fool for Love* the final emphasis on the figure of the Old Man pointed toward the possibility that the truth of a narrative is relative to its teller and auditor. Here, though—despite Putzel's claim—the realm of fiction making seems to be even less privileged. Rather, those who see such fictions as lies and those who find wholeness in pretending, as Beth tries to, are equally likely to survive or to dissolve back into emptiness. Thus, the play itself is continually creating and then destroying its own fictions/lies—a typical postmodernist tactic—in order to arrive at some version of its truths at the same time, if such a version even exists in the first place.

As the fantasist (to use the Old Man's description of Eddie) who "dreams up" these plays, Shepard places himself in the precarious position of being at the same time a teller of truths and a teller of lies. The result is that, despite the trappings these late plays have of confessional family dramas or even of oedipal tragedies, narrative moments of revelation and recognition are always just out of reach in the postmodern refusal of closure. Perhaps the closest any of these characters comes to such a moment occurs after May completes Eddie's story in *Fool for Love,* but even that is undercut by the reappearance of the Countess and the reassertion of the Old Man's status as problematic narrator. Given the continual absence or displacement of "insight," it makes sense that these plays tend not to include traditional soliloquies. Instead, as we have seen, characters seek to repair their fractured subjectivity through storytelling. For monologic language continues to assert a peculiar power over both the characters and the larger narratives of the plays themselves, as the monologues in these pieces continue to insist upon the primacy of the verbal over the visual—even when, as in *Buried Child* or *A Lie of the Mind,* that which can be represented physically onstage is made to compete with the narrative language. When narrative is implicitly "privileged" even as it is constantly displaced and disrupted, then the postmodern perspective of the plays inevitably seems to play tricks on the spectator. As Hoss says in *The Tooth of Crime:* "It's like looking down a long pipe. All the time figurin' that to be the total picture. You take your eye away for a second and see you been gyped" (233). It is precisely Shepard's refusal to totalize the picture in his plays, though, to force them within the strictures and structures of a balanced realism, that gives them their astigmatic grace.

The Theater as "House of Games": David Mamet's (Con) Artistry and the Monologic Voice

David Mamet's characters, like Shepard's, are unstoppable storytellers; their monologues dominate his plays so fully that words replace and even subvert the physical and visual elements of the productions. And, like Shepard, Mamet creates storytellers who are always on some level conscious that they are performing: to engage in monologue is to take center stage (figuratively, although not necessarily literally). But Shepard's monologues, even in his later plays, rarely serve as pathways to psychological revelations of character: they are, above all else, the projections of Shepard's theatrical imagination.

Mamet's case, however, is somewhat more complicated, as he simultaneously embraces and rejects the Shepardian notion of character. In an essay in *Some Freaks* (1989), Mamet writes, "*Characterization is taken care of by the author . . .* [who] will avoid it like the plague, and show us *what the character does. . . .*"[1] He nevertheless claims a concern with the inner lives of his characters; yet, as Bigsby says, Mamet "seems to be arguing for the necessity of a humanism for which he cannot always find space within the plays."[2] One might say that Mamet's works perpetuate a tension between this apparent *drive* for a traditional humanism and the constant *denial* of such a vision in favor of postmodernist "tricks" and "devices," which, as has been shown, actually promote a Brechtian refusal of immersion in the characters and "story" in favor of alienation from them.

Chapter 2 mentioned Lyotard's interest in the game (specifically, the "language game," a term he derives from Wittgenstein) as a "pagan" (i.e., postmodernist) trope and discussed the appropriateness of such a metaphor in the arena of play constituted by the contemporary theater. Jameson, in his foreword to Lyotard's *The Postmodern Condition,* writes that from the postmodernist perspective, not only is language "an unstable exchange between its speakers," but these exchanges themselves are

> now seen less as a process of the transmission of information or messages, or in terms of some network of signs or even signifying systems, than as (to use one of Lyotard's favorite figures) the "taking of tricks," the trumping of a communicational adversary, an essentially conflictual relationship between tricksters.[3]

One theatrical version of the trickster is the charlatan figure, a fast-talking con artist who attempts to "direct" the action of the play; the tradition of such a character extends back to ancient Roman comedy. The postmodernist attraction to the charlatan lies in the sense that language itself is based on manipulations and shared (mis)understandings, coupled with the Lyotardian dynamic wherein language games are inherently theatrical and performative. Mamet's fascination with characters who play language games by manipulating others with monologic language (which, after all, provides the opportunity for the quintessential "sales pitch") naturally invites us to consider the ways in which trickery operates in his own narratives, for Mamet ultimately throws into relief the ability of the theatrical work itself to "con," or persuade, its audience.

The Sanctity of Storytelling

> Maj . . . the maj . . . the *majesty* of it. Its strength come (*Pause.*) From repetition. It is a tale that we know.
>> —David Mamet, *The Spanish Prisoner*

> If you're going to talk to somebody, why fuck around the bush, right? . . . Why lie?
>> —David Mamet, *Lakeboat*

Mamet's early works are both metadramatic and "catechistic."[4] While their structure is not overtly metadramatic in the style of Pirandello or even of early Shepard, Mamet calls attention to the theatricality of these pieces by making frequent use of "stock" dramatic devices, always presented with an ironic twist, such as the chorus, the soliloquy, and so on.

These works are also catechistic because they rely on pairs of characters, frequently cast into a mentor-disciple relationship, who appear to have retold each other their narratives many times over (the catechism is itself a form of performance or recitation). Pascale Hubert-Leibler establishes a model of student-teacher relationships rather than one of catechism to discuss Mamet's work; following Foucault, she emphasizes that such relationships are based, above all, on the manipulation of power.[5] Lyotard says that, in language games,

> the partners, the people who are assigned their roles by the language games in which they are caught, occupy positions that are incommensurable to each other. Not only is there an incommensurability within a game between the position of recipient and that of utterer . . . but, from game to game . . . [:] it is not the same thing to be the recipient of a narrative, and to be the recipient of a denotative discourse with a function of truthfulness, or to be the recipient of a command.[6]

The unbalanced relationship between speaker and listener suggests that, even though characters' meetings are cast as dialogic exchanges, the operative force in these early works is primarily a monologic one: the storyteller may become a listener, and vice versa, but only one character at a time serves as the dominant speaker who controls the play's narrative space. This is not to imply that the presence of the "listener" character is superfluous; often, as in The Duck Variations (1972), Dark Pony (1977), and the later Prairie du Chien (1985), the auditor's presence is what sets the monologist's story—and, by extension, the play itself—into motion.

The Duck Variations is naturalistic in its setting but formally theatrical in structure.[7] As the musical conceit of its title (and scene divisions) shows, the piece is intended to be a number of reworkings of a single theme; Dennis Carroll writes that Mamet was apparently influenced by Aaron Copland's What to Listen for in Music in designing the form of the play.[8] The central characters are Emil Varec and George S. Aronovitz, two elderly men who sit on a park bench near Lake Michigan and pass their time by talking about the life cycles of ducks (and related topics). It becomes evident in the course of the "variations" that the two men are using their observed world as the stepping-off point for their own mythology, a mythology based partially on vaguely remembered nature "facts" from the Reader's Digest and other sources and partially on the unintentional poetry that arises from their own commentary about the permutations of nature. Of the two men, George is the most anxious to validate his stories by saying that he "read . . . [them] *somewhere.*"⁹ These declarations of "sources" seem to be a way for George to assert that his contributions are somehow more valid than Emil's because they already have an existence as texts, as stories that can rest upon the authority of an outside creator.

Unlike in Mamet's later plays, though, where fraud becomes a genuine issue, the impulse of collaboration overrides the desire to ascertain a story's "validity." As Steven Gale says, "ultimately the importance of their conversation lies not in occasional insights but in the fact that they are conversing."¹⁰ In the final scene Emil creates an analogy (though not on a conscious level, one suspects) between his watching the ducks with George and the similar activities of the ancient Greeks:

> These were the Ancient Greeks. Old. Old men.
> Incapable of working.
> Of no use to their society.
> Just used to watch the birds all day
> First light to Last light.
>
> (124)

Emil's misreading of "Ancient Greeks" as "Old men" is comic, but the parallel to his and George's own status is obvious. Emil's words resonate further in terms of Mamet's own sense of the storytelling in this work. The reference to the ancient Greeks evokes an image of the chorus figures in Greek drama—frequently, "old men"—whose role was to observe, narrate, and comment on the action of the play. In Greek drama the Chorus figures were in the position of declaiming on the events of the play yet were powerless to act on these events or to influence their outcome; so, too, have George and Emil become marginalized narrators of a world that excludes their presence.

At the same time there is a key difference between the Emil/George tandem and the choral figures of Greek drama. The latter react to the behavior of a central protagonist (e.g., Oedipus); in one sense Emil and George have taken over as the protagonists, but in another sense they remain choral figures, commenting on the ducks (or on nature in general) as stand-in "protagonist(s)." One might take this possibility one step further and point out that this is, then, a play with choral figures but without a protagonist. In other words, in postmodern fashion the center of the play is marked with a void or absence, while the discourse shifts to the ex-centric figures (Emil and George). Without a genuine protagonist, the center does not hold, and Emil's and George's narrating status as chorus figures becomes unstable when they have no "real" story to narrate. As a result, the exchanges between the two men are tinged with a comic desperation; Bigsby characterizes their interactions as "like a vaudeville act, each relying on the other to keep the patter going, to avoid the dangerous silences."[11] Such an image evokes Vladimir and Estragon of *Waiting for Godot,* or perhaps Stoppard's version of Rosencrantz and Guildenstern, in the attempt to fill an increasingly threatening silence with words and more words.[12]

While *The Duck Variations* is in some ways about the performance of nature, *A Life in the Theatre* (1977), which involves two actors who play actors, is more overtly concerned with the nature of performance. In the original production of this play the stage was designed with two curtains so that the audience saw the two players from the front during the backstage sequences and from the back during their play-within-a-play sequences—"in effect," says Mamet, "a true view from back-stage."[13] Robert, the older actor, seems to be caught within this double staging as if within a Pirandellian box: even when he is offstage he is always acting. In a teacher-student relationship that follows many of Hubert-Leibler's Foucauldian paradigms,[14] Robert instructs John, the younger actor, that theatrical tradition needs to be passed from one generation to the next; he feels that the theater is "a closed society" (66) to such an extent that he has virtually no life outside of the theater. Although he tells John that "life on stage" is nothing but "attitudes" (67), these attitudes, or poses sustain Robert in his everyday behavior.

As in *The Duck Variations,* however, the two characters are not simply metadramatic commentators. A more traditional playwright's approach would culminate in a validation of Robert as a tragic hero of sorts, a representative of the generation that understood the true essence of the theater. The tensions between Robert and John that emerge in the course of the play, however, reveal that, even though John certainly may see Robert as a mentor—and even though Robert's speeches expressing his love for the craft of acting are indeed moving—Robert is in the process of becoming a cipher, a character, an empty sign that has a floating referent. His pursuit of "life" through the theater is ultimately an impossible one; the characters, like the stage open from both the front and the back on which they perform *A Life in the Theatre* itself, can rely only on illusory and invisible "backgrounds."

With its parodic examples of different theatrical styles (dispatched with varying degrees of success by the two performers),[15] and with its commentary on the theatrical process itself—despite the fact that the fourth wall is never genuinely broken—*A Life in the Theatre* is in some ways a perfect example of a postmodernist drama. Mamet chooses and then problematizes theatrical devices more overtly here than in any of his other works; this is particularly true of the soliloquy, an "outmoded" theatrical form that, as we have seen, is overtly metadramatic because the soliloquizer implicitly or explicitly addresses the audience. A fleeting, but pivotal, moment of soliloquy in *A Life in the Theatre* occurs in scene 2 when Robert and John are on their way out of the wardrobe area and John hands Robert his hat; Robert looks down at it and pauses, then (the stage directions tell us), "*soliloquizing,*" says, "My hat, my hat, my hat." He turns to John for approval: "Eh?" and John's reply is an ambiguous "*Mmm*" (27). Here soliloquizing is the self-conscious impulse of an actor who is always "onstage"; it is a natural outburst for a histrionic character. When Robert extends the soliloquizing impulse into a speech about his makeup in the dressing room, John tells him in exasperation to "shut up" (65). But it is clear by the end of the play that Robert turns again and again to soliloquizing not simply because he is always "on" but also because the form reflects his isolation in perpetual characterhood, as it were—an ultimately lonely "existence." The soliloquizer speaks to a captive audience yet dares not wish for a reply. In the final scene, a reversal of the earlier moment in which Robert insisted on staying while John rehearsed his speech, Robert speaks to an empty house as John eavesdrops:

> You've been so kind. . . . Thank you, you've really been so kind. You know, and I speak, I am sure, not for myself alone, but on behalf of all of us . . . (*composes himself*). . . . All of us here, when I say that these . . . *these* moments make it all . . . they make it all worthwhile. (94–95)

Robert's rehearsal of what is obviously intended to appear to a later audience (if he presents this) as an extemporaneous speech, along with the immediate situation of his delivery to a theater full of empty seats, renders ironic his insistence that "these moments" make it all worth-while. Yet he does have not only John as a listener but also the filled seats (one would hope) of the actual theater in which the actor who plays Robert is performing. Mamet thus uses the moment to foreground the paradoxical nature of the soliloquy: the presence of the audience is both ignored in the intimacy of the moment and acknowledged in the vocalization of the speaker's thoughts.[16]

In *Lakeboat* (written in 1970 and revised extensively for production by the Milwaukee Repertory in 1980), when Fred speaks alone on the deck in scenes 11 and 13, Mamet specifically indicates in the stage directions that he "soliloquizes" (57). Yet there seems to be something tongue-in-cheek about the application of this consciously theatrical term to Fred's remarks about Giugliani's mugging and about horseracing. It is true that in both of these soliloquies, Fred arrives at a decision, or revelation, by voicing his thoughts aloud with no explicit audience present, and so the speeches fit my original definition of the soliloquy.[17] A modernist playwright, such as O'Neill, might write this type of scene to suggest—with no intended irony—that Fred is indeed a "poet" of the ordinary. Mamet, however, as a postmodern dramatist, does not intend for us to see Fred as possessing a poetic voice; rather, he creates a disparity between the *design* of the two scenes as soliloquies (which the staging might suggest in performance so that the contrast is not dependent upon reading the directions in the text) and the content of the speeches. Furthermore, he invites a heightened (in these moments almost Brechtian) awareness of our position as members of a real audience who observe Fred as he speaks both to himself and to an *imaginary* audience. Fred is no poet, then, but he is also a less distant relative of *A Life in the Theatre*'s Robert than one might initially think.

While language games sustain the friendship between Emil and George and provide the source for Robert's and John's (and perhaps Fred's) theatricalized interactions, Mamet implies in *Sexual Perversity in Chicago* (1974) that they may also be the basis for the perpetuation of potentially destructive mythologies about men and women. The narratives that the characters exchange in the play are comic in their exaggerated claims, but they are also infused with a deep distrust and fear of sexuality, implying that the characters live in a profoundly alienating world. The play's structure reflects this alienation, for all of the characters talk to themselves and talk at rather than with each other. Each of the four characters delivers at least one soliloquy (or facsimile thereof)

at some point in the play. Bernie speaks to a set of imaginary compan-
ions at the Health Club, Danny to an imaginary coworker, Deborah to
herself, and Joan to her imaginary nursery school students. In the stage
directions for Bernie's, Danny's, and Joan's soliloquies, Mamet indicates, by using the word *imaginary* in reference to their listeners, that the
characters have an actual audience, which *we* must imagine seeing. It is
also possible, though, that they are pretending to speak for an audience;
in any event, there are no extra characters visible on stage. The effect is
to call into question the extent to which these speakers find themselves
in a naturalistic play and therefore to heighten the emphasis on the narrative impulse. Even if the characters are holding forth for "invisible,"
rather than purely imaginary, listeners, we might conclude that their
desire to do so is yet another sign of their inability to engage in actual
dialogue with one another. In Deborah's brief soliloquy, which is the
only one in which the speaker is undoubtedly onstage alone, she asks
questions aloud ("You see? What is a sublimation of what? . . . What
signifies what?")[18] as if there were a listener present; her words evoke
both the futile reaching toward the dialogue that seems to be a way out
of monologic isolation and the awareness on some level that she *is* addressing (the play's) spectators—but they are incapable of participating
in dialogue.

Bernie is the play's principal monologist/storyteller, and he special-
izes in elaborate accounts of his own and others' sexual exploits. In fact,
the outrageousness of his stories seems to increase in direct proportion
to his inability to succeed with women. At the beginning of the play
Bernie tells Danny of an encounter that he claims to have had with a
woman who, dressed up in a flak suit, requested that he make combat
sounds during sex and ended up setting the hotel room on fire. Douglas
Bruster insists that, since Bernie is one of Mamet's "charlatan" characters, Danny is his "gull" who "believes . . . [the story] completely."[19] I
would argue, however, that there is no evidence that Danny "buys"
Bernie's narratives; rather, Mamet seems more interested in showing us,
through the rhythm and repetitions of their exchanges, that the language
game with Bernie as speaker and Danny as auditor, or "prompter," is a
familiar, even ritualized, part of their interactions:

DANNY: So tell me.
BERNIE: So okay, so where am I?

DANNY: When?
BERNIE: Last night, two-thirty.
DANNY: So two-thirty, you're probably over at Yak-Zies.
BERNIE: Left Yak-Zies at one.
DANNY: So you're probably over at Grunts.
BERNIE: They only got a two o'clock license.
DANNY: So you're probably over at the Commonwealth.
BERNIE: So okay, so I'm over at the Commonwealth. . . .

(10–11)

John Ditsky provides a helpful characterization of the pattern established by this opening sequence: "One character constantly defines himself as dependent, inferior, questioning, eager to learn—even going to the point of asking questions or making repetitions that merely continue the rhythm of the scene, allowing the other character to invent again."[20] (Indeed, if Danny intentionally "allows" Bernie to keep inventing his narrative, this would suggest a far greater *awareness* of fraud than Bruster sees in this sequence.) Bernie, as he does in his later story about King Farouk's sexual exploits, veils the fantastic in the ordinary and attempts to appear as a type of mentor (even if his success in convincing Danny of this is questionable) to the younger, less "experienced" Danny. He uses monologic language to create a more glamorous self; Bernie's identity, as Robert Storey aptly notes, "has long been determined by his speech."[21] Hence, when he tries to pick up Joan in a bar by launching into a story about the loneliness of his job as a meteorologist for TWA, he is caught off balance when Joan responds bluntly that she does not find him attractive.

The last scene of the play, in which Bernie and Danny (who has ended his romance with Deborah) sit on the beach and comment on the women who walk by them, shows that the two men have returned to the same fiction-based realm as the opening sequence. They comment extensively on the anatomy of the women around them, but it is also evident at this point that, in the midst of their bravado, they want to consider themselves "victims" of female sexuality as well:

BERNIE: . . . I mean who the fuck do they think they are all of a sudden, coming out here and just flaunting their bodies all over? (*Pause.*) I mean, what are you supposed to think? I come to the

beach with a friend to get some sun and watch the action and . . . I
mean a fellow comes to the beach to sit out in the fucking sun,
am I wrong? . . .
DANNY: Are you feeling all right?
BERNIE: Well, how do I look, do I look all right?
DANNY: Sure.
BERNIE: Well, then let's assume that I feel all right, okay?

                                                                (68)

With the play's return to the rituals with which it began, it becomes clear
that the "sexual perversity" of Mamet's title is not so much the material
in Bernie's wild stories as it is the perversity of the characters themselves
in their refusal or inability to transcend the myths about the "right" way
to deal with the opposite sex. Nor is the audience excluded from complicity in this "perversity," for, as Bigsby insists, we are seduced on
some level by the play's energy and images.[22]

"Fiction," says Bigsby, "is a fundamental strategy and consolation
to characters who could scarcely survive the knowledge of their own
marginality."[23] Mamet begins to provide a hint, then, of an idea he will
make overt in his later plays: the creation of narrative may be a way of
surviving in a world that is depicted as essentially hostile, but its fraudulence and its attractiveness render it troubling and appealing at the same
time. Early in *Lakeboat,* when Joe asks Collins how long they could
survive if they were to fall overboard, Collins reassures him that there
would be lifejackets and a rescue helicopter; Joe remarks, "I guess the big
problem wouldn't be the drowning as much as the boredom, huh?" (77).
Without intending to do so, Joe creates an equation between two forms
of oblivion—and it is precisely as a protection from oblivion, from a
metaphorical drowning, that the crew members (like Mamet's characters
in these other early plays) hold tightly to the narrative wreckage, the
fragments of stories, that keeps them afloat.

Americans Buffaloed: Monologue and the Strategies
of Deception in Mamet's "Business Plays"

TEACH: Don, Don, I see you're put out, you find out this guy is a
    cheat. . . .
DON: According to you.

TEACH: According to me, yes. I am the person it's usually according *to* when I'm talking.

—David Mamet, *American Buffalo*

FORD: You were going to con me out of my money.
MIKE: It was only business.
FORD: It was only business, huh?
JOEY: It's the American Way.

—David Mamet, *House of Games*

The characters in Mamet's early plays argue about whether the stories they tell one another are true, yet their dependence on the *recounting* of their narratives takes priority over the possibility that a speaker has the power to perpetrate a kind of fraud by engaging a listener who is willing to believe the tales he or she tells.[24] But Mamet's "business" plays— *American Buffalo* (1975), *The Water Engine* (1977), and *Glengarry Glen Ross* (1983)—are all preoccupied with the connections between narrative (especially monologic) language and deception. In these three works Mamet draws upon the world of American business to create a metaphorical structure that has double-dealing and double-crossing at its core. Bigsby offers a valuable description of the way the myths of American success in business, rooted in the "founding" of the country, contain both the lure of achievement and the image of greed:

> The supposed frontier virtues of a sturdy masculine self-sufficiency that took by force what was denied by right are echoed in . . . [Mamet's] plays by people who deploy that rhetoric and dispose those myths in a world that has lost its epic dimensions. Perhaps the myths were always crude rationalizations, but at least the sheer scale on which they were enacted sustained the elevated language and concealed the extent of the moral affront. But, mimicked in his plays by the petty gangster and the salesman, they become ironic as well as immoral, while their deforming effect on the individual and the culture becomes more clearly apparent in the pettiness of their projects and the patently self-destructive nature of their fantasies.[25]

The storytellers who inhabit the shady side of the business world derive much of their power to deceive others (and sometimes themselves) from monologic speech. This type of discourse, with its ability to control time, space, and attention, gives them the capacity for manipulation and distortion of the truth—if such a truth is even available in a postmodern world in which deceptions are layered upon one another in the intricate and theatrical structures of language games.

The characters in *American Buffalo* construct their experience according to the narratives they have internalized about such American "ideals" as "initiative," "ambition," "friendship," "success," and the like, only to find that the myths valorizing such terms are merely facades to cover over the fundamental ways in which they are alienated from one another. Don's early praise to Bobby of Fletcher's "skill and talent" (4), for example, sours when Teach claims later in the play that Fletcher actually won his four hundred dollars in the poker game by cheating. Similarly, when Teach enters the junkshop he is fuming because he says that Grace and Ruthie have abused the generosity of his friendship by complaining when he helped himself to a piece of toast off Grace's plate: "This hurts me in a way I don't know what the fuck to do. . . . The only way to teach these people is to kill them" (11). Teach has depended on the myth that one's friends can always be trusted, but on some level he seems to be aware of the tenuousness of that myth, for the smallest of actions is enough to make him feel that it has been destroyed. His keenest sense of alienation comes from the realization of, and yet the dependence on, the ability that narrative language has to conceal and distort.

I have mentioned Shakespeare's use of homiletic soliloquies;[26] through the ironically named Teach, Mamet does a postmodern take on the homily as Teach attempts constantly to instruct the other characters yet is utterly blind to his own shortcomings. For instance, he confuses "free enterprise" with a more metaphysical type of freedom:

> You know what is free enterprise? . . . The freedom . . . of the *Individual* . . . To Embark on Any Fucking Course that he sees fit. . . . In order to secure his honest chance to make a profit. . . . The country's *founded* on this, Don. . . . Without this we're just savage shitheads in the wilderness. . . . Sitting around some vicious campfire. . . . And take those fuckers in the concentration camps. You think they went in there by *choice*? . . . They were *dragged* in there, Don . . . Kicking and screaming. (72–73)

For Teach free enterprise is the glue that holds civilization itself together; from an individual perspective, too, he sees himself as nothing if he is deprived of the chance to participate in this enterprise as he defines it. At some level Teach views himself as a deeply moral human being; to find confirmation that the world does not meet his expectations—as is the case at the end of the play, when the robbery plans go haywire—is, for him, to look into the abyss. As Hubert-Leibler points out, Teach "fails to understand that the total egotism he is promoting also implies the frightening consequences he will bitterly deplore at the end of the play."[27] Mamet writes Teach's final litany of disavowal in the form of "pronouncements":

> My Whole Cocksucking Life. . . .
> The Whole Entire World.
> There Is No Law.
> There Is No Right and Wrong.
> The World Is Lies.
> There Is No Friendship.
> Every Fucking Thing. [*Pause.*]
> Every God-forsaken Thing. . . .
> We all live like the cavemen.
>
> (103)

In Teach's paradoxically nihilistic and didactic vision, the myths of freedom, profit, friendship, and so forth are the principal forces of order in the universe itself. As a postmodern Polonius, though, Teach lives in a world in which one's survival cannot be assured merely through the formulation of "principles" that one passes on to others; Mamet's irony demands that a homiletic narrative will ultimately point the spectators toward the shortcomings of the speaker rather than simply toward a vision of his or her "wisdom."

The paradox, then, is that the same myths that sustain the characters also destroy them, and vice versa; Mamet allows this paradox to be reflected in the structure of the play itself. *American Buffalo* ends almost the same way as it begins, with Bobby apologizing to Don and Don reassuring him that it is "all right" (106); this construction resembles a frame or a circle that, as Beckett's *Godot* shows, is also a metatheatrical image, reflecting the status of a play that is performed again and again. The play's junk shop set, laden with strange and ordinary pieces of culture from 1933 Chicago World's Fair souvenirs to a dead pig sticker, establishes a connection between the myths that nurture/torture the characters and the literal and figurative "foundation" of the play, which therefore has an "architecture" of fraud. Ultimately, while the action of *American Buffalo* comes through its language, the language conceals and eventually is transformed into the physical violence that seems to be the inevitable consequence of language's capacity for misrepresentation.

The Water Engine, which was written as a radio play and then reshaped for stage production in 1977, continues to theatricalize the relationship between narrative and trickery as embodied in the language games of the American business culture. The staged version of the piece retains a great deal of the radio version's reliance on verbal narrative rather than visual action.[28] Mamet notes of the first theatrical production that

> many scenes were played on mike, as actors presenting a radio drama, and many scenes were played off mike as in a traditional, realistic play. The result was a third reality, a scenic truth, which dealt with radio not as an electronic convenience, but as an expression of our need to create and to communicate and to explain— much like a chainletter.[29]

This "third reality" operates in terms of multiple narrative levels: interwoven like musical themes throughout the play are the radio voices (e.g., the Announcer's), the interactions of the protagonist Lang and others, the chain letter, the Hall of Science voices, the overheard conversations, the knife-grinder and train conductor, and the soapbox speakers.

As the spectators of this play are beseiged with stories—some in the form of gossip (the stories in the elevator) and some in the form of declamatory address (the speakers in Bughouse Square)—they are placed almost in the position of "jurors" as the central narrative undertakes the revelation of fraud. Mamet renders this postmodernist collage of stories (all of which have different levels of realism) even more complicated by framing Lang's actions as the plot of a radio story in itself. At the beginning the Annnouncer says: "Chicago 1934. The Century of Progress" (5). And at the commencement of act 2 he states, "You'll remember when we last saw the inventor, Charles Lang . . ." (43). The Announcer's words imply that Lang's own adventures serve in themselves as a larger "story"—yet within the play, as we see it, Lang's interactions are validated as representing a central reality off of which the other narrative modes play.

Another textual complication is the presence of the chain letter, bits of which are narrated throughout the play. Although the Barker reads Lang the letter at one point, Lang himself is (without knowing it) already part of the chain, for very early in the play the chain letter "voice" says, "In September, 1934, a young man in Chicago, Illinois designed—built an engine which used distilled water as its only fuel" (8). This implies that the chain letter itself has a narrative privilege that goes beyond superstition and therefore calls into question the separation of "story" and "science." To place Lang's experience within the context of the other stories in the chain letter is simultaneously to render the chain letter itself more credible and to hint that the saga of the water engine has entered the "folktale" realm, which the Barker mentions (71). Since the play itself enacts just such a folktale, the art of telling—in all of its magnificent and frustrating forms—is granted an urgency in itself. Linda Hutcheon's description of the narrative paradoxes of the postmodernist novels she calls "historiographic metafiction" is to some degree applicable to the competing narrational modes in *The Water Engine*. Hutcheon says,

> The interaction of the historiographic and the metafictional [read: metadramatic] foregrounds the rejection of the claims of both "authentic" representation and "inauthentic" copy alike, and the very meaning of artistic originality is as forcefully challenged as is the transparency of historical referentiality.[30]

The point is, though, that in the process we are not asked to validate one type of narrative over another; rather, the play implies that all of the ways information is transmitted involve a certain level of fraudulence inherent in the act of transmission. The "scenic truth" to which Mamet refers, then, is actually a carefully designed scenic *deception,* a deception that has as its ironic parallel the central narrative's revelation of fraud (Lang is swindled out of his rights to the water engine he has invented by a lawyer and a representative of corporate interests). Guido Almansi extends this picture by arguing that the play's multiple narrative voices reflect the "American dream . . . of communication," which is actually a hoax: "Mamet's characters pretend to speak, to communicate, and to relate with other people, in a world where everyone is isolated. The wires have been cut."[31] The play's multiple voices thus offer us different "layers" of fiction, and Mamet plays with our (in)ability to determine which, if any, can be considered reliable or authoritative. He writes, "The only profit in the sharing of a myth is to those who participate as storytellers or as listeners, and this profit is the shared experience itself, the *celebration* of the tale, and of its truth."[32] For Mamet the transmission and reception of a narrative form the basis of a profitable (though still possibly duplicitous, as with the chain letter) communicative act, rather than the judgment of the narrative's essential plausiblity. The "*celebration* of the tale, and of its truth" overrides the "objective" content of the tale itself.

While the presence of a manipulator, or huckster, character remains relatively marginal to *The Water Engine,* in *Glengarry Glen Ross* (1983) Mamet foregrounds the presence of this figure, for the major characters in this work are real estate salesmen who attempt to pawn off worthless pieces of Florida swampland on unsuspecting buyers. All of the salesmen play language games, and their narratives show their adeptness at taking advantage of the monologic voice to "sell" an idea, a dream, or a personality. Again monologic language enacts the consummate sales pitch: not only does it preclude interruption, but it also allows the speaker to appear "personal" and "confessional" even when he or she is only acting.

As this type of narrative commands a listener, moreover, the listener is drawn in to the point where buying the story means agreeing to buy whatever the story is selling. Moss, for example, takes advantage of this knowledge when he draws Aaronow into his plan to steal the sales leads from the office: almost imperceptibly, he moves the discussion from the hypothetical robbery to the actual plan for one, finally telling Aaronow that he will have to face the consequences if he refuses to do the job for him. When Aaronow asks why, Moss replies, "Because you listened."[33] Without realizing it, Aaronow catches himself in the very snare into which he tries to lead his own customers: after a certain accumulation of speech has occurred, to listen is implicitly to comply.

The play sets up two of its manipulator figures, Shelly Levene and Richard Roma, as examples of salesmen who are, respectively, on their way "down" and on their way "up." Levene ultimately falls victim to a "con" himself by believing that the Nyborgs, to whom he thinks he has made his big "comeback" sale, are legitimate customers. He also gives himself away as a perpetrator of the robbery of the sales leads; ironically, it is Levene's inability *not* to betray the truth that proves to be his undoing. Unlike Levene, though, Roma survives because he remains securely within the business's parameters of deception.[34]

The first time we see Roma he is seated in a Chinese restaurant, delivering a long and peculiar monologue to James Lingk—a man alone at another table—and moving almost undetectably into a sales pitch. He begins on a perversely, abruptly personal level, telling Lingk that, rather than being hypocrites, people should live with their actions: "You fuck little girls, so *be* it" (47). Lingk barely responds to Roma's questions, which seem purely rhetorical, and so Roma continues by moving from a description of his most memorable sexual encounter to a more "philosophical" plane:

> I do those things which seem correct to me *today*. I trust myself. And if security concerns me, I do that which *today* I think will make me secure. . . . Stocks, bonds, objects of art, real estate.
> Now: what are they? [*Pause.*] An opportunity. . . . They're an *event.* A guy comes up to you, you make a call, you send in a brochure, it doesn't matter. . . . All it is is THINGS THAT HAPPEN TO YOU. . . . Some poor newly married guy gets run down by a cab. Some *busboy* wins the lottery. [*Pause.*] All it is, it's a carnival. What's special . . . what *draws* us? [*Pause.*] We're all different. . . . I want to show you something. . . . [*Pause. He takes out a small map and spreads it on a table.*] What is that? Florida. Glengarry Highlands. Florida. "Florida. *Bullshit.*" And maybe that's true; and that's what *I* said: but look *here:* what is this? This is a piece of land. Listen to what I'm going to tell you now: (49–51)

The scene ends, mid-sentence, with Roma's "now:"—and we can infer that at this point the monologue has Lingk transfixed, and so Roma can move from there to the details of the sale. But Roma's monologue itself is striking on several counts. As he draws his listener in, Roma indicates that he *lives inside* his own fictions. His personal "philosophy" and his need to sell are inseparable, for he has sold himself on himself. Bigsby suggests that the audience, like Lingk, has been seduced and then "betrayed" by the discovery that this is a sales pitch when it has appeared that genuine contact was occurring.[35] Roma's words, on the surface, indicate a philosophy of passivity—"THINGS HAPPEN TO YOU"—but this is a mask for a philosophy of gratification and acquisition, a capitalist carpe diem. "The point," Mamet says in an interview with David Savran, "is not to speak the desire but to speak that which is most likely to bring about the desire."[36] Certainly, Roma is creating a character for the purpose of making a sale—but, like a Method actor, he rejects the idea of pure surface acting, and (at least convinces us that) he has internalized his role.

Indeed, Roma carries through with the theatrical aspect of his salesmanship when Lingk comes into the office to try to cancel the contract he has signed. Immediately and unflinchingly, Roma enlists Levene in a "routine" in which Levene becomes an out-of-town client whom Roma must rush to the airport so that he will not have time to talk with Lingk. He follows this with a large dose of "psychology" regarding Lingk's need to be able to do things independently of his wife without feeling unfaithful, a tactic that is on the verge of success until Williamson ruins it. We receive confirmation in these scenes that Roma is intuitively connected to the procedures for deception; he slides from story to story so effectively that he even begins to persuade Levene to be his partner so that he will be able to profit from Levene's sales as well as his own. No principles of friendship or of business ethics, it seems, will prevent Roma from getting what he wants, yet he bases his persuasive narratives on the proposition that he is a man who has done a considerable amount of soul-searching. He does not have to play at being sincere, for he has made his world-weary cynicism into part of his routine—or, more aptly, he is entirely *sincere* about his full-fledged immersion in deception. Thus, he is able to say in so many words that the Florida land is "bullshit," but his readiness to say this becomes part of the reason that his sales pitch is successful.

Roma succeeds where others (such as Levene) fail, then, because he has internalized the capacity for fraud, and so he can sustain the fictions he creates. In the world of these hucksters the ability to maintain one's stories is a survival tactic, and the play, on one level, makes an obvious judgment about the unethical nature of those who rob others by practicing such deception. But it is crucial to realize that, on another level, Mamet is *not without admiration* for the capacity for dissembling that such a figure as Roma has acquired. The "D. Ray Morton" scene that Roma and Levene perform to save Roma's deal makes manifest the connection between the salesmen's fraudulent stories and the theater itself, for the sequence—even with its qualities of shtick—functions as a play-within-the-play, and we delight in seeing the two characters act under pressure.

If storytelling constitutes a kind of fraud, Mamet seems to say, then to act in the theater is to seduce and persuade with one's stories in the same way that the salesmen use their narratives to lure customers (and indeed, to extend the metaphor of the real estate salesmen, the actors, too, must sell the audience on the tangibility of their "properties").

The Magician Behind the Curtain: Textual "Trickery" in the Later Plays

> JOE: Did you make this up?
> MIKE: No. I mean, you know, I *embellished* it. Yeah. I made part of it up.
> JOE: Uh-huh.
>   —David Mamet, *Film Crew*

> The cards may be diverting, or dangerous, or destructive. They are never neutral.
>   —David Mamet, "Black as the Ace of Spades"

The power of the planned robbery in *American Buffalo,* the chain letter in *The Water Engine,* and the sales contest board (or, for the customers, the descriptions of the real estate) in *Glengarry Glen Ross* resides in the promise that the characters will come one step closer to transforming their inner narratives of achievement into actuality; as a result of their readiness to believe in the viability of myth, though, the characters are caught in a matrix of self-perpetuating deceptions.[37] Yet the theater itself is just such a matrix of *intentional* deceptions. The imaging of such characters as Roma and Levene as actors or as "directors" of others' theatricalized actions leaves us with the sense that Mamet's movement toward a validation of "fraud"—at least in theatrical terms—is perhaps inevitable. Such later pieces as *Prairie du Chien, The Shawl* (1985), and *Speed-the-Plow* (1988) are not without the violence, paranoia, crossed rhetoric, and scheming visible in the business plays; the difference is that these elements are integrated more fully into the theatrical narratives rather than functioning as the attributes of *characters* who deploy narratives. As such, they invite consideration in terms of metaphoric structures that foreground narrative, particularly structures that allow a place for the free play of deception as it figures in the workings of the imagination.

Like *The Water Engine, Prairie du Chien* (written for radio in 1979 and rewritten for the stage in 1985) retains a "radio" quality even in its staged adaptation, for the play highlights spoken narrative rather than the poetics of the visual; moreover, as a piece that is *about* the process of telling a story that may or may not be true (counterpointed by the progress of a card game that may or may not involve cheating), its emphasis on listening points both to the mutability of the story and to the "trust" that the listener (for whom the Listener character in the play is a surrogate figure) must place in the Storyteller. *Prairie du Chien* simultaneously privileges monologic narrative, as in Mamet's early plays, and calls its possible "fraudulent" qualities into question, as in the business plays. These seemingly polar impulses are reconciled as Mamet allows the play's narrative to encompass the metatheatrical meeting of subject and structure.

Mamet's decision to situate *Prairie du Chien* on a train underscores the relationship between the progress of the narrative and the train's movement (the same is true of the car ride in *Dark Pony*). The "subdued"[38] voices of the speakers also call attention to the play's narrative as a form of extraordinary discourse—that is, a tale that is told at 3 A.M. in a hushed voice has the quality of myth, of a ghost story, and so the Storyteller's rhetorical mode points to the possibility that his narrative is a fabrication. It is not simply the macabre, Gothic quality of the tale of adultery and vengeance that the Storyteller relates, though, that makes it hover in the realm of pure fiction; the events in the narrative are composed of multiple levels of hearsay, of stories-within-stories.[39]

Just when the Storyteller reaches the culmination of his narrative—the point, one might say, at which he must depend on having captured the trust of the Listener in order to make the lurid vision he has conjured believable—the Gin Player accuses the Dealer of cheating. It is at this juncture that we begin to see the implicit relationship between the Dealer's card game and the Storyteller's language game. As the Storyteller relates his tale, the exchanges between the Dealer and the Gin Player, though largely intended to serve as muted background to the Storyteller's and Listener's voices, occasionally emerge in ironic relationship to the central narrative; for example, as the Storyteller tells of the jealous man's plan to murder his wife, the Dealer refers to "Soo–cide jacks, Man with the Ax" (65). When the Gin Player accuses the Dealer of cheating and fires a shot at him, the Dealer extricates himself from the accusation and compels an apology (and the money) from the Gin Player by acting affronted at the suggestion of fraud. The Gin Player's apology reveals how readily he—like the Listener—can be "taken" by the authority of a dominant speaker. But the Dealer's departure from the train with his bags when the train stops for water may imply that he needs to escape while the "game" is in his hands. A final indication of the symbolic link between the Storyteller and Dealer comes in the Storyteller's announcement that he, too, intends to step off the train when it stops; the two "confidence men" thus enter and exit the actual stage where the narrative takes place (i.e., the car of the train) together, almost as if they were one character divided into two parts. If the Dealer has indeed been cheating the Gin Player and if the Storyteller's narrative has indeed been a fabrication, then the two characters are linked by their propensity for deception—but the connection is not necessarily that simple. Just as we have no direct evidence that the Dealer was cheating at cards, we have no possibility of "confirming" the Storyteller's narrative; this ambiguity places us in the same position as the Gin Player and the Listener, who are "taken in" by the card/language game but who also seem to *choose* to be convinced, an idea that Mamet pursues in greater detail in *The Shawl* and in his 1985 screenplay and subsequent film *House of Games*.

Finally, the play's recurrent images of sleep and dreaming suggest that one way of responding to the question of fraud in the work is to consider the oneiric qualities of its storytelling, a possibility that suits the setting and the hushed (dreamlike?) voices. While the sheriff within the Storyteller's narrative refuses to awaken from his dream world, the Storyteller himself experiences insomnia because he cannot escape from the story that constitutes the dream. In his afterword to Lyotard's and Thébaud's *Just Gaming*, Samuel Weber suggests that dreams constitute a variety of language game wherein the narrative resolution is always indeterminate, and so the act of narration takes precedence over the narrated material itself.[40] If this "dream" is also the larger narrative of the play, then Mamet has provided a subtle response to the possibility that the Listener/listeners will experience the play as yet another "confidence game"—for a dream, like the theater, is *experienced* as both real and unreal at the same time, constituting a third reality like that which Mamet mentions in his note for performance of *The Water Engine*. In fact, Mamet writes in "A National Dream Life" that "the life of the play is the life of the unconscious. . . . As in our dreams, the law of psychic ecomony operates. In dreams . . . we seek answers to those questions which the conscious mind is incompetent to deal with. So with the drama. . . ."[41] The dream/drama is a kind of fraud in its ephemerality and its ability to break rules of chronology and consistency—but it is also a kind of fraud we will tolerate and will sometimes even, like the Gin Player, pay to have perpetrated upon us.

The main character of *The Shawl,* John, is apparently another one of Mamet's manipulators: as a "psychic," or "spiritualist," he professes to divine the answers to his clients' questions, insisting to Charles, his lover, that doing so is simply a matter of knowing how to read the signals that the client provides unwittingly. When Miss A comes to John for advice, Charles convinces him (under duress) to try and use his "powers" to get her money; the scheme falls through, but, as John continues to talk with Miss A at the end of the play, the possibility that John does indeed possess some type of psychic ability hovers over their closing exchange. Just as the central monologic narrative of *Prairie du Chien* emerges from myriad levels of "hearsay" to constitute an experience for the listener that has the disturbingly real/unreal quality of a dream, *The Shawl*'s preoccupation with trances and clairvoyance—counterpointed with the assertions that the psychic phenomena are merely akin to a magician's tricks of the trade—leaves the spectators feeling as if they have witnessed a curious type of doubled event that is at once mystifying and a demystification (a typically postmodern refusal of clarity and closure).

The opening encounter between John and Miss A has somewhat the effect, if not the rhythm, of Roma's verbal seduction of James Lingk in *Glengarry Glen Ross.* John, like Roma, uses the elaboration of a philosophy as an inroad to obtaining the potential client's interest then consent: both of these "con men" move from an image of the body (John says, "When you awaken, it is . . . to be hungry")[42] to a metaphysical question ("And what powers DO exist? And what looks after us?" [5]), closing the "pitch" with a seemingly concrete "answer" that demonstrates what is being "sold" ("And you have come to *ask* me. If you should contest the will" [15]). In one sense, then, John and Roma are both charlatans, salesmen who ply their trade through words and through their ability to detect and promise to fill the emptinesses in their clients' lives. But Roma, as we have seen, has too much at stake to risk living outside the persona he has created for even a moment, and so his sales pitch is foremost a way of *being.* John, though, goes to the opposite extreme: so eager is he to assert the transparency of his trickery and his alleged power's grounding in simple observation that, by the end of the play, we may wonder if John has a talent of which he himself is largely unaware—or if we, too, have been taken in by his magicianship.

The play's central monologue occurs in John's "séance" with Miss A; using the research he has done at the library, he seems to speak through the voice of a character he calls the Boston Woman as a vehicle for establishing "contact" with Miss A's dead mother. The resulting monologue, with its echoes of Joyce and Faulkner, can be seen simultaneously as parodic pastiche and as rich invention:

> Afternoons by the docks, by the waterfront I went there to his room he rented and it smelt of sweat, the curtains blowing on the dock, we saw the curtains blow, the ship commands from down, men working men on the wharves, do your bidding on the sea but what's here? . . . (34–35)

The diction and syntax suggest John's immersion in an intertextualized voice of otherness; he may have culled the narrative from library books, but the primary effect is that of an actor playing a role, or even of someone "possessed" by a spirit. The audience, in one respect, has the advantage over Miss A in knowing the duplicitous motivation of the monologue—yet in the process of its performance, the spectators are placed in a position not unlike Miss A's of witnessing the presentation of a hitherto suppressed character in the play. In a sense the doubleness of the monologue reflects the doubleness of the play as a whole: the performance privileges as a virtuoso solo the very mode of narrative that the characters' interactions have sought to deconstruct.

Mamet complicates this position by adding one final twist: just when it seems, by the end of the play, that every aspect of John's trickery has been exposed, John tells Miss A that she burned the shawl, "in rage. Standing somewhere by the water, five years ago" (53). Since the play ends here, we have no more "explanations" forthcoming about how John gathered this information: thus abandoned, we are placed in the same position as Miss A, believing not simply because we want to but because we have no choice. The audience has thus been "gulled," like Miss A—or, alternatively, John is unable or unwilling to admit the existence of his actual powers; Mamet's own game here is the refusal to leave his spectators with a clear resolution.

Early in the play John tells Charles that the problem Charles has in accepting his techniques is due to his lack of experience in seeing the operation from the inside out, as it were:

> I *show* you the trick "from the back" and you're disappointed. Of course you are. If you view it as a "member of the audience." One of the, you will see, the most painful sides of the profession is this: you do your work well, and who will see it? No one, really. . . . To say, to learn to say, I suppose you must, to just say what separates us, finally, from them is this: that is we look *clearly*. (26–27)

In *The Shawl,* as in *A Life in the Theatre,* we see "the trick 'from the back,'" as John tells Charles. The implication is that to do so is to risk a split between one's immersion in and one's "dis-illusionment" in the "art" one is witnessing. In some respects, as Bigsby contends, the passage thus stands as a justification of Mamet's own art: "From the deceits of art are born truths," but that realization should be combined with a sense of "the poetry that lies behind the calculation."[43] The magic that this art constitutes, John claims, comes simply from the ability to "look *clearly*"—but even these words suggest a pun that reaffirms the doubleness of his vision, for *look clearly* is also a translation of *clairvoyance*—which underscores the very psychic ability John seeks so ardently to deny. *The Shawl* tells a story, then, that Mamet feels can be seen "from the back" without losing the simultaneous acknowledgment of the unseeable, the intangible; in effect, it insists upon a recognition of theatrical narrative's power to "conjure" images even in the face of skepticism about the possible fraudulence of such power.

    As a theatricalized form of illusion, the movies—and, specifically, the workings of the Hollywood "machine" behind the movies, which also fascinated Shepard in *Angel City*—serve as a compelling way for Mamet to satirize our predisposition for being conned or conquered by the conjuring of images. Mamet's work both in film (*House of Games, Things Change* [1988], *We're No Angels* [1990]) and in *Speed-the-Plow* (written in 1985; first produced in 1988), a play *about* the movies, extends his fascination with charlatans and their language games. In *Speed-the-Plow*, Mamet complicates the role of the charlatan by making the play's principal "con man" into its principal victim as well.

    Bobby Gould, recently promoted to Head of Production at a movie studio, gloats with his friend Charlie Fox about their ability to manipulate others. They parody the "touchy-feely" clichés of the Hollywood industry:

GOULD: 'Cause, people, Charlie. . . . Are what it's All About.
FOX: I know.
GOULD: And it's a People Business.
FOX: That it is.
GOULD: It's *full* of fuckcn' pcople . . .
FOX: And we're gonna kick some ass, Bob.
GOULD: That we are.[44]

The manipulation in business is paralleled by (and conjoined with) sexual manipulation, as Gould bets Fox five hundred dollars that he can get Karen, the temporary secretary, to go to bed with him. Throughout the play power and sexuality are linked: Fox and Gould refer to each other as "Two Whorcs" who work in a "bordello" (26); Gould jokes to Fox that, when they mcet for lunch, they will "talk about boys and clothes" (33); and, after Gould says he plans to renege on his deal with Fox, Fox calls him "Menopaus[al]" (69), an "old woman" (70), and a "whore," or "chippy" (71), who thinks he is a "ballerina" (72). The characters project their feelings of emasculation or castration as pawns of the Hollywood gamc onto their images of one another as female. They redirect their feelings of powerlessness and impotence onto the target of an abstract femininity.

Yet, ironically, Bobby's attempt to win the sexual bet that he makes with Gould results in his being conned by Karen, who induces him to drop Fox's project in favor of the book on radiation that Gould has offered her the task of reading, both as an apparent favor for her and in order not to have to read it himself. Mamet juxtaposes Gould's reactions to the book—it "Won't Make A Good Movie" (53)—with Karen's monologues, which consist of reading excerpts from the text:

And he says that, that these are the Dark Ages . . . they are now. We're living them. [*Reads:*] "In the waning days . . . in the last days." . . . "Yes," he says, it's *true,* and you needn't deny it . . . and I fclt such *fear,* because, of course, he's right . . . when you read it, the story itself . . . written with such love. . . . (49–50)

The textual excerpts that Mamet gives us are just cryptic enough so that it is difficult to tell whether the radiation book is genuinely "profound," with an apocalyptic commentary that reflects the decadence and self-absorption of the movie industry, or whether we, like Karen and (temporarily) Bobby, are likely to be "suckers" for its ostensible literary "value."

At the end of the play Fox reasserts both masculine dominance (he calls Karen a "Tight Pussy wrapped around Ambition" [78]) and control over Bobby's cooperation in his project. Perhaps anticipating Mamet's sequel *Bobby Gould in Hell* (1989), Fox tells Gould, "And what *if* this fucken' 'grace' exists? It's not for you. You know that, Bob. . . . You have a different thing" (81). By the closing sequence, Fox—true to his name—has outsmarted the other characters and taken control of the language game. Whereas Gould was the "directive" speaker in the play's earlier exchanges, Fox takes the potentially monologic lead at the end:

> GOULD: I wanted to do Good. . . . But I became foolish.
> FOX: Well, so we learn a lesson. But we aren't here to "pine," Bob, we aren't put here to *mope*. What are we here to do [*pause*] Bob? After everything is said and done. What are we put on earth to do?
> GOULD: We're here to make a movie.
> FOX: Whose name goes above the title?
> GOULD: Fox and Gould.
> FOX: Then how bad can life be?
>
> (81–82)

Fox plays parodically upon the "evangelical" tone of the radiation book (see Karen's earlier "I've been bad" [58]) by describing their jobs as a mission of sorts; it is what they are "put on earth to do." Bobby, then, whose last name conflates the desire to be or to do "good" and the temptation of "gold," ultimately embodies his name's additional pun, for he is doubly gulled by Karen and by Fox. Fox's words to Gould—"I know you, Bob. I know you from the *back*" (34)—suggests simultaneously another sexualizing of dominance (in homoerotic terms) and an echo of *The Shawl*'s "trick from the back": as in *The Wizard of Oz,* seeing behind the curtain reveals the workings of a machine that is finally both a fraud (because its machinery is human and not truly "magical") and an effective ideological apparatus (because its workings can be imitated or replicated for a public that will believe whatever it sees).

If the traditional definition of metadrama presupposes that theater is capable of an internal mimesis, an ability to duplicate and imitate its own processes, then Mamet engages in the postmodern practice of tricking these processes. To leave us uncertain about whether John is a charlatan or a spiritualist at the end of *The Shawl,* or whether the text of the radiation book in *Speed-the-Plow* is fraudulent or meaningful, is to play at the abstractions of theater's potential to "dupe" its audience. Lyotard, in his essay on "The Unconscious as Mise-en-Scène," argues: "Works must not be taken as symptoms symbolically expressing a concealed discourse, but as attempts to state perspectives of reality. Interpretation must in turn give way to descriptions of devices."[45] Indeed, Mamet's metadrama foregrounds the existence of "devices" and allows the energy of these devices to power his staging and characterization without being blocked by a concern with the extent to which the manipulation involved in these devices is *genuinely* conning the audience. If the recent *Bobby Gould in Hell* foreshadows an increasing preoccupation with the "trappings" of Renaissance drama (it contains everything from trap doors to lightning to an exit "pursued by a bear"), it may be because his next phase is an explicit test of what happens when metadrama turns to trick playing—when the theater is a "house of games" that we enter with an awareness of our desire to watch ourselves being fooled.

Wordscapes of the Body: Performative Language as *Gestus* in Maria Irene Fornes's Plays

If the stage is a place where, as Hélène Cixous claims, "it is possible to get across the living, breathing, speaking body,"[1] does that body constitute a text in and of itself? In performance art an often cited example of the female body "as" text is Carolee Schneeman's *Interior Scroll* (1975), in which she appeared naked before her audience, extracted a long scroll from her vagina and read aloud the words on the scroll.[2] More recently, Karen Finley has used her body as the site of transgressive (some might say counterpornographic) acts: by arousing the mechanisms of disgust in her audience, her performances parody and subvert the associations between the female body and its role as sexually evocative signifier.[3] As this chapter's discussion of Maria Irene Fornes's work will show, the text/body question is integral to an examination of monologue's role in feminist drama.

Brecht, Feminist Monologue, and the "Embodied" Text

Current theoretical debates about the staging of the female body return repeatedly to the problem of whether privileging the "textual" body is a reductive strategy that risks biological essentialism. The body's role in theatrical representation poses some particularly complex issues for materialist feminists because, despite the extent to which "gender" and "character" may be social and/or theatrical constructions, the facticity of the actor's biological sex always reinscribes the performer with the cultural codes associated with his or her gender. Jill Dolan notes that "the female body is not reducible to a sign free of connotation. Women always bear the mark and meaning of their sex, which inscribes them

within a cultural hierarchy."[4] At the same time it is at the moment of
entry into discourse (here theatrical discourse) that the body acquires the
multiple sources of signification associated with the *speaking subject*. Julia
Kristeva, for instance, emphasizes the speaking subject's remarkable
ability to "multiply," "pulverize," and "revive" meaning.[5] Janelle
Reinelt and others, however, have criticized Kristeva's ultimate reliance
on "bipolarities" (male-female, maternal-paternal) that ignore the
"polyvocal" nature of the female subject.[6] Re-visions of Kristeva favor
polyvocality as a means for describing the processual nature of subjectivity; this metaphor of the voice, simultaneously bodied and textual, is an
apt one for consideration of the theater's unique status as an arena for the
enactment, or "voicing," of multiple subject positions.

To show the subject-in-process, or the nonunified subject, though,
is to begin breaking the "rules" of what happens to the speaking body
on stage. Traditional theater uses the actor's immersion in a character,
and the audience's resultant empathy, as a way of closing up the occasional gaps between the languages of the body (both explicit and implicit) and the spoken language of the character: costumes, voice modu-
lations, even lighting and music work to create an illusion of coherence
that is sustained by the complicity of the spectators. Brechtian theory,
as chapters 1 and 2 remarked, often serves as a paradigm for challenging
or displacing these conventional strategies of representation. In Brecht's
"A-effect," the ongoing refusal to permit audience empathy—or the
concomitant distinctions between actor/character and story/history—allows for a constructive disengagement (or, more accurately, a historicized "reading" of) the speaking body and its signifiers. Elin Diamond's
feminist revaluation of Brecht proposes that the *Gestus* serves as an especially powerful agent for this spectatorial disengagement without wholly
subsuming the possibility of spectatorial pleasure; her conclusion is that
a "gestic feminist criticism would 'alienate' or foreground those moments in a playtext in which social attitudes about gender could be made
visible."[7] It is in this realm of *Gestus* that Diamond invites an exploration
of new modes for a feminist theatrical discourse, as the term refers both
to critical theory and to the discursive aspect of the female body as it
appears within staged representation. As Brecht would have it, *Gestus*
may occur through language as well as or instead of in the moment of
physical enactment. In fact, Patrice Pavis sees *Gestus* as the "radical"
displacement, or splitting, of the two elements:

Instead of fusing logos and gestuality in an illusion of reality, the *Gestus* radically cleaves the performance into two blocks: the shown (the said) and the showing (the saying). Discourse no longer has the form of a homogenous block; it threatens at any moment to break away from its enunciator. Far from assuring the construction and the continuity of the action, it intervenes to stop the movement and to comment on what might have been acted on stage. *Gestus* thus displaces the dialectic between ideas and actions; the dialectic no longer operates within the system of these ideas and actions, but at the point of intersection of the enunciating gesture and the enunciated discourse.[8]

Monologic speech, we might say, takes on "gestic" qualities as it forces the creation of the same moment of "splitting" between *énoncé* and *énonciation* that Pavis describes. As an extended discourse, monologue continually threatens to halt the "continuity of action" and to "break away from its enunciator." The gestic monologue is an almost literal seizing of the word. To take such a step can be, as Cixous and Frieden have argued in different contexts, a transgressive, or "deviant," act.[9] Perhaps this is one reason why so many female playwrights have been drawn to the monologue form: to some extent the gestic monologue marks a locus for the struggle for female subjectivity as it enacts the drama of the gendered speaking body and its polyvocal signifiers. The monologue's conquest of narrative space might thus be viewed as a reification of the feminine subject-in-process.

Fornes's plays provide a striking opportunity for illustrating the nature of gestic language, especially gestic monologue, in feminist drama. Her works emphasize the creation of embodied characters—that is, characters who enact the movements toward and away from female subjectivity in which corporeality locates itself as the site of culturally conditioned "meanings." While these characters may reflect the "broken"-ness and isolation that are inevitable in their repressive environments (see, e.g., Julia in *Fefu and Her Friends* [1977], Sarita in the play by that name [1984], or Marion in *Abingdon Square* [1987]), the fact that their "impulses" as such are communicated in the gestic, self-narrated discourse of Brechtianism allows a partial recuperation of this fragmentation.

The (Dis)placement of Language

Surprisingly, despite Fornes's insistence that the Method helped her to locate an autonomy for her characters,[10] the figures that populate her earliest works (including *Tango Palace,* written in 1963 before Fornes studied drama formally) are noticeably lacking in corporeal identity: Isidore in *Tango Palace* is neither completely male nor completely female, the characters in *The Successful Life of 3* (1965) are identified by names that are at once universal and anonymous ("He," "She," "3"), and the very plot of *Promenade* (1965) hinges on the notion that outer trappings determine and transform character, such as it is: "Costumes/Change the course/Of life," sing 105, 106, and The Servant.[11]

At the same time the physical movement and activity in these plays is nearly relentless, as if the characters were brought to life, puppetlike, only when they moved about onstage (a technique Fornes returns to in *Mud* [1983] and in *The Danube* [1982–84]). Similarly, the language used by the robotic characters in these early plays is continually mechanized, "alienated," or formalized as a game, or stage device; its failures and shortcomings are invoked repeatedly. Isidore in *Tango Palace,* for example, tosses out card after card upon which "he" has written (and almost simultaneously recites) a multitude of clichés, anecdotes, and encyclopedic information, so that the words that pour out of his mouth actually appear to fill up the stage space. At one point Isidore tells a story about a man who loved his white rat, lost it, and fell in love with the rat's picture, then became desperate and smashed the picture, thereby killing the rat that had been hiding beneath the picture all along. Like the man in this story, the Jailer in *Promenade* confuses the signifier and signified when he arrests the Driver and Injured Man simply because they are wearing the jackets that have the numbers of the fugitives (105 and 106) on them. And at the beginning of *The Successful Life of 3,* 3 says he is glad to have discovered that He (the other character) was waiting for 3 to drop his shoe because "it starts action." When He asks, "What action did you start?" and 3 replies, "We're talking," He retorts, "That's nothing. We could as well be waiting for the shoe to drop."[12]

Dr. Kheal (1968), a piece for a solo actor, reflects an even more overtly metatheatrical direction in which Fornes takes the potential for language to "detach" itself from its speaker. The play itself consists simply of Dr. Kheal's lecture to a classroom of "students" (who may or may not be the members of the audience). Dr. Kheal asks his listeners:

But who, tell me, understands the poetry of space in a box? I
do. . . . Abysmal and concrete at the same time. Four walls, a top,
and a bottom . . . and yet a void. . . . Who understands that? I, Pro-
fessor Kheal, understand it clearly and expound it well![13]

His description of the box—"Four walls, a top, and a bottom . . . and yet
a void"—evokes an image of the theater, or theatrical space; as the actor,
Dr. Kheal appears to "understand" and "expound" its function. Yet, the
more he says to expound upon his points, the more obvious it becomes
that Dr. Kheal himself is an almost laughably insignificant figure in
relation to "the poetry of space in a box" itself, as is reinforced by the
opening stage direction: "He [Dr. Kheal] is small, or else the furniture
is large" (129). In other words, as Dr. Kheal's monologic discourse
becomes increasingly circular and solipsistic in the course of the play, it
reflects Kheal's own comment that "words change the nature of things.
A thing not named and the same thing named are two different things"
(132). In his encounter with the vision of Crissanda, she not only speaks
a language that is incomprehensible to him ("She speaks in riddles, like
the gods. 'ksjdnhyidfgesles'"), but he lacks the language for recounting
his experience of her: "I know what happened and yet I cannot say. I do
not know the words to speak of beauty and love. I, who know everything . . . some things are impossible" (133). The play, then, poses the
possibility of a fundamental contradiction between the apparent agent
of signification (Dr. Kheal) and the attempted decreation, or destabiliza-
tion, of that agent suggested by Crissanda's alternate language. In fact,
Dr. Kheal's words about the "arithmetic of love" might be read as a gloss
of this point:

Don't you know that you can take a yes and a no and push them
together, squeeze them together, compress them so they are one?
That in fact is what reality is? Opposites, contradictions com-
pressed so that you don't know where one stops and the other
begins? (134)

Like Brecht, Fornes refuses wholly to engage the language of these early
plays in the seamlessness of traditional narrative—but she takes this to
the point where the characters themselves seem at times to be oblivious
to the story that they are supposed to be in.[14]

Fefu and Her Friends and the Controlling of Discourse

Leopold in *Tango Palace* instructs Isidore to make his mind a blank with the paradoxical advice, "Don't imagine orange groves or anything";[15] Dr. Kheal tells his audience that the moment one "names" truth it disappears (132). Fornes's predilection for these slightly fractured moments of *énonciation* reflects her interest in the *im*possibilities of the discourse of theater itself: how can the theater provide us with signs and assume that they have stable referents? While her early works seem to address this question more generally, the plays dating from *Fefu and Her Friends* locate the female speaking subject—itself a site for complex oscillations of signifier and signifieds—as a medium for pursuing this question at the level of theatrical language, especially monologic language.

Fornes has said that writing *Fefu* was, for her, a "breakthrough" in her sense of her characters' autonomy; she comments, "The style of *Fefu* dealt more with characters as real persons rather than voices that are the expression of the mind of the play."[16] Much has also been made of the play's nonlinear structure and its relation to a feminist perspective: after the first act the audience divides into four groups and moves from scene to scene so that each group experiences the four scenes (each of which is repeated four times) in a different order; this structure is further complicated through the presence (made possible by meticulous timing) of two of the characters in more than one of the four scenes. As a result, when the spectators join back together as a single group to watch the third act of the play, they bring varying senses of the play's narrative into their experiences of the closing sequence.

Nearly all of the monologues in *Fefu,* up to Emma's lecture, involve the characters' senses of identity as defined in relationship to (or, more accurately, in contradiction to) their view of men. Cindy relates a dream in which she is being confronted and chased by a doctor, two policemen, and other figures; when she tells the doctor to stop cursing her, all present in the dream admire her forcefulness, but, when she tries to determine "whether the words coming out of my mouth were what I wanted to say,"[17] she and her sister must run to escape being murdered by the doctor. Cindy's inability to control her own discourse in her dream resembles the way that all of the characters have their language controlled or silenced by the patriarchal world represented by Fefu's husband and the other men, who remain outside the women's meeting place of Fefu's country house for the duration of the play. Emma, for instance, tells the story of Gloria, who was sent to a psychiatrist at school because the instructors could not believe that the brilliant paper she wrote was indeed her own work.

The most extreme victim of this male-controlled discourse is Julia, who hallucinates that she has torturers who force her to utter and reiterate a "prayer" consisting of precepts about the evils of the female gender:

> There are Evil Plants, Evil Animals, Evil Minerals, and Women are Evil.—Woman is not a human being. She is: 1-A mystery. 2-Another species. 3-As yet undefined. 4-Unpredictable: therefore wicked and gentle and evil and good which is evil.—If a man commits an evil act, he must be pitied. The evil comes from outside him, through him and into the act. Woman generates the evil herself. . . . Man is not spiritually sexual, he therefore can enjoy sexuality. His sexuality is physical which means his spirit is pure. Women's spirit is sexual. That is why after coitus they dwell in nefarious feelings. Because that is their natural habitat. . . . (25)

After she recites this monologue, Julia adds that she is supposed to be able to forget her torturers once she believes the prayer, and vice versa: "They say both happen at once. And all women have done it. Why can't I?" (25). She is at once unable to resist and to acquiesce, and her paralysis between the two is reflected in the physical paralysis that confines her to a wheelchair. To some extent Julia's condition is a representation of the oppression suffered by all of the women in the play; in this sense her paralysis has a gestic quality. W. B. Worthen, writing of the scar in Julia's brain (from a hunting accident) that apparently causes her spells of madness and her delusions of the speaking male "guardians," says: "The women of *Fefu and Her Friends* share Julia's invisible 'scar,' the mark of their paralyzing subjection to a masculine authority. . . . [Her] internalized 'guardian' rewrites Julia's identity at the interface of the body itself, where the masculine voice materializes itself in the woman's flesh."[18]

Indeed, the play resonates with instances of the division of the mind and the body caused by this "authority" as we see that the characters inhabit a society (the work is set in 1935) that insists on denying the validity of female sexual energy. When Emma remarks that heaven must be a place "populated with divine lovers" ("in heaven they don't judge

goodness the way we think" [19–20]), Fefu responds that she is fre-
quented by a foul, black cat, mangled and diseased, to whom she gives
food because "I thought, this is a monster that has been sent to me, and
I must feed him . . . . I am afraid of him" (20). The black cat is perhaps
an extension of herself, the part of her that agrees with her husband's
assessment of women as "loathsome," her "revolting" sexuality, which
she must feed and yet finds frightening.

Fefu, at the same time, seems somewhat cognizant of the challenges
involved in admitting the existence of the female body in a society that
views it as a decorative, useless, or inherently loathsome commodity;
after explaining to Christina and Cindy that she has learned how to fix
a toilet herself, she leaves the room with the comment, "Plumbing is
more important than you think" (13). The gestic implications of Fefu's
proficiency as a plumber and of this line work on several levels. Most
literally, Fefu has learned a "man's" activity and has therefore guaranteed
herself a greater degree of autonomy. But "plumbing," the inner pipes
that sustain a system—here, specifically, the toilet—also represents the
unmentionable and mysterious plumbing of the female body, which Fefu
has in a sense reappropriated from the patriarchy by "learning" its workings for herself. Finally, her admonition that it is "more important than
you think" suggests that the women as a group have been taught (as is
evident in Sue's and Emma's anecdotes about their education) to under-
value their femaleness, their "plumbing," in both the literal and the
metaphorical senses.

Most of the characters in *Fefu* have difficulty accepting the body as
a possible site for the inscription of their subjectivity because their bodies
have already been (in)scripted for them by the male codes of their culture. The play's third act invites a possible reinscription on their own
terms, which will come about through ending their physical/verbal paralysis and joining together as a community of women. Emma has to
some extent urged the dissolution of the artificial barriers of authority
from the beginning of the play: when the women are discussing their
upcoming fundraising presentation, she says, "If we're showing what
life is, can be, we must do theatre. . . . It's not acting. It's being. It's
springing forth with the powers of the spirit. It's breathing" (17). And
Emma's monologue in part 3, a lecture taken from Emma Sheridan Fry's
"The Science of Educational Dramatics," provides some indications for
a new realm of subjectivity. Emma urges her listeners (the speech is
actually part of the women's rehearsal, but here they listen to one an-

other) to resist indifference, to give in to the "Divine Urge," and to allow "Environment" to come rushing in. Both of the Emmas (the author and the character) call for an end to the type of paralysis that Julia embodies. The "lecture" demands, in effect, an awareness of acting in both its theatrical and ontological senses: again, "It's not acting. It's being."

As they applaud Emma's speech, the other women share the sense of being a community of listeners (replicated to some degree by the intimacy that results from the small groups of audience members entering the characters' spaces in part 2) who have much to give to one another. Such a community is transgressive and is capable of generating enormous power. In this sense Fefu's earlier comment that, if women "shall recognize each other, the world will be blown apart" (13), proves to be somewhat prophetic as Julia, after refusing Fefu's exhortations to overcome her paralysis, "dies" from an apparent gunshot wound at the same moment that Fefu shoots her gun to kill a rabbit. Perhaps, as Beverley Pevitts suggests, this moment marks the new female identity defined by the end of the play, and this identity must emerge from the sacrifice of the old.[19] Evidently, in view of the odds that these characters face, individual strength in itself is insufficient for the assertion of identity. Cecilia's words at the beginning of part 3 might serve as the keynote for the communal nature of such an assertion, bound as the women in this play are to their specific sociohistorical limitations and circumstances:

We must be part of a community, perhaps 10, 100, 1000. It depends on how strong you are. But even the strongest will need a dozen, three, even one who sees, thinks and feels as they do. . . . Thoughts, emotions that fit all, have to be limited to a small number. That is, I feel, the concern of the educator—to teach how to be sensitive to the differences, in ourselves as well as outside ourselves, not to supervise the memorization of facts. (29)

The last line of this speech gathers additional force by Cecilia's injunction to eschew the "supervising" and "memorization" of the traditional (i.e., patriarchal) order. When we remember the "facts" that the characters must memorize—women are loathsome, "the human being is of the masculine gender," and so on—it is clear that a community with an awareness of sexual difference refuses ultimately to "supervise the memorization of facts" and resists the coercion of dominant ideology.

The Textual Body: *Mud*

In *Mud* (1983) Fornes places a single female character, Mae, in a world
that is just like the play's title: primitive, dingy, mundane, smeared, and
dulled by hopelessness and routine. The set itself consists of a run–down
room filled with household items that allude to incompletion and bro-
kenness (unpressed trousers, old shoes), attempts at creating a domestic
space (stacked plates and spoons), and barely suppressed brutality (an
ax and rifle). This room, in turn, is placed "on an earth promontory . . . five feet high . . . red and soft . . . [with] no greenery."[20] This
earthen setting (reminiscent of Hamlet's "sterile promontory"?), along
with the white mud-stained clothes worn by the characters in the original Padua Hills production,[21] gives the play a stylized quality in spite of
the essentially naturalistic description of the room: these elements imply
that "mud" has permeated the play at its essence and that the characters
are visually marked or stained with all that the mud comes to represent.
As in *Fefu,* the structure of the play replicates, or "enacts," its content:
at the end of each extremely brief scene, Fornes has the actors freeze for
several seconds (in the 1983 Theater for the New City production directed by Fornes, one could see the actors "drop" their characters then
pick them up when the next scene resumed).[22] While the intention of
this freeze-frame was initially a practical one, since the outdoor staging
at Padua Hills prevented the use of blackouts or curtains between
scenes,[23] the effect is of a series of cinematic-style "shots" that reflect the
repetitive, clumsily violent lives of the characters themselves. They not
only enact a Beckettian tragicomic vaudeville, but the tableaux are also
a reminder that the characters stand before us imprisoned in their bodies
for the duration of each scene.

Mae, a woman with little education, seeks a way out of this imprisonment ("I work," she says, "I wake up and I work. Open my eyes and
I work. I work" [19]) by learning how to read and write. She lives with
two men: Lloyd, who is essentially "good-hearted" but who only functions at an animal-like level (14), and Henry, who initially possesses a
scant amount of the "knowledge" that Mae covets so earnestly but who
becomes paralyzed, inarticulate, and helpless after he suffers a fall. When
Mae decides that she has had enough of Lloyd and Henry, she announces
her intention to leave them both, and Lloyd kills her with his rifle; the
play ends with the two men sobbing near Mae's body, which is out-
stretched on the kitchen table.

The gestic quality of Mae's language in *Mud* emerges from her efforts to possess what she considers a more elevated form of discourse than her typical exchanges with Lloyd ("Fuck you, Mae. / Fuck you, Lloyd" [18]). Her duties in the house are to feed Lloyd (and Henry), to wash and press their clothes, to attend to their bodily needs. Written texts seem to her to be part of a realm of knowledge and beauty into which she longs to escape. She cries when Henry says grace ("For he satisfies the longing soul, and fills the hungry soul with goodness") because, she says, "I am a hungry soul. I am a longing soul. I am an empty soul. . . . It satisfies me to hear words that speak so lovingly to my soul" (27). For Mae language—which she connects with spirituality—is central to subjectivity to the extent that it takes on an almost material quality as "food" for spiritual hunger, and yet its power for her lies in its ability to let her transcend her earthbound existence. When, for example, Mae struggles to read a passage about the starfish aloud from a book, it is the very clumsiness and concentration of her effort that allows us to feel the *physical* process by which she tries to transform her world:

> The starfish is an animal, not a fish. He is called a fish because he lives in the water. The starfish cannot live out of the water. If he is moist and in the shade he may be able to live out of the water for a day. Starfish eat old and dead sea animals. They keep the water clean. A starfish has five arms like a star. That is why it is called a starfish. Each of the arms of the starfish has an eye in the end. These eyes do not look like our eyes. A starfish's eye cannot see. But they can tell if it is night or day. If a starfish loses an arm he can grow a new one. This takes about a year. A starfish can live five or ten years or perhaps more, no one really knows. (27)

The luminousness of this moment comes not from the passage itself, which resembles an excerpt from a biology textbook, nor from Mae's skill in delivering it, for she can barely read. Yet Fornes indicates in the stage directions that Mae's reading of the passage is "inspired" (27). In fact, it should be the very *difficulty* with which she reads that gives her recitation this quality. Brecht, similarly, has written of the ways that he found an "almost unreadable 'stumbling'" translation of Shakespeare preferable to a smooth one for more aptly expressing the "tussle of thoughts" in the gestic monologue.[24]

Just as Emma in *Fefu* urges the conflation of acting and being, Mae acquires an identity and even a corporeality as she reifies herself through a text. Dolan argues that Mae's "entry into discourse" is in fact marked by Henry, who, as we have seen, possesses the ability to move Mae with his language.[25] Certainly, it is true that Mae sees Henry's usefulness as existing only to the point where he can teach her or she can listen to his words; after Henry's fall distorts his ability to speak, she tells Lloyd, "Kill him if you want.—He can't talk straight anymore" (34). While Henry may indeed be a catalyst for Mae's inspiration, I would suggest that her point of entry into discourse is, more fundamentally, the act of reading from her textbook. First, the stage language establishes the centrality of Mae to the play and the centrality of the text both to Mae and to the staging; Fornes has said in an interview:

> I feel that what is important about this play is that Mae is the central character. It says something about women's place in the world, not because she is good or a heroine, not because she is oppressed by men or because the men "won't let her get away with it," but simply because she is the *center* of that play.[26]

Mae is framed onstage by Henry and Lloyd because she differs from them in gender, and her physical appearance onstage reflects the position of being "at the center of the universe," which Fornes says is integral to the portrayal of Mae's mind. Correspondingly, throughout the play we are told that Mae's textbook is placed "in the center" of the kitchen table (27, 29).[27] To the extent that Mae refigures herself as a text, the parallel centricity is evocative, for this moment of *Gestus* embodies Mae's liberation from the representational limits within which she has been confined.

Dolan further claims that, since Henry represents Mae's possibility for learning discourse, the accident that reduces him to a sexual body leaves Mae "outside the register of language."[28] Certainly, Mae's death occurs before she is fully able to find the realm of language she has been seeking, but her somewhat formally presented closing speech after she has been shot indicates that to some extent, her text *has* "given" her a language:

> Like the starfish, I live in the dark and my eyes see only a faint light. It is faint and yet it consumes me. I long for it. I thirst for it. I would die for it. Lloyd, I am dying. (40)

This is a moment in which Mae experiences a brief flash of the lucidity she has longed to attain; in the speech, her identification with the starfish of her text (present to some degree in the earlier passages) becomes manifest, but it is also infused with a voice that clearly comes from her own associative and poetic powers and thus moves *beyond* the mechanical prose of the biology textbook. This linguistic recourse allows Mae the power of self-demonstration, the ability to articulate her bodied subjectivity. The somewhat "presentational" and overstated quality of the sequence as a "closing speech" figures it as a Brechtian-style didactic epilogue, as in *The Threepenny Opera:* to some extent Mae stands "outside" of her character to reveal to the audience the nature of her assimilation of language through the starfish text, marking the speech as the closing *Gestus* of the play.

Recoding Subjectivity in *The Conduct of Life*

The Conduct of Life (1985) is set in the more overtly political context of an unnamed Latin American country in which prisoners are tortured routinely and in which those who are victims of oppression become, in an endless cycle, oppressors themselves. Orlando, an army lieutenant later promoted to lieutenant commander, tortures political prisoners, maintains his marriage to Leticia only because she keeps house for him, and has as a secret prisoner an impoverished young girl named Nena whom he uses to satisfy his sexual appetite. Leticia, Nena, and Olimpia (the maid) are all women who must exist within the power structures of both Orlando's dominance and the ongoing repressive violence in the country itself. As in *Mud,* Fornes uses monologic discourse to show the gestic role of language in the constitution of the subject-in-process. Again female subjectivity is constricted by powerful social and historical forces, and yet there are ways for the speaking subject to emerge.

Unlike *Fefu* or *Mud* (except perhaps for Lloyd's brief self-introduction near the beginning of the latter), this play includes monologues spoken by a male character that counterpoint the speeches of the female characters. Orlando's monologues differ from those of the three women in *Conduct* because he uses language to justify a previously defined and circumscribed identity, or "role," rather than being in the position of creating subjectivity *out* of language. He "narrates," or "performs," himself with Brechtian aplomb, and the result is an elaborate series of rationalizations for his own behavior:

Man must have an ideal, mine is to achieve maximum power. That is my destiny.—No other interest will deter me from this.—My sexual drive is detrimental to my ideals. I must no longer be overwhelmed by sexual passion or I will be degraded beyond all hope of recovery.[29]

The irony, of course, is that the more Orlando tries to control his actions by setting them forth in language and then expecting his body (i.e., his "sexual passion") to follow suit, the more obvious it becomes to the audience that Orlando's own words betray him. Although he uses Nena to satisfy his sexual desire, the result is the very degradation he has tried to avoid. He attempts to justify his brutalization of Nena as "love" (82), just as he rationalizes the death of a political prisoner whom he tortured as being due to "fear, not from anything I did to him" (79).[30] He believes, then, that he can change an actuality simply by expressing it in different words; one might say that he tries to exert the same domination over language that he does in "marital" terms over Leticia and in sexual terms over Nena. Olimpia's description of Orlando is amusing, but apt: "Like an alligator, big mouth and no brains. Lots of teeth but no brains. All tongue" (79).

As the maid, Olimpia is the play's most "invisible" character, but she is the speaker of the play's longest monologue, when she launches into a lengthy narrative about the tasks she has to complete every morning:

You can't just ask me to do what you want me to do, and interrupt what I'm doing. I don't stop from the time I wake up in the morning to the time I go to sleep. You can't interrupt me whenever you want, not if you want me to get to the end of my work. I wake up at 5:30. I wash. I put on my clothes and make my bed. I go to the kitchen. I get the milk and the bread from outside and I put them on the counter. I open the icebox. I put one bottle in and take the butter out. I leave the other bottle on the counter. I shut the refrigerator door. I take the pan that I use for water and put water in it. I know how much. I put the pan on the stove, light the stove, cover it. I take the top off the milk and pour it in the milk pan except for a little. . . . Like this. For the cat. I put the pan on the stove, light the stove. I put the coffee in the thing. I know how much. I light the oven and put bread in it. [She continues in detail.] . . . I go upstairs to make your bed and clean your bathroom. I come down here to meet you and figure out what you want for lunch and dinner. And try to get you to think quickly so I can run to the market and get it bought before all the fresh stuff is bought up. Then, I start the day. (71)

The amount of detail that accumulates in Olimpia's monologue renders it humorous in effect, especially as it is followed by Leticia's "So?" and Olimpia's response, "So I need a steam pot" (71). At the same time the delivery of the speech is deliberately difficult and unaesthetic to listen to; the stage directions indicate that Olimpia has a speech defect and that she speaks the monologue "in a mumble" (71). In the 1987 Organic Theater production in Chicago the actress who portrayed Olimpia used an atonal voice resembling that of a deaf person, and the repeated lines ("I know how much . . . ") took on the quality of an untuned musical instrument repeating an off-key chorus. Again Fornes's emphasis on the "unlistenability" of the monologue—its rough and grating rhythms and sounds—resembles Brecht's insistence that the *Gestus* not be created through smoothly flowing poetry. Here, the gestic quality of Olimpia's monologue is shaped out of her insistence on transforming domestic space into narrative space to affirm her place in an environment in which (as the servant) she is marginalized. One might say that Olimpia's use of language is the opposite extreme of Orlando's: while the latter attempts to make his behavior follow from his language, Olimpia's language *is* her behavior. Perhaps more so than any of Fornes's other characters, Olimpia depends upon her discourse (which embodies her actions, and vice versa) in order to establish that she even exists: hence her monologue's repeated invocation of the actual and grammatical subject, the "I."[31]

Although she is impatient with Olimpia's monologue, Leticia, too, struggles to find ways of "speaking herself." She resembles Mac in *Mud* in her desire to "be knowledgeable," for she equates appearing as an "ignorant person" with "being ignored" (70). Indeed, her most powerful desire is to command an audience; she tells Orlando's friend Alejo, "I would like to be a woman who speaks in a group and have others listen" (70). At moments Leticia does attempt to enter this taboo territory, such as when she speaks movingly and eloquently, but to no effect, to Orlando and Alejo about the condition of their country ("We're blind. We can't see beyond an arm's reach . . . " [75]). But for the most part

Leticia's only opportunities to speak for an audience are when she talks to her friend Mona on the telephone; at one point she even pretends to speak "to Mona in her mind" (81) in order to express herself. Even her monologues, then, are thwarted and reshaped as incomplete dialogues. When Leticia endeavors—like Mae, or like Marion in *Abingdon Square*— to memorize a passage from a book, we see the cumulative effect of her frustration (as well as, perhaps, the limitations of Leticia's own class consciousness) when she slaps Olimpia for pretending to know how to read in order to help with the memorization. At some level Leticia's furor at Olimpia masks her rage at herself for her own lack of knowledge and her inability to receive sufficient attention.[32]

In the "legal, social superstructure" that Dolan characterizes as the source of hierarchical power in Fornes's works,[33] Nena is most overtly and painfully a victim of oppression. Orlando controls her to such an extent that she is barely even able "to speak words" and only "whimpers" (80).[34] In a later scene with Olimpia, though, Nena gives voice to a narrative about her earlier experiences doing ironing to earn her keep and about her grandfather's life in a camp for the homeless. Her description of the ways she would like to fix up the box where her grandfather stays is, once again, an effort at existing (or, in her case, surviving) through the creation of a linguistic reality; her verbal construction of the box is like an architecture of the self. Yet even her ability to reside within this verbal framework has been destroyed, for her narrative turns into a re-evocation of her imprisonment and rape by Orlando. He beats her, she says, because "the dirt won't go away from inside me" (84). Nena's speech, and the scene itself, ends with the chilling words:

> I want to conduct each day of my life in the best possible way. I should value the things I have. . . . And I should value the kindness that others bestow upon me. And if someone should treat me unkindly, I should not blind myself with rage, but I should see them and receive them, since maybe they are in worse pain than me. (84–85)

The moment is particularly unsettling because Fornes seems to be deliberately unclear about whether Nena is reciting words that Orlando or another authority figure has taught her to believe or whether the passage emerges from Nena's own idea that she should pity those who victimize her because they are probably victims themselves. Worthen sees the speech as emblematic of Nena's learned helplessness: "Rather than taking a resistant, revolutionary posture, Nena accepts a Christian humility, an attitude that simply enforces her own objectification, her continued abuse. . . . [She] finally adopts a morality that—grotesquely—completes her subjection to . . . [Orlando] and to the social order that empowers him."[35]

Perhaps, though, Worthen stops a bit short with the pinpointing of Nena's "acceptance" and "adoption" of the doctrine that her words announce. Apparently Nena, like Julia in *Fefu,* possesses a fragment of text to which she must cling for survival, even if the text itself perpetuates her oppression. So great is the gulf between Nena's text and what we know of her physical brutalization by Orlando that Nena must disconnect herself from her body and from the pain that Orlando inflicts upon it. Her sense that she is indeed, as Orlando says, "dirty" reflects the extent to which she has had to alienate herself from the physical and to hold on tightly and desperately to language because it is all she has. The spectator, though—one might assume—remains aware of the disjunction of logos (Nena's words) and *gestuality* (the physical moment of her enunciation), and so the speech is a gestic one in spite of or even because of Nena's inability to own her body—or even her language, if the words she speaks are ones she has been forced to learn.

Jeanie Forte, writing about debates over the use of the female body in performance art, argues that, "through women's performance art, the body speaks both as a sign and as an intervention into language; and it is further possible for the female body to be used in such a way as to foreground the genderization of culture and the repressive system of representation."[36] Forte's point, which emphasizes that the (re)inscription of corporeality in the female speaking subject is not a priori "biological essentialism," is also true of Fornes's work. Whereas a more self-consciously Brechtian feminist playwright such as Caryl Churchill might choose to alienate the gendered body as a social formation existing almost solely in the realm of language,[37] Fornes allows the potential readings and misreadings of the body-as-sign to counterpoint and participate in the linguistic emergence of the subject. She recognizes language as the crux of subjectivity, but, just as language creates and deploys a body/corpus of words, the body/corpus creates and deploys a language. As a final example, at one point in *The Danube,* Eve says:

I feel how my face quivers. And my blood feels thin. // And I can hardly breathe. And my skin feels dry. // I have no power to show something other than what I feel.[38]

Eve is using language to "give voice to" her body: she suggests that her body has a sign-system (face quivering, blood feeling thin, difficulty breathing, skin dry) of its own, yet it is actually at the moment of transference to language that her body becomes the site of a readable text. The moment also is a gestic one because, in the context of the play, these "symptoms" figure both Eve's perceived pain in her alienation from Paul and her radiation sickness from what we assume is a nuclear explosion. Thus, Eve's decoding of her body foregrounds Fornes's larger indication of nuclear war's ability to encode, to usurp control of the body.

Fornes, then, presents what Catherine Belsey calls the "crisis of subjectivity,"[39] a crisis set in motion at the moment of entry into the symbolic order embodied in the mode of performance. A reclamation of the speaking body's ability to act (in its dual theatrical/existential senses) comes through recodifying this symbolic order; as Belsey says, "in the fact that the subject is a *process* lies the possibility of transformation.[40] The *Gestus,* with its multivalent moments of highlighting the competition of logos and gestuality, insists on an attention to this process. The female bodies on stage in Fornes's plays may not "speak" with the comic literalness of Schneeman's interior scroll, but her theatricalization of the subject-in-process through the use of gestic monologues suggests a similar preoccupation with the scripting/inscription/conscription of a textualized voice, playing ironically, like Schneeman, off the notion that language "originates from" the body of the speaking subject.

Chapter 6

"Takin a Solo": Monologue in Ntozake Shange's Theater Pieces

> . . . bein alive & bein a woman & bein colored is a metaphysical dilemma/i havent conquered yet/ do you see the point my spirit is too ancient to understand the separation of soul & gender/ my love is too delicate to have thrown back on my face
>
> —Ntozake Shange, *for colored girls who have considered suicide / when the rainbow is enuf*

Role-Playing and the Creation of Narrative Voices

Ntozake Shange's works refuse traditional "generic" categories: just as her poems (published in *Nappy Edges* [1978], *A Daughter's Geography* [1983], and other volumes) are also performance pieces, her works for the theater defy the boundaries of drama and merge into the region of poetry. Her most celebrated work, *for colored girls who have considered suicide / when the rainbow is enuf* (1977), is subtitled "a choreopoem." Similarly, she has written *Betsey Brown* (1985) as a novel and then again (with Emily Mann) in play form, and her first novel, *Sassafrass, Cypress & Indigo* (1982), incorporates recipes, spells, and letters into its free-ranging narrative modes. Perhaps more so than any other practicing playwright, Shange has created a poetic voice that is distinctively "hers"—a voice that is deeply rooted in her experience of being African American and female but also one that, again, refuses and transcends categorization. Her works articulate the connection between the doubly marginalized social position of the African-American woman and the need to invent and appropriate a language with which to constitute subjectivity.[1]

The key here is the complexity, for Shange, of the performative experience. In her plays, especially *for colored girls* and *spell #7* (1979), Shange relies primarily on monologic speech to develop her theatrical narratives because monologue, as we have seen, inevitably places the narrative weight of a play upon the *énonciation,* the moment of transference into spoken language, which is also the signal of the movement toward the voicing of a subject position. Whereas Fornes turns toward monologic language in order to define and embody her characters as subjects, though, Shange draws upon the performative qualities of monologue to allow her actors to take on *multiple* roles and therefore to foreground narrative itself, the act of storytelling, in her work. This emphasis is crucial to Shange's articulation of a postmodernist aesthetic that is feminist/Afrocentric (and that echoes the call to humanity to accept that "black women are inherently valuable") on two counts.[2] First, the incorporation of role-playing reflects the ways in which African Americans (as "minstrels," "servants," "athletes," etc.) and women (as "maids," "whores," "mothers," etc.) are expected to fulfill such roles on a constant basis in Western society.[3] Second, the space between the audience's experience of Shange's theater pieces as "spectacle" (through the recitation of the monologues and through the dancing and singing that often accompany them) and their awareness of Shange's urgent call for a black female subjectivity free of stereotypes serves as a "rupturing" of the performance moment; it is the uncomfortableness of that space, that rupture, that is alternately moving and disturbing.

In "takin a solo / a poetic possibility / a poetic imperative," the opening poem of *nappy edges,* Shange suggests that, just as the great jazz musicians each have a recognizable sound and musical style, so too should the public develop a sensitivity to the rhythms and nuances of African-American writers as the writers themselves cultivate distinctive "sounds":

> as we demand to be heard/ we want you to hear us. we come to you the way leroi jenkins comes or cecil taylor/ or b.b. king. we come to you alone/in the theater/ in the story/ & the poem. like with billie holiday or betty carter/ we shd give you a moment that cnnot be re-created/ a specificity that cannot be confused. our language shd let you know who's talkin, what we're talkin abt & how we cant stop sayin this to you. some urgency accompanies the text. something important is going on. we are speakin. reachin for yr person/

we cannot hold it/ we dont wanna sell it/we give you ourselves/ if
you listen.[4]

Although Shange's remarks were intended to address larger concerns in
African-American writing, her words hold true for the speakers of
monologue in her plays as well, for the monologue is another way of
"takin a solo." For Shange's actors/characters (it is sometimes difficult
to draw a distinction between the two, as the actors frequently portray
actors who in turn portray multiple characters), monologues issue forth
with the same sense that "some urgency accompanies the text" and that,
in delivering the speeches, they are "reachin for yr person." In this
respect the characters seem to aspire toward a specificity that would
make them stand as if independent of their author. But the hallmark of
the very "imperative" that Shange has announced in the first place is the
unmistakable sense that all of the speakers' voices are ultimately parts
of Shange's own monologic voice (in this respect, Shange is closer to
such performance artists as Spalding Gray and Karen Finley, whose
works will be discussed later, than she is to the more "characterological"
Fornes).

All of Shange's theater pieces, even *a photograph: lovers in motion*
(1977) and *boogie woogie landscapes* (1978), unfold as collections of stories
rather than following the linear/oedipal narrrative continuum. John
Timpane points out that Shange's use of fragmentation and collage
stands in deliberate resistance to the emphasis on closure and completion
linked to the "white European theatrical tradition."[5] The events are generated less from actual interactions as they unfold in the "present" of the
play (except perhaps in *a photograph*) than from the monologue speakers'
re-creations of separate dramas. The implied privilege of the storyteller
to create alternate worlds, as well as the fluidity of the narratives themselves and the characters in them, relies heavily upon the immense power
African-American culture has assigned to the spoken word. As
Geneviève Fabre explains in *Drumbeats Masks and Metaphor*:

For slaves (who were often forbidden to learn to write) . . . [the oral
tradition] was the safest means of communication. It provided basic
contact with Africa as a homeland and a source of folklore, a contract also between ethnic groups unified under a common symbolic
heritage, between generations, and finally, between the speaker and

his audience. . . . Because the oral tradition has long remained a living practice in Afro-American culture, the dramatic artist has been tempted to emulate not only the art and techniques of the storyteller, but also his prestigious social function—that of recording and reformulating experience, of shaping and transmitting values, opinions, and attitudes, and of expressing a certain collective wisdom.[6]

Shange takes the notion of exchange and collectivity among storytellers even further in her use of the space in which her pieces are performed. Monologue, as we have seen, creates "narrative space"; more than most of the other playwrights discussed up to this point, Shange depends upon this space within her plays to create scenes without the use of backdrops and other theatrical effects. *for colored girls* is the most "open" of the plays in this sense, as its set consists only of lights of different colors and specific places for the characters to enter and exit the stage. *boogie woogie landscapes* conjures up the mental images of the title within the confines of Layla's bedroom: "there is what furniture a bedroom might accommodate, though not too much of it. the most important thing is that a bedroom is suggested."[7] Although the sets of both *spell #7* and *a photograph* are fairly specific (a huge minstrel mask as a backdrop and, later, a bar in lower Manhattan for the former, a photographer's apartment for the latter), they still call for this space to be reborn in different nonconcrete ways as the characters come forth and relay their narratives.

for colored girls and Communal Performance

for colored girls, Shange's first major theater piece, evolved from a series of poems modeled on Judy Grahn's *Common Woman.* The play received its first performances in coffeehouses in San Francisco and on the Lower East Side of Manhattan; eventually, it attracted critical and public attention and moved to the New Federal Theater, The Public Theatre, and then to Broadway in 1976. *for colored girls* draws its power from the performances—in voice, dance, and song—of its actors as well as from the ways it articulates a realm of experience that heretofore had been suppressed in the theater; the "lady in brown" speaks to the release of this suppression when she says near the beginning of the piece:

sing a black girl's song
bring her out
to know her self
. . . she's been dead so long
closed in silence so long
she doesn't know the sound
of her own voice
her infinite beauty

                                                    (2–3)

The instruments for releasing and expressing the "infinite beauty" of the "black girl's song" become the characters, who do not have names and specific identities of their own (except through their physical presences) but, rather, take on multiple identities and characters as the "lady in brown," "lady in red," "lady in yellow," and so on. These "ladies" put on the metaphorical masks of various characters in order to enact the "ceremony" of the play, which gathers them together in a stylized, ritualistic fashion. The ritual is "religious" insofar as the participants turn to the "spirit" that might be best described as the black female collective unconscious; it is also celebratory in that their immersion is ultimately a source of joy and strength. In this sense the ritual is a festival that depends as much upon the bonds of the group as it does upon individual expression; Fabre makes this connection explicit when she says that "the group . . . takes possession of space and enlarges it to express communion."[8]

As the characters assume their different "masks," we see them enact a complex series of microdramas. So it is that the "lady in purple" narrates the tale of Sechita, who "kicked viciously thru the nite/ catchin stars tween her toes" (26), while the lady in green "plays" Sechita and dances out the role. Both of these performers "are" Sechita, for the identity of this character within a character merges in the spoken narration and the accompanying movement. Yet it also becomes clear in the course of the play that these actors/characters are not simply assuming masks or roles for the sake of a dramatic production; they must enact the "dramas" and wear the masks of African-American women every day of their lives. Shange has taken on the difficult task, then, of universalizing her characters in the play without allowing them to fall into roles that are essentially stereotypes. She discusses the problem of balancing the "idiosyncratic" and the symbolic, or "representative," in an interview with Claudia Tate:

> I feel that as an artist my job is to appreciate the differences among my women characters. We're usually just thrown together, like "tits and ass," or a good cook, or how we can really "f——" [*sic*]. Our personalities and distinctions are lost. What I appreciate about the women whom I write about, the women whom I know, is how idiosyncratic they are. I take delight in the very peculiar or particular things that fascinate or terrify them. Also, I discovered that by putting them all together, there are some things they all are repelled by, and there are some things they are all attracted to. I only discovered this by having them have their special relationships to their dreams and their unconscious.[9]

Throughout *for colored girls* Shange's storytellers put on masks of humor, which they wear, as part of the assumption of a role, or character, in order to redeploy fear and anger in a "performative" mode. This masking creates the play's complex emotional alternations, as a passage from the beginning of the piece shows:

> distraught laughter fallin
> over a black girl's shoulder
> it's funny/it's hysterical
> the melody-less-ness of her dance
> don't tell nobody don't tell a soul
> she's dancin on beer cans and shingles
>
> (1–2)

The images associated with the word *hysterical* in this passage show the multilayered and interdependent qualities of the "black girl's" experience: *hysterical* connotes a laughter that has gone out of control, a madness connected with femaleness (as in T. S. Eliot's poem "Hysteria"). Moreover, the admonition "don't tell nobody don't tell a soul" suggests the call to silence, the fear that to speak of her pain will be to violate a law of submission. The onlooker will aestheticize the dance (convert it to spectacle) or call attention to its comic qualities rather than realize the extent to which the dance and the laughter are a reaction against—and

are even motivated by—the uncovering of pain. Similarly, in one monologue the lady in red expresses the pain of a rejected love with a sardonic
"itemization" of what she has been through:

> without any assistance or guidance from you
> i have loved you assiduously for 8 months 2 wks &
>   a day
> i have been stood up four times
> i've left 7 packages on yr doorstep
> forty poems 2 plants & 3 handmade notecards i left
> town so i cd send to you have been no help to me
> on my job
> you call at 3:00 in the mornin on weekdays
> so i cd drive 27 1/2 miles cross the bay before i go to
>   work
> charmin charmin
> but you are of no assistance . . .
>
>   (13)

The disruptive power of this and other "comic" narratives in the
play comes from the realization that the same material that provokes
laughter has a bitter, even tormented underside. Often the monologues
in the play swing with extreme abruptness from humor to anger, causing
us to feel almost as if we have been slapped, which is precisely the way
Shange describes the transition to the narrative on "latent rapist bravado":

> we cd even have em over for dinner
> & get raped in our own houses
> by invitation
> a friend
>
>   (21)

As Helene Keyssar points out in *The Curtain and the Veil*, the spectator
is likely to overlook the pain in favor of the humor in the play's earliest
vignettes. When *for colored girls* moves into such narratives as the lady in
blue's story of an abortion, though, we begin to feel increasingly uncomfortable with our own laughter. The candor of the speakers combined
with the persistent irony, says Keyssar, "prevents the display of emotion

from becoming melodramatic and allows the spectators a vulnerability
to their own feelings that can renew their ability to act with others in the
world outside the theater."[10] But there is also another way to view this
generation of "vulnerability": as a result of the disjunction between the
guise of humor and the realization that such moments in the play are
actually imbued with pain and anger, the spectator enters an uncomfortable and disruptive "space" between the two strategies of performance.
Like Brecht, Shange seems to believe that inhabiting such a space causes
the audience to question its own values and beliefs; unlike Brecht,
though (and in a manner markedly different than Fornes), she engages
the emotions directly in this process. She says in her interview with Tate,
"I write to get at the part of people's emotional lives that they don't have
control over, the part that can and will respond."[11]

The most complicated and controversial monologue in the play in
terms of this vulnerability is the "beau willie brown" sequence, the only
narrative with a male protagonist. It concerns beau willie, a Vietnam
veteran who beats up crystal, the mother of their two children, so many
times that she gets a court order restraining him from coming near them.
When beau willie forces his way into crystal's apartment and insists that
she marry him, she refuses, and he takes the children away from her and
holds them out on the window ledge. In the devastating final moments
of the monologue, the lady in red, who has been narrating the story,
suddenly shifts from referring to crystal in the third person to using "I":

> i stood by beau in the window/ with naomi reachin for me/ &
> kwame screamin mommy mommy from the fifth story/ but i cd
> only whisper/ & he dropped em. (63)

Though subtle, the transition to "I" is a crucial change in the positioning
of narrative voice, for it highlights the relationship established in the play
between acting or telling and subjectivity. It is as if, in this moment, the
lady in red has abandoned the sense that she is "acting out" a story; she
merges with the character she has been narrating. As she closes the space
between her role as narrator and the character of crystal, this moment
of the monologue itself shifts away from the distancing effect created
by Shange's use of spectacle up to this point: the piece is no longer
simply an "entertainment" but also a ritualization that is didactic yet one
that also engages the emotions and so moves beyond the surface characteristic of performance.

Because of the resonance of the beau willie brown narrative, *for colored girls* seems on the brink of an abyss; as part of a politicized strategy of feminist theatricality, though, the lady in red's / crystal's narrative serves to bring the "colored girls" together to acknowledge the strength they derive from one another. Their final affirmation simultaneously echoes African-American church tradition and radically reinvents the deistic in terms that emphasize the speaking subject ("I") yet emerge as a collective voice:

> a layin on of hands
> the holiness of myself released
> . . . i found god in myself
> & i loved her/ i loved her fiercely
>
> (66–67)

Janet Brown rightly indicates the need for a movement toward such a point when she says that the "successful resolution to the search for autonomy is attributable first to the communal nature of the struggle."[12] These last two sequences of the play have come under fire by some critics, however, because they feel that Shange ultimately has failed to translate the personal into the political. Andrea Benton Rushing criticizes Shange's isolation in *for colored girls* "from salient aspects of black literary and political history," the "shockingly ahistorical" way it seems to ignore "white responsibility for our pain," and its final "rejection of political solutions."[13] Similarly, Erskine Peters is appalled by the apparent manipulativeness of the beau willie brown monologue:

> This climax is the author's blatantly melodramatic attempt to turn the work into tragedy without fulfilling her obligations to explore or implicate the historical and deeper tragic circumstances. There is a very heated attempt to rush the play toward an evocation of pity, horror, and suffering. The application of such a cheap device at this critical thematic and structural point is an inhumane gesture to the Black community.[14]

Rushing and Peters raise a valid issue when they say that *for colored girls* is not a direct and forceful indictment of white racism, at least not in as immediate a sense as *spell #7*. But Peters's accusation that crystal's story constitutes a "cheap device" that turns the play into a pseudotragedy seems unfounded, for such an argument ignores the declaration of community that comes at the end of the play in response to the emotions expressed in the individual monologues, which reached their peak in the beau willie brown narrative. Indeed, one might argue that the placement of this narrative before the play's closing "ritual" sequence indicates Shange's attempt to avoid having the spectator convert the final moments into cathartic ones, for (as Augusto Boal argues so convincingly in *Theater of the Oppressed*), catharsis can have the "repressive" or coercive effect of lulling the spectator into complacency.[15] Or, as Michael W. Kaufman says of the Black Revolutionary Theater of Amiri Baraka, Ed Bullins, and others, "The very notion of catharsis, an emotional purgation of the audience's collective energies, means that theatre becomes society's buffer sponging up all the moral indignities that if translated into action could effect substantial change."[16] If the ending of the play is dissatisfying because it seems to be administering a palliative to the audience, that is precisely the point: Shange is suggesting the sources of possible strength and redemption by having the characters *perform* the play's closing ritual. But since the beau willie brown sequence has closed the gulf between narrator and narrative, this final performance cannot be only a "show." Just as the "ladies" collapse the identities of character, narrator, and (to a certain extent, although the actors are, of course, still acting) performer, and no longer play multiple roles, the spectacle of their concluding ritual conveys a sense of urgency that—coupled with the shock of the beau willie brown narrative—prevents the audience from experiencing the ending as cathartic.

Parodic Masking in *spell #7*

Kimberly Benston discusses African-American theater's movement away from Western structures and toward Afrocentric ones in terms of the shift from mimesis to *methexis*/ritual. Benston claims that the foregrounding of ritual creates a sense of community (as I have mentioned); moreover, it breaks down the barriers that have traditionally existed between performers and spectators.[17] This is perhaps why, in the opening of Shange's *spell #7*, there is a "huge blackface mask" visible on the stage, even while the audience is still coming into the theater. Shange says that "in a way the show has already begun, for the members of the audience must integrate this grotesque, larger-than-life misrepresentation of life into their pre-show chatter."[18] We might say that she thus attempts to blur distinctions between play and audience: not only does the performance address the spectators, but in this case the spectators are also forced to "address" the performance. At the beginning of the play the performers parade in minstrel masks identical to the huge one that looms overhead; they eventually shed their masks and pose instead as actors (or actors playing actors who, in turn, play at being actors), but the image of the minstrel mask is a sign, a postmodern historicized parody that implies that even contemporary black actors are still often conceived of as little more than minstrels. Shange thus engages in what Hutcheon calls the "postmodern ironic contesting of myth as master narrative."[19] As the actor/character Bettina complains, "if that director asks me to play it any blacker/ i'm gonna have to do it in a mammy dress" (14).

Shange, then, makes the minstrel masking into a simultaneous parody and a ceremony of sorts in the opening scene of *spell #7*, for the resemblance of the giant minstrel mask above the stage to an African voodoo mask is also evident. The blackface masks that the actors wear at the beginning of the play invoke, as a result, the *travesty* of a ceremony, for the masks represent the "parts" each must play (in the Western tradition) in order to get a job. Shange connects this to her feelings about her own masking in an interview with Tate:

> It was risky for us to do the minstrel dance in *spell #7*, but I insisted on it because I thought the actors in my play were coming from pieces they didn't want to be in but pieces that helped them pay their bills. Black characters are always being closed up in a "point." They decided, for instance, that *spell #7* by Zaki Shange is a feminist piece and therefore not poetry. Well, that's a lie. That's giving me a minstrel mask. . . . We're not free of our paint yet! The biggest money-makers—*The Wiz, Bubblin' Brown Sugar, Ain't Misbehavin'*—are all minstrel shows.[20]

In the course of the play, though, the actors/characters also use masking in a different way: they try on various roles, as in *for colored girls*, to perform the monologues and group narratives that provide both mirrors of and alternatives for the multiple, often fragmented subject positions they create under pressure from a society governed by white values and images. So, for instance, one of the nameless and faceless performers behind a minstrel mask at the beginning becomes the actor Natalie in the next scene, who in turn "becomes" Sue-Jean, a young woman who desperately wants a baby, as she and Alec (another of the "minstrels" revealed as actor/character) alternate in narrating her story, while she mimes it out.

Unlike *for colored girls, spell #7* makes the somewhat Brechtian use of a central storyteller figure, Lou, who "directs" the monologues that are performed in the course of the play. It is appropriate that Lou is a magician, for even the title of *spell #7* (the subtitle of which is "geechee jibara quik magic trance manual for technologically stressed third world people") refers to magic making. In his opening speech as "interlocutor," though, Lou warns of the power (and danger) of "colored" magic:

> my daddy retired from magic & took
> up another trade cuz this friend a mine
> from the 3rd grade/ asked to be made white
> on the spot
> . . . . . .
> all things are possible
> but aint no colored magician in his right mind
> gonna make you   white
> i mean
>   this is blk magic
> you lookin at
> & i'm fixin you up good/fixin you up good & colored
>
> (7–8)

The image of the narrator as "magician" implies that the storytellers themselves will be under the control of a certain "authorship"; yet, as the actors perform their pieces, the narratives seem at times to slip away from a guiding narratorial force. In a sense, the performers threaten to overpower the narrator in the same way that the third grader's request to be made white is beyond the power of Lou's magician father: the "magic" of the narratives is independent of their director, and yet to enter this narrative realm may be painful and perilous. Lou, then, embodies a surrogate author who is responsible for the content of the play but who also cannot fully control what happens to it once the performers begin to take part.[21]

Lou's position in relation to the performers is most fully evident

when, after Lily becomes wholly absorbed in her monologue about the
network of dreams she has constructed around the image of her hair, he
stands up and points to her. Shange indicates in the stage directions that
Lou "reminds us that it is only thru him that we are able to know these
people without the 'masks'/ the lies/ & he cautions that all their thoughts
are not benign. they are not safe from what they remember or imagine"
(27). He says, partly to Lily and partly to the audience:

> you have t come with me/ to this place where magic is/
> to hear my song/
> . . . & in this place where magic stays
> you can let yrself in or out
> but when you leave yrself at home/ burglars & daylight thieves
> pounce on you & sell your skin/ at cut-rates on tenth avenue
>
> (27)

The "place where magic is" means, within the most literal context of the
play, the bar where the actors meet and feel free to try on various roles.
But it is also the theater, and the implication is that, as such, it is both a
"safe" place and an "unsafe" place: certain inhibitions are lifted and certain feelings can be portrayed, but one risks vulnerability in exposing
one's memories and emotions. Finally, "this place where magic is"
marks the space in which the actor/writer/artist allows creativity to
happen. The impulse to safeguard it—"lately i leave my self in all the
wrong hands" (27)—echoes the fear of loss that Shange turns into a
similar set of metaphors in the "somebody almost walked off wid alla
my stuff" poem in *for colored girls*. But something interesting occurs as
the result of Lou's delivery of this speech: although he "designs" it to
reinforce his power as the play's magician/narrator, its effect is to establish *him* as being in a position not altogether different from that of the
other characters, for the speech reveals his vulnerability, his disguises
and defenses, and his need to inhabit a safe place in which to create.

If Lou is indeed addressing the audience as well as Lily, the implication is that he is inviting the spectator to become similarly vulnerable.
Not surprisingly, then, the play's two "centerpiece" monologues attempt—as in *for colored girls*—to take hold of the spectator in the gap that
the performers create between the safe region of spectacle/entertainment
and the unsafe region of pain and emotional assailability. In the first of

the two monologues Alec tells of his wish for all of the white people all over the world to kneel down for three minutes of silence in formal apology for the pain that they have given to black people:

> i just want to find out why no one has even been able to sound a gong & all the reporters recite that the gong is ringin/ while we watch all the white people/ immigrants and invaders/conquistadors & relatives of london debtors from georgia/ kneel & apologize to us/ just for three or four minutes. now/ this is not impossible . . . (46)

There is a certain absurdity to this image, and Lou calls attention to this when he responds to Alec, "what are you gonna do with white folks kneeling all over the country anyway/ man" (47). The humor in Alec's proposal is undercut, however, by the suffering that stands behind such a request. Perhaps the most extreme example of anger transferred to the realm of the comic, though, and one that will no doubt disturb the audience, is Natalie's "today i'm gonna be a white girl" monologue. She takes on the voice of the vacuous and hypocritical "white girl" who flings her hair, waters her plants, and takes twenty Valiums a day:

> . . . i'm still waiting for my cleaning lady & the lady who takes care of my children & the lady who caters my parties & the lady who accepts quarters at the bathroom in sardi's. those poor creatures shd be sterilized/ no one shd have to live such a life. cd you hand me a towel/ thank-you caroline. . . . (49)

Freud says in *Jokes and Their Relation to the Unconscious* that the ability to laugh at something is interfered with when the "joke" material also produces a strong affect and so another emotion "blocks" one's capacity to generate laughter;[22] for this reason the "white girls" in the audience at whom this monologue is aimed may feel too angry at Natalie's speech to consider it funny. Or they may laugh because they distance themselves from the reality of her words. Similarly, the very intensity of Natalie's emotions as she speaks this piece shows both the amount of pain that gradually interferes with her ability to sustain the joking tone of her own speech at the end and the intensified need for release through humor that her bitterness engenders.[23]

It is also striking that the play's final monologue, spoken by Maxine, comes forth because she is "compelled to speak by natalie's pain" (i.e., after Natalie delivers the white girl monologue [49]). As in *for colored girls,* the play's penultimate sequence seems to be different in tone from the earlier monologues—and, again, the effect is a noncathartic closure of the "gaps" I have discussed. Here Maxine speaks of the way her world was shattered when she realized as a child that African Americans were not exempt from the diseases, crimes, and so on that white people experienced. She closes with a description of her decision to appropriate gold chains, bracelets, and necklaces as a symbol of "anything hard to get & beautiful./ anything lasting/ wrought from pain," followed by the shattering remark that "no one understands that surviving the impossible is sposed to accentuate the positive aspects of a people" (51). Lou, as director of the action, freezes the players before they can fully respond to Maxine's words, and he repeats the closing portion of his opening speech: ". . . & you gonna be colored all yr life/ & you gonna love it/bein colored/ all yr life." As the minstrel mask reappears above them, he leads the actors in the chant "colored & love it/ love it/ bein colored" (52).

Shange notes in the stage directions that the chant is a "serious celebration, like church/ like home" (52). Her words are entirely appropriate to the dual nature of the ending: it is true that the characters are celebrating themselves, but the resonance of the preceding monologue, which was fraught with pain—as well as the overwhelming presence of the minstrel mask—recalls the anger and frustration that also underlie their chant. The characters, then, are imprisoned in the stereotypes and social position that the world has assigned to them, but, like the women in *for colored girls,* they call for unity as a source of strength (and ultimately, perhaps, a source of subjectivity). Their chant of "colored & love it/ love it/ bein colored" suggests that they intend to escape from their prison by redefining it so that it is no longer a prison. But the possibility remains that for the time being the escape (and the consequent movement from marginality to subjectivity) may be only a partial one. As Shange writes in "unrecovered losses/ black theater traditions," the minstrel face which descends is "laughing at all of us for having been so game/ we believed we cd escape his powers."[24]

spell #7's ultimate vision may be more cynical than that of *for colored girls,* but its call for redefinitions is one that echoes throughout Shange's theater pieces. She invites a reconsideration of role-playing that suggests that in the process of acting out the various masks that African Americans and women are *expected* to assume, one undergoes an experience of interior drama different from that explored by the theater of Chekhov, O'Neill, and other modernist playwrights. Liberated through monologic language and by dance, song, and so forth, which release different, richer, more complex characters and experiences, the very nature of role-playing has been appropriated as a tool for performing the subject. As chapter 5 suggested, Fornes's characters never "act"—they simply present themselves—but Shange sees role-playing as a way simultaneously to give her characters a nonproscriptive fluidity and to confront role-oriented stereotypes. On some level Shange's characters are, like Brecht's, always aware that they are speaking to an audience; perhaps this emphasis is an acknowledgment of the sense that women—as John Berger discusses in *Ways of Seeing*—are always the objects of vision and so are constantly watching themselves being watched.[25] Fornes seems to decenter authorship in her plays by shifting the emphasis to the textualized bodies of the characters; Shange, though, appears to share Michelene Wandor's view that deliberate attention to the author's role as "storyteller" provides a controlling structure for the play.[26]

Interwoven with this is a re-vision of spectacle as more than simply a vehicle for amusement: Shange's interpretation of spectacle insists upon a deconstruction of both the *genre* of performance, which lures the audience's attention (as in the postmodernist reconfiguration of the minstrel show at the beginning of *spell #7*), and the *(sub)text* of the spectacle itself. The monologue, then, is both an object for transformation and a means by which transformations can occur. Above all, Shange feels passionately that "we must move our theater into the drama of our lives."[27] Her works attempt to speak, in the way that she says Layla's unconscious does in *boogie woogie landscapes,* of "unspeakable realities/for no self-respecting afro-american girl wd reveal so much of herself of her own will/ there is too much anger to handle assuredly/ too much pain to keep on truckin/ less ya bury it."[28]

Chapter 7

Crossing into Autoperformance: Spalding Gray and Karen Finley

I think, finally, that everyone is playing themselves.

—Spalding Gray

Postmodernism and Beyond: Monologue in Performance Art

The contemporary playwrights considered up to this point in this study—Shepard, Mamet, Fornes, Shange—have all participated in a revolution of sorts, an emancipation of the monologue's narrative roles. As postmodern artists, they have encouraged us to move beyond plot-oriented and characterological uses of the monologic voice and to appreciate the roles of the parodic, the metatheatrical, and the Brechtian in shaping a "new" conception of what monologue can accomplish onstage. Above all, the monologue becomes with these artists a focal point for the complicated fragmentation and continual reformation of subjectivity suggested by a postmodern world. Yet it is crucial to add that none of these playwrights challenge the essentially fictional framework of theatrical performance (although Shange comes the closest); that is, while Shepard and other dramatists may break the previously established "rules" of dramatic discourse and narrative, the works remain fairly separate from their authors. Fornes, Mamet, and Shepard do not appear as characters in their plays, nor do their characters (despite the playwrights' forays into the metatheatrical) make reference tó an awareness of their own status as creations of these writers.

As I have mentioned, postmodern fiction makes frequent use of the paradoxes of self-conscious authorship; John Barth, John Fowles, Kathy

Acker, Salman Rushdie, and others recurrently "write themselves" (or, at least, their metafictional personas as "authors") into their novels, following the earlier, anachronistically postmodern examples of Laurence Sterne and similar writers. In contemporary drama performance artists provide the closest parallel to this technique of "autofiction"; in fact, the reality of the performer's physical presence may even bring these artists one step closer to challenging the limits of fictionality than metafictional novelists—always inevitably "behind the scenes" of a text rather than physically *there*—would be able to do.

Performance artists urge their audiences to reconsider the traditional boundaries between performance and reality, art and life, fiction and autobiography. Their creations are not necessarily limited to theatrical stagings: in one of performance artist Linda Montano's pieces, for example, she spent a year tied by a piece of rope to a male artist, Tehching Hsieh, and so the audience became both the onlookers who would see the pair on the street and by chance, and the mirror of the participants' own reactions (the lack of privacy, etc.) afforded by the experience.[1] Performance art often seeks to question the limits of "enactment" wherein the performer is not necessarily "pretending"; in several infamous pieces in the 1970s Chris Burden designated events such as shooting himself in the arm (with a real gun) as performance art creations.[2] Most important for our purposes, performance artists (as inspired by the works of the Open Theater, the Living Theatre, and other experiments discussed in chapter 2) do not necessarily create characters that they subsequently enact; rather, they deliberately confuse their real-life "selves" with the persona(s)—since, to some extent, even a "real self" is, once theatricalized and narrated, a persona—in their works of performance.

One example of the roles that monologue can play in such creations is John Malpede's work with the inhabitants of Los Angeles' "Skid Row" in a performance group called the Los Angeles Poverty Department (LAPD). The members of this group, most of whom are homeless and many of whom experience serious mental illness, physical disabilities, and alcohol or drug addictions, create monologues and other works that question the boundaries between life and text.[3] Due in part to the particular nature of the group's members and in part to the political need to avoid fictionalizing as "escape" or catharsis, the creations of LAPD lack the ironic distance that one might see in such a performer as Spalding Gray, as I will discuss shortly. Rather, storytelling becomes a way of reclaiming the past and creating the accessibility of a future; the concept of acquiring the requisite confidence to perform is made literal. Since monologue is part of an oral tradition, the performers do not need to be "literate" in order to create: one man tells stories about his 108-year-old grandmother, and his narratives "change each time he tells them—because he can neither read nor write."[4]

Monologue in itself also has what might be termed a "therapeutic" value for the performers; Malpede has said that, although he would like to see LAPD create more ensemble work (which they have subsequently done as they have visited other groups and made collaborative performances in Miami and other places), allowing each member to perform a monologue in the group's showcase *South of the Clouds* was a process for "self-affirmation."[5] The narratives for this work were the result of an exercise in which, according to Linda Burnham, "Malpede asked them [LAPD members] to recall an action that makes them feel good when they do it (partly, he says, to help them recognize that they can produce that good feeling when they want to)."[6]

The work of Malpede and the LAPD, like that of similar theater groups in other urban centers (e.g., Rebecca Ranson's theatrical cocreations with PWAs in Atlanta)[7] suggests that the monologic voice, while seemingly a hallmark of isolation, can also participate in the acknowledgment of a community, as Shange's work also shows. In a sense, Frank Christian, one of the performers in LAPD's *South of the Clouds,* enacts the simultaneously solo and communal process of monologic (inter)subjectivity in his piece itself, which is about a boxer who is transformed by the civil rights movement. Christian says in the last section of the monologue:

> For the first time, solid, I saw Whitey as a victim and right then and there, solid, I dedicated myself to the whole human race, to prove I's mystical. Can you dig it? Hoo!! Now my body's on the line too, Dudes, and I'm still fightin'. But there is one thing I won't fight no mo' for; I won't fight no mo' for trophies that rust.[8]

Performances in this mode, moreover, underscore monologue's unique status as both theatrical (i.e., containing boundaries that designate performance) and personal (i.e., the first-person narrative is a point of departure for autobiography or subjectivity), granting it a narrative flexibility that makes it succeed initially where other types of theater activity may not.

Spalding Gray and Karen Finley, the two artists to be considered at greater length in this chapter, create solo theatrical works that, like those of their peers Leeny Sack, Rachel Rosenthal, and others, fall generally into the category of "autoperformance" in the sense that their creations challenge the traditional separations between actor and character. While Gray plays at narrating a self, Finley (who, unlike Gray, does not assume an overtly autobiographical stance) uses the monologic voice to demand a reconsideration of the limits of performance/theatricality itself by crossing repeatedly into the realm of the "taboo."

Spalding Gray and the Autobiographical Imperative

> My turn comes in the circle and I say: "Oh great spirit, my name is Spalding and I would like to say a prayer about privacy: that this event today could be a private, sacred act for me, not something that I would feel that I would compulsively have to turn into a story and lose the meaning of the event before I experienced it fully. Let this be a private act for me today. I have spoken.
>
> —Spalding Gray, "Gray's Anatomy"

The work of Spalding Gray merits consideration as one example of the "monologue beyond monologue"—that is, of a way in which a contemporary performance artist has pursued the challenge of using monologic language to greater narrative "extremes" than the playwrights discussed in earlier chapters.[9] Originally a member of Richard Schechner's Performance Group, Gray (along with Elizabeth LeCompte and others) formed the Wooster Group in 1980; already, for several years prior to that, Gray, LeCompte, and their coperformers/-creators had been working on the Rhode Island trilogy (*Sakonnet Point* [1975], *Rumstick Road* [1977], *Nayatt School* [1978], and an "epilogue," *Point Judith* [1979]), which was based on material from Gray's life. In *Cast of One*, a history of American solo performance, John Gentile makes an important point about the difference between Gray's autobiographical monologues and those of earlier artists. Whereas other raconteurs drew initial audiences largely as the result of their previously established status, Gray—as Gentile points out—"had no public image" (except perhaps within a limited "downtown" theatrical circle), but, "through the process of exposing his private self in performance, Gray actually created a public self as a role to assume with an audience."[10] Gray explains his movement into autoperformance, the theatricalization of the self rather than of a character, as having been motivated by Schechner's insistence in the Performance Group that the performer is more important than the role. In an essay for *The Drama Review* Gray writes:

> Could I stop acting, and what was it I actually did when I acted? Was I, in fact, acting all the time, and was my acting in the theatre the surface showing of that? Was my theatre acting a confession of the constant state of feeling my life as an act? What was the reality of myself on the other side of that "act"? . . . These identity questions become a foundation for more personal work. . . . The conflict between acting (active interpretation) and non-acting (just doing the actions) created a new thesis, a new "act." . . . It was a dialectic between my life and theatre rather than between role and text. . . . I was not so much interested in changing or curing my self-consciousness but, rather, redirecting it into my work in theatre, into the act of seeing myself in front of others.[11]

Inspired by the power of the sequence in *Rumstick Road* in which he sat at a table and spoke directly to the audience about himself,[12] Gray went on to create monologue pieces that did not have texts per se but which he improvised based on a particular autobiographical theme. As David Savran puts it, "for Spalding Gray, all performance is autobiographical, not because it re-creates the performer's past, but because the performer can play himself, can project only the diversity within."[13] Among such pieces are *Sex and Death to the Age 14* (1979), *Booze, Cars, and College Girls* (1979), *India and After (America)* (1979), *A Personal History of the American Theatre* (1980), and *Swimming to Cambodia* (1984). Devices including randomly selected index cards with play titles on them (*A Personal History of the American Theatre*) and the choosing of dictionary words upon which to base a portion of a given night's monologue (*India and After*) are designed to keep the improvisational quality of the works alive from performance to performance.[14] This technique also enacts, to an even greater extent than other works, the postmodern refusal of closure that I have mentioned in earlier chapters. Any given performance of *India and After,* for example, only provided partial access to a much larger text or story—and, of course, that text itself was not a fixed entity. In his discussion of *India and After* Savran writes that "the piece can never be complete. . . . There will always be fragments left over, unexplored and unexplained, that elude the play of rationality and the game of chance, loose ends that resist incorporation. . . . "[15]

Of course, a good deal of this spontaneity is lost in the published texts of Gray's more fully "scripted" monologues, but even these are based on taped transcripts of performances. More than Shepard, Fornes, and the other playwrights discussed thus far, then, Gray's theater is embodied in the *moment* of enactment. Theodore Shank provides a useful characterization of the importance of this present tense to Gray's work:

> Ending with the present moment is just one of the means Gray uses to bring focus to the present so that the performance is not merely a relating of past events. It is important that the spectator does not have the sense that Gray is "acting," but rather that he is speaking to them about real events. His style of delivery is flat, uncoloured, and candid. He really looks at spectators, especially when they react to something he has said. He actually reflects while in front of them rather than speaking memorized lines and pretending to reflect. . . . Ideally, says Gray, a performance would deal with the present in the room where the performance is taking place. He would simply enter and start talking about the events taking place in the room. . . . his monologues are the most literally autobiographical work that has been presented in the theatre. Although talking about past events, he is present as himself before the audience, living the most recent segment of his life.[16]

This insistence on the immediate present adds a new twist to our consideration of the monologue's ability to suspend or alter time or the audience's perception of time. One might say that, by making the present-tense Spalding Gray into his subject, Gray literalizes the notion that drama unfolds in a perpetual present—but, by using his past to create the text of his monologue, he simultaneously participates in the text as actor and creates a distance from it by transposing his experience into the realm of narrative; that is, despite the realism of his autobiographical discourse, the monologue that he narrates renders him (paradoxically) a fictionalizer or a "work of fiction" himself. Savran says, "The character Spalding and the performer Gray both appear before us, not to reinforce a distinction between the 'theatrical' and the 'real,' but to demonstrate that the former is necessarily inscribed within the latter."[17] Thus, Gray continually reinforces the monologue's status as a storytelling technique even while he locates his performance within boundaries that are ostensibly anti-"textual."

The ongoing paradox of Gray's decision to perform "himself" and to present his texts as autobiographical, then, is that the traditionally maintained separations between the fictional and the nonfictional are continually being challenged in characteristic postmodern fashion, yet, to some degree (since Gray is always inevitably textualizing and performing), "genuine" self-revelation is denied by the performance frame of this work. One of the most fascinating aspects of Gray's artistic situation, then, is the difficulty of locating "him" inside or around his autobiographical persona. For instance, in the version of *Terrors of Pleasure* filmed for HBO in 1987, Gray makes a remark that is not in the published text of the work: "Did I do it? Did I really do it? Did I really buy this piece of shit house just to make a monologue about it?"[18] In saying this, Gray mocks his own impulse to "collect" experience for the sake of monologue material; yet even an acknowledgment of the pitfalls of such impulses is relegated to part of his performance, almost as if the chain of experience-narrative cannot be broken. Similarly, after spending the day with Gray in an attempt to "document" his formulations of experience, *New York Times* writer Alex Witchel expresses some frustration at the apparent impenetrability of Gray's monologic voice:

> It's a clever disguise, talking constantly, keeping people entertained—and distracted—enough not to ask too many questions. You can listen to Mr. Gray for hours and still not find the him behind the story. On the other hand, you can't knock the form. It imposes the order and sense on life that most people expect religion to provide. No detail is too small, no coincidence too outlandish. A monologue is the best defense.[19]

The performance of any type of monologue inescapably calls maximum attention to the voice and body of the speaker; for Gray, to create monologues that also foreground the speaker in terms of *content* is to risk accusations of promoting a narcissistic theater. William Demastes sees the ironic interplay between the various "levels" of performance for Gray (the "private citizen," the "artist," the [seemingly] "naive. performer") as a device that ultimately marks a political presence rather than indicating, as some have suggested, a retreat from the awareness of a world outside his own subjectivity. According to Demastes,

> While Gray's work may *appear* supportive of the status quo, it presents a persona who ironically utilizes an empowered naivety to undermine itself and the authority it seems to uphold. . . . Reaching beyond both written authority and physical presence is the design of Gray's works. Each consumes the other, leaving a void that forces the audience to doubt the power of either and search within itself for a replacement, empowering the audience, then, in the process . . . . Gray the performer is immersed; it is the behind-the-scenes artist Gray who is ironically detached and subtly confrontational.[20]

Still, the charge that Gray's work resists an identification with a "community" is not wholly unfounded.[21] Gray offers a partial response:

> There is nothing larger than the personal when it is communicated well. The very act of communication takes it into a "larger vein" and brings it back to the community. The personal confessional, stripped of its grand theatrical metaphors, is what matters to me now. . . . This personal exploration has made me more politically aware because now that I've come to myself as authority I have found that I still feel repressed and because of this feeling of repression I am forced to look further into the outside world for its source.[22]

Much of Gray's recent work (including *Monster in a Box* [1990]) shows this effort to use the realm of subjective experience for purposes that also address his part in a manic-paranoiac, terrifying, and seductive postmodern culture that seems bent on its own destruction; his responses to and articulation of this ethos run throughout *Swimming to Cambodia* and even emerge as the dominant theme in *Rivkala's Ring* (1986), the monologue he wrote as an adaptation of Chekhov's story "The Witch" as part of the Acting Company's seven-author revue *Orchards*. So dependent are Gray's monologues on overall form and rhythm that it is difficult to provide an excerpt, but this particular piece closes with the following words:

And for one brief instant, we were one as that nuclear wind tore at the palms and split the moon through the Venetian blinds. I closed my eyes to it and saw just before sleep, I saw the last images spin out like a wheel of life and death. All spinning and mixed together. I saw the sacrificial blonde, sprawled, broken in her leaking blood. I saw the wild green money spinning in the wind above her, and above that, high up, a Chinese 747 was about to fall from the sky. And above all this shedding rays of silver light was that ring. Rivkala's ring. That blessed ring. And beyond that, black, black, dark black. Oh dark dark dark, forever dark. We all go into the dark.[23]

More consciously "literary" than his improvisation-based monologues, the piece marks a more overt acknowledgment of Gray's own status as fictionalizer, especially since the piece was inspired by a Chekhov text. Yet such an acknowledgment is partially Gray's way of creating room to generate theatrical works that express the tension between monologic isolation/fragmentation and the desire to achieve an affinity with an audience. The portion of *Monster in a Box* in which Gray narrates his experiences playing the Stage Manager in a Lincoln Center production of Wilder's *Our Town* (a play parodied, interestingly, by Gray's own Wooster Group in *Route 1 & 9 [The Last Act]*)[24] again addresses such a tension. Gray recounts (and, at one point, stands and pretends to reenact) the role, but in a way that underscores the struggle between his pleasure in interpreting Wilder's text and his comic effort not to lose the "feel" for his own performance as various mishaps threaten to undermine it.

As we have seen, it is precisely Gray's refusal of coherence, of a "plot" or linear form for his monologues, that takes his work in the direction of a postmodern antagonism toward perfect form. Yet, to some degree, the increased "mainstreaming" of Gray's work for a general audience, while bringing his cultural commentary into popular culture itself (e.g., HBO), has played against the more radical manifestations of this postmodernist impulse. For example, despite the *lack* of closure to the monologue of *Terrors of Pleasure* itself, the HBO production added a subtitle at the end, after the credits, that read: "On May 1, 1987, Spalding Gray miraculously found someone to buy his house."[25] Of course, as with all of Gray's autobiographical statements, we do not know if the "fact" being presented to us is indeed truth or if it is manufactured—and so the sentence may be a *parodic* form of closure. Yet the inclusion of such a subtitle partially undermines the sense that Gray's monologues, like the 1,900-page manuscript of his novel *The Impossible Vacation* (1992) that forms the subject of *Monster in a Box,* enact a battle with the practice of textual "containment." The tantalizing subversiveness of Gray's work lies ultimately in his simultaneous embracing and rejection of the actor, the role, and the story, or text—and such a paradoxical process suggests even further realms of possibility for the postmodernist monologue.

Karen Finley's Defiant Enactments

> Words are something you can't buy
> Language has no boundaries
> Words can kill with no blood
> Words inspire change, overthrow
> Overthrow governments and systems
> That's why they try to censor us.
>
> —Karen Finley, *Modern Prayers*

Karen Finley's performances have become notorious for their "shock" value and their intensely visceral/corporeal emphases; Finley considers no subject, from castration to incest, to be off-limits.[26] In one interview she comments that "people are scared of my information. They really don't know what I'm going to do, they don't like me dealing with sexual issues or political issues."[27] In fact, her most recent pieces have responded directly to her denial of a grant by the National Endowment for the Arts due to her alleged obscenity; in *We Keep Our Victims Ready* (1990), she refers, for example, to "our religious fanatics who try to destroy and distort the artist . . . Wildmon, Robertson, and Helms."[28] Ironically, Finley's career may have been bolstered by the media attention she received after the NEA controversy; *We Keep Our Victims Ready* played to a full house at Lincoln Center as part of its summer "Serious Fun" series in 1990, as did *A Certain Level of Denial* in the summer of 1992.

In an early essay on feminism and postmodernism, Craig Owens's metaphorical reference to staging can be taken literally in order to invoke the subversive political and theatrical power of Finley's work. Owens writes, "It is precisely at the legislative frontier between what can be represented and what cannot that the postmodernist operation is being staged—not in order to transcend representation, but in order to expose that system of power that authorizes certain representations while blocking, prohibiting or invalidating others."[29] Like other avant-garde female performance artists and writers (e.g., Holly Hughes, Kathy Acker), Finley addresses both the need to alter previously established "boundaries" of representation—especially as such boundaries have been assigned to the female voice/body—and the urgency of reappropriating discursive forms (e.g., pornography) to give them new definitions, new languages and stagings. Finley's work, as Lynda Hart points out, challenges traditional constructions of the "unitary, coherent humanist subject."[30]

It is difficult to read the textual versions of Finley's monologues, as printed in *TDR*, in an anthology of female performance artists (*Out from Under* [1990]) and in the collection *Shock Treatment* (1990)[31] without experiencing a vicarious form of the performances' shock value. The minimal stage directions are sometimes humorous in their matter-of-factness, as the following excerpt from *The Constant State of Desire* (1988) shows:

> *Easter baskets and stuffed animals sit on table. Take off clothes. Put colored unboiled eggs from basket and animals in one large clear-plastic bag. Smash contents till contents are yellow. Put mixture on body using soaked animals as applicators. Sprinkle glitter and confetti on body and wrap self in paper garlands as boas.*[32]

The recipe-like style of these stage directions becomes even more ironic with the knowledge that, as Nancy Davidson points out, it is unlikely that another performer besides Finley would actually "follow" them and perform the piece.[33] Such lines also make it clear that Finley's work relies on the physical body to such an extent that *seeing* her pieces performed is central to appreciating them, as is the case with Gray and other performance artists. But recent criticism of Finley's oeuvre has focused on these visual elements almost to the exclusion of their verbal texts;[34] as a result, we still have much to gain from taking a closer look at how Finley's physical stagings *and* her spoken enactments form a postmodern monologic voice that is, above all, a "transgressive" one.[35]

Finley's work is both Brechtian and Artaudian: she engages in the Brechtian practices of "alienating" the actor from the text, acknowledging the performance moment (particularly in her ad-libs and asides), making the familiar strange and vice versa, and avoiding catharsis. Herbert Blau makes a convincing argument that, while we now tend not to consider works that go to the physical and linguistic extremes of Finley's pieces as relevant to Brecht's *Verfremdungseffekt,* there is indeed a "tradition of the scatological grotesque" wherein "the critical power of the obscene" is precisely a technique of Brechtian alienation. Blau writes:

> Heavy as the words are, Finley's technique is to let the obscenity carry her away, but there is for all that a kind of clinical cool in the apparently rapt vision of her foul-mouthed *jouissance.* Cutting up (with) the sexual organs, jerking off and putting on, she is not only reversing gender roles but, in the ecstatically scabrous outburst of bilious Alienation, upending the last taboos. . . . As we consider . . . the extremities of Finley's performance, we might also remember that the technique of Alienation, for all its famous rational distance, comes out of the history of aesthetic violence, only overmatched by the violence of the culture from which it was eventually distanced.[36]

Blau might have also pointed out, though, that, despite the sometimes conflicting tenets of Brecht's and Artaud's approaches to the theater, Finley's work also contains elements of the Artaudian vision expressed throughout *The Theatre and Its Double:* the violent assaults upon the spectators' senses, the denial of romantic textualization (as in Artaud's *Jet of Blood* [1925], moments of melodrama are parodic or are undercut by the moments that follow), and above all the breaking of taboos in the movement into a redefinition of the "stageable."

It is in this last realm—the challenge to taboos—that Finley's work is the most interesting. Her confrontations not only with the NEA but also with her audience members themselves simultaneously violate theatrical conventions and conventions of "femininity" as Finley defies every imaginable rule of how women are to conduct or display themselves in staged representation.[37] Reportedly, when male spectators heckled Finley at a recent performance, she responded, "I've got female intuition—all you've got is a dick."[38] A comment such as this reflects Finley's subversive and parodic response to the male gaze as she demands a reconstruction of the female's/performer's status as object. As Jeanie Forte says, the challenge to a woman who wishes to "generate subversion of . . . [patriarchal] language from within" is that our culture has inculcated a "psychoanalytic model of subject construction" wherein desire belongs to the male domain, and so "it is female desire that is most disruptive."[39] Blau comments that, "in defying the rules of representation and displaying her body as biodegradable or disposable flesh, an already consumed object . . . [Finley] thwart[s] the male spectator who wants in the system of reproduction a passive womb of desire."[40] By playing literally with the notion of spectatorial "consumption" (as when she covers her body with chocolate in *We Keep Our Victims Ready*) and spectatorial "desire" (as when she challenges the audience's voyeurism by enacting *A Certain Level of Denial* as a kind of reverse striptease), Finley forces us to acknowledge our greed as consumers of theatrical pleasure—and, by extension, our role in happily digesting the products of our own oppression. For instance, she makes these metaphors explicit in one moment of *The Constant State of Desire* in which she speaks of making chocolate-covered candies out of the balls of Wall Street traders:

> Then I roll the scrotum, manure, chocolate-coated balls into fancy foiled papers from found Eurotrash cigarette boxes. Now I've got gourmet Easter egg candy to sell. I sell these Easter eggs to gourmet chocolate shops. And I love to see nine-year-old boys who only communicate with their computers eat their daddies' balls. I love to watch all of you Park Avenue, Madison Avenue know-it-alls eating your own chocolate-covered balls for twenty-five dollars a pound. (62–63)

It would be too easy to criticize Finley's work by saying that she intends merely to shock her audience; such an accusation, in emphasizing this aspect of the political nature of her work, underestimates the responses that her pieces offer to the effects of *oppression*. She says in an interview with Richard Schechner, "In *The Constant State of Desire* I wanted to show vignettes of capitalist, consumer society where people go far out, stretch the boundaries—but still they never can be satisfied. So they take things into themselves, and this is what incest or abuse are about."[41] The aggressiveness of Finley's imagery (as in the "chocolate balls" quotation) directs an enormous amount of rage and pain toward various types of victimization, as the title of *We Keep Our Victims Ready* indicates. Whereas Shange's characters laugh to keep from crying,[42] using humor as a mask for their outrage, Finley conflates *outrage* and *outrageousness* such that anger pulls her language (and visual theatrics) into extremes that we tend to interpret as satirical, as a form of self-protection (i.e., for the audience, not the performer).

At times in performance Finley will even say directly to her audience after hearing (nervous?) laughter in response to a sequence on a topic such as rape or incest, "That's not funny."[43] In other words, by refusing to signpost her material as explicitly "fictional," "satirical," "autobiographical," and so forth, Finley forces her spectators to move uneasily among multiple options for response, and the result is an instability of the normally protected relationship between the speaker/text and the audience that receives it, for there is probably no safe distance at which one can simply derive aesthetic "pleasure" from her works. Forte sees the refusal of aestheticism as a further feminist strategy to confront voyeurism and the insistence that women create "'pretty' images"; she writes, "The violence and/or 'disgust' factor . . . fuels the exploration of aesthetics as an ideological trap, one which subjugates women in particular but which also dictates the numbed and plastic tastes of dominant culture.[44]

This is not to imply that Finley refuses identification with others' pain; one might even say that the entire text of *A Certain Level of Denial* has to do with empathy. Finley has openly expressed a desire to establish some connection to suffering and has said that she is aware of the feelings that some of her pieces about such topics as incest elicit in her audience members.[45] In fact, although it would be a mistake to read such sequences as the description of the father hanging himself in the first act of *The Constant State of Desire* from a literal autobiographical viewpoint, Finley has remarked that she began performing as a way of confronting her own emotions after her father's suicide; she says that it "put an effect on me that reality is stronger than art."[46] Throughout her pieces the figure of the abusive father emerges repeatedly, enlarging in resonance from a familial/sexual figure (e.g., the "Refrigerator" sequence in *The Constant State of Desire*) to an image of oppressive patriarchal political authority (e.g., *Quotes from a Hysterical Female* [1990]: "We were proud to be white men. Carrying on the traditions of our fathers and forefathers—lynchings, beatings, rapes."[47]). The father also represents a textualized version of theatrical and psychological or literary authority, the perpetuation of patriarchal myths about women—particularly through Freud, the "father" of psychoanalysis. In the "Freud" sequence of *The Constant State of Desire,* for instance, the speaker says:

I'm sick and tired of your asking me about my headaches, my ways, my life. Don't you know that my illness is all I have? That my headaches are my only form of nurturing? My disease is my life, my health. Sure, I take Valium. But how can I look at my daughters and sons and try to dispel the myths that have been a tradition for centuries? To just say, "Sure, we're all created equal." I've never been treated equally my entire life. That I'm supposed to be so excited that Mary Boone Gallery signed up two women. Wow. Yeah, big fucking deal. Like I'm supposed to be *so* thankful 'cause a chick is on the Supreme Court. You can read your fucking books. But nothing's changed. Nothing has changed. (64–65)

In this sequence Finley establishes the competing voices of the questioner/analyst (printed in boldface type in the version published in *Shock Treatment*) and the female respondent(s), all of which emerge from her speaking body as the performer. The female voices here move among several different identities, including the "housewife" who takes women's studies courses ("But if it ever got in the way of me being a proper hostess for Richard's business I'd give it up in a minute" [64]) and the politically charged voice that seems to be more directly connected to that of Finley herself (as in the comments about the gallery and the Supreme Court in the passage cited above). As a result, Finley refuses both dialogue and character in their conventional manifestations, enacting instead an extreme version of the Brechtian splitting between performer and character (particularly as revised in feminist form by Elin Diamond, as chapter 5 discusses).[48] In Finley's postmodern Brechtianism identity is not fixed, and character is not stable, and so the narrative sequences themselves jump across time and space; the little girl who is an incest victim at the beginning of "Refrigerator" becomes a man dying of AIDS at the end of the same sequence, but both voices (if they are indeed separate voices) are addressing "the father in all of us" (69).

Just as the same speaker creates the questioner/analyst voice in "Freud" and the responding women's voices, it is worth noting that the speaker here addresses the father *in,* not *of,* "all of us." Jon Erickson comments that

the obsession that Finley articulates is indeed a constant state of desire, a socially imposed value that infects all other relations—the desire for absolute control and mastery which in turn promotes abuse at every level, sees other human beings as means for satisfying one's insatiable appetites, eventually turns inward to devour the family itself and ends in suicide. It seems that she is appropriating the male voice to push it to its limits as a despotic force. But when she says, "It's the father . . . in all of us," is she seeing the "father" as the enemy, or as a[n] inevitable aspect of behavior found in both sexes?[49]

By embodying constantly the voices of both the oppressors and the oppressed, Finley implies that the nature of social responsibility ultimately rests not in deflecting blame for oppression onto an all-powerful other, but, instead, in reappropriating and transforming the others' voices. Rather than being inviolable, their texts are therefore open to destruction, reconstruction, and deconstruction. The monologic voice thus allows Finley the opportunity, as a solo performer, for assuming multiple and sometimes conflicting subject positions; while Gray uses the semiautobiographical persona/character of "Spalding Gray" as an elusive, problematic repository of narrative "experience," Finley uses the explicit *denial* of character (except insofar as her visual presence and textual style create a character out of Karen Finley the performer) as a vehicle for her narratives to venture freely from one forbidden territory to the next.

Afterword

Postmodern culture seems at present to be fascinated with the display of written texts as images: at the 1992 Democratic National Convention in New York video screens projected key words as speakers exhorted the crowd to support their platform (e.g., as Jesse Jackson spoke, the screen behind him read "Hope");[1] Barbara Kruger's signature red and white graphics pasted on black and white photographs have spawned a league of imitations (even the June 29, 1992 issue of *Theater Week* announced, using Kruger's style, "The Tony Massacre"); television commercials now rely routinely on juxtaposing video imagery with textual graphics (e.g., "Why ask why? Try Bud Dry"). And Leslie Frankish's design for Niagara-on-the-Lake, Ontario's 1992 Shaw Festival production of *Pygmalion* included a church column made up of the letters C-O-L-U-M-N, a fireplace with the word *fireplace* on it, and other Brechtian winks appropriate to this play about language and artifice.[2]

Of course, the temptation to play with lettering and textuality goes back to the modernist interest in collage and montage, as is evident in some of the works of Picasso, Braque, and others.[3] Deconstruction, though, which David Harvey sees as "a powerful stimulus to postmodern ways of thought," encourages us to see texts (which I would extend to mean the various texts of the theatrical experience as well) by means of pluralistic re- (or de-) configurations:

> Cultural life is then viewed as a series of texts intersecting with other texts, producing more texts. . . . This intertextual weaving has a life of its own. Whatever we write conveys meanings we do not or could not possibly intend, and our words cannot say what we mean. It is vain to try and master a text because the perpetual

interweaving of texts and meanings is beyond our control. Language works through us. Recognizing that, the deconstructionist impulse is to look inside one text for another, dissolve one text into another, or build one text into another.[4]

As Elinor Fuchs explains in "Presence and the Revenge of Writing," Derrida's interest in exploding the various layers of the (inter)textual has brought us to a point where writing, or the act of writing, is no longer treated as the means toward the mystified end of representation. In the theater, in particular, Fuchs argues, "it is no longer clear that the text is the *outside* of which the *inside* is the representation of the life of characters in action."[5]

These poststructuralist redefinitions of textuality and the resulting parodies of the relations between language and image reflect the directions in which theatrical monologue has moved during the postmodern era. The monologic voice, often split from the speaking body and even from the mimetic apparatus of dramatic (re)presentation, creates playful juxtapositions with the play's scenography and physical enactment so that—in effect—these uttered texts (like the textual portions of Kruger's photographs) open up narrative spaces that both compete with and complicate the accompanying visual iconography. Shange, for instance, has used recent pieces (such as *Ridin' the Moon in Texas* [1987] and *The Love Space Demands* [1991]) to orchestrate the interactions between visual artworks and the monologues that speak to, at, and within them. Finley's most recent works, like Shepard's early plays, also provide vivid examples of this impulse. In Finley's *A Certain Level of Denial,* she delivers several of her monologues standing before a triptych of slides of her paintings; at one point, in the midst of a speech about AIDS and women, the word *PAIN* from one painting can be seen projected onto her body, even while her shadow seems to become part of the painting. The monologic (spoken) text and the visual iconography thus engage with each other to create new texts for the audience that underscore the double meaning of the "graphic." If Fornes calls attention to the body as text, then Finley plays even more caustically with the text as body.

I should emphasize, however, that my description of the relationships between spoken and visual texts in these artists' works is not meant to imply a "dialogue" between the two forms of representation; rather, the postmodern theatricalizing of monologue and image is competing, ironic, and fragmented. The two texts do not "complete," or "answer," each other—instead, though they occasionally intersect, they only *play* at being dialogical. More to the point, they do not strive to achieve any kind of formal coherence or balance. In this respect, Gilles Deleuze and Félix Guattari's distinction between the "fragment" (in the sense of a part broken off from a missing but implicit whole) and the "partial object" is helpful:

> We live today in the age of partial objects, bricks that have been shattered to bits, and leftovers. We no longer believe in the myth of the existence of fragments that, like pieces of an antique statue, are merely waiting for the last one to be turned up, so that they may all be glued back together to create a unity that is precisely the same as the original unity.[6]

This characterization of the refusal of unity also points the way toward the refusal of master narratives, the Lyotardian *grands récits* that so often follow (as chapter 3's discussion of Shepard's late plays emphasized) the oedipal continuum. By celebrating the replacement of oedipal narrative with nonlinear narrative fragments (and/or with narrative forms that *parody* the oedipal pattern), postmodern drama reinvents subjectivity (and the ideology of the subject) as multilayered texts reflect polyvocal, nonunified subject positions. The monologic voice, then, as I have illustrated in this study, both attempts to enter and enact, or embody, those subject positions yet keeps them (with that postmodern predilection for teasing) just out of reach; one need only recall Spalding Gray's playfully elusive autopresentation—as "artist," "performer," "neurotic," "New Englander," and so forth—that emerges through the assumption that the figure we see on stage may (or may not) be "just" Spalding Gray, "just" talking to the audience. Gray presents his texts as digressions on digressions on digressions, all of which pretend to return to a framing narrative line (finding a house in *Terrors of Pleasure,* completing his book in *Monster in a Box,* etc.) but which really divide the subject/protagonist and reweave or split the text's threads so many times that the very idea of the narrative's original focal point becomes more of a joke than anything else. In one's most cynical moments it is possible to view Gray's hypereloquence as another version of that manifested by Mamet's salesmen and con artists: when the speaker of monologue plies text upon text upon text, language is foregrounded as performance or game, and the *act* of utterance is what taunts and challenges the listener, perhaps even more than the texts themselves. Certainly, this is what happens to James Lingk when he meets Richard Roma in the Chinese restaurant at the opening of *Glengarry Glen Ross*.

The playwrights I have focused on in this study all create works that represent some of the different forms that the postmodern theatrical monologue can take, but I want to emphasize in closing that they are still only a small sample from among myriad contemporary American theater artists who have demonstrated an attraction to monologic voices (I have mentioned some of these other writers in passing). Among many recent "established" playwrights who have been drawn to monologue, David Rabe, John Guare, Tina Howe, and Adrienne Kennedy all stand out in terms of their consistent interest in experimenting with the form. To give just a few examples, the monologues of the characters of Rabe's Vietnam trilogy (*The Basic Training of Pavlo Hummel* [1971], *Sticks and Bones* [1971], *Streamers* [1976]) tend to confront myths of masculine self-invention, which in turn reflect on the various forms of deception associated with American involvement in Vietnam.[7] Guare's penchant for monologues that address the audience directly (as in *Six Degrees of Separation* [1990]) resembles the parodically metatheatrical moments in Shepard's early works. Howe, like Fornes, seems to associate female monologue with the problematics of subjectivity and the speaking body; in her case, however (in such works as *The Art of Dining* [1979] and *Painting Churches* [1983]), the characters' relationships between food and creativity provide the catalyst for monologic texts that are at once grotesquely disturbing and wildly comic.[8] Kennedy's works literalize the "splitting" of female subjectivity as her monologue speakers divide and subdivide their fractured utterances (in *Funnyhouse of a Negro* [1964], *The Owl Answers* [1965], *A Movie Star Has to Star in Black and White* [1976], and other plays) such that character, like voice, is not a fixed construct: in *The Owl Answers*, we see "SHE who is CLARA PASSMORE who is the VIRGIN MARY who is the BASTARD who is the OWL."[9]

Like Gray and Finley, other writer-performers prevail upon the monologue form to challenge the boundaries between "enactment" and "reality." Some of the current artists whose work has been particularly innovative in this respect include Eric Bogosian, Reno, David Drake, Richard Elovich, Rachel Rosenthal, and the other members of the "NEA Four," who, along with Finley, were denied government grants for their controversial performance pieces: Holly Hughes, Tim Miller, and John Fleck. Bogosian and Reno are probably the most well known of this list, having made successful forays into film and cable television. Their work

owes part of its popularity to stand-up comedy, yet it retains a political
bite and an edgy (rather Brechtian) theatricality (consider, e.g., Bogosian's homeless man in *Sex Drugs & Rock'n'Roll* [1990]) that keeps their
material somewhat on the subversive side.[10] Marginalized voices, often
subversive, speak loudly in solo performance: Drake (*The Night Larry
Kramer Kissed Me* [1992]) and Elovich (*Someone Else from Queens Is Queer*
[1990]) address aspects of gay male experience in the age of AIDS, and
Rachel Rosenthal's powerful, strikingly physical persona attempts, like
Finley's, to question received ideas about sexual taboos and femininity—
a questioning that Holly Hughes extends, in *World without End* (1989)
and the pieces she has written for the group Split Britches, to include
lesbian sexuality. Finally, Miller and Fleck (whose works also convey
an explicitly gay sensibility) combine Gray's affection for the (apparently) autobiographical anecdote with Finley's sense of outrageous theatrical visuals: Miller's *Stretch Marks* (1990) and Fleck's *BLESSED Are All
the* Little *FISHES* (1990) rely (like many of Shepard's plays) on a pastiche
of pop culture imagery yet infuse it with a highly histrionic aggressiveness. At one point in *BLESSED,* for example, Fleck has an Angry Man
from the audience confront him in the middle of a sequence in which he
has been smothering a goldfish with bread; this leads to a lengthy monologue in which Fleck (identified throughout the piece as "Man") berates
the audience for its hypocrisy—"What about the 12,000,000 dolphins
dead in the nets 'cause you had to have your tuna fish???"[11]

Fleck and Miller, like the other vanguards of monologic performance, cull the texts of popular culture and produce material that elicits
pleasure precisely because somewhere in its shock value is an uncanny
sense of familiarity; as in Terry Gilliam's postmodern film *Brazil* (1985),
one has the Brechtian experience of being in a world that is enormously
warped and funny yet disconcertingly similar to (and thus a brisk parody
of) the world one already recognizes. Yet what emerges is a *different* kind
of vision, a critical—not nostalgic—perspective of the world that has
been historicized or narrativized in this manner. This critical vision is
expressed in the ongoing creation of new texts, new theatric(k)s, that
illuminate the stage(s) of postmodern culture. As Lyotard writes,

> The powers of sensing and phrasing are being probed on the limits
> of what is possible, and thus the domain of the perceptible-sensing
> and the speakable-speaking is being extended. Experiments are
> made. This is our postmodernity's entire vocation, and commen-
> tary has infinite possibilities open to it.[12]

Notes

Introduction

1. Harold Pinter, *Monologue*, in *Plays: Four* (London: Methuen, 1981), 272.

2. Ken Frieden, *Genius and Monologue* (Ithaca, N.Y.: Cornell Univ. Press, 1985).

3. Ruby Cohn, *Dialogue in American Drama* (Bloomington: Indiana Univ. Press, 1971); Andrew K. Kennedy, *Dramatic Dialogue: The Duologue of Personal Encounter* (Cambridge: Cambridge Univ. Press, 1983).

Chapter 1

Chapter epigraph is from William Shakespeare, *Henry V*, in *The Riverside Shakespeare*, ed. G. Blakemore Evans (Boston: Houghton Mifflin, 1974), 936. All future citations from Shakespeare's plays refer to *The Riverside Shakespeare* and will be indicated parenthetically in the text.

1. Ken Frieden, *Genius and Monologue* (Ithaca, N.Y.: Cornell Univ. Press, 1985), 17.

2. Sam Shepard, *Icarus's Mother*, in *The Unseen Hand and Other Plays* (New York: Bantam, 1986), 68–70.

3. Keir Elam, *The Semiotics of Theatre and Drama* (London: Methuen, 1980), 90.

4. Bernard Beckerman refers to this type of moment as "crux." See *Dynamics of Drama* (New York: Drama Book Specialists, 1979), 86–87.

5. Erving Goffman, *Frame Analysis* (Cambridge, Mass.: Harvard Univ. Press, 1974), 233.

6. William Congreve, *The Double Dealer*, in *The Comedies of William Congreve*, ed. Eric S. Rump (Middlesex: Penguin, 1985), 123.

7. Goffman, *Frame Analysis*, 231.

8. Elam, *The Semiotics of Theatre and Drama*, 182–83.

9. Frieden, *Genius and Monologue*, 20.

10. Susanne K. Langer, *Feeling and Form* (New York: Charles Scribner's Sons, 1953), 307.

11. Peter Szondi claims that "if soliloquies followed one another without any dialogue, time would stand still" (*Theory of the Modern Drama,* ed. and trans. Michael Hays [Minneapolis: Univ. of Minnesota Press, 1987], 83).

12. Elam, *Semiotics of Theatre and Drama,* 56.

13. Langer, *Feeling and Form,* 72.

14. Ibid., 314.

15. In *Canters and Chronicles* Kristin Morrison argues that words thus become action in Beckett's and Pinter's works; her words are applicable to the monologues of such playwrights as Shepard as well: "the phenomenon of telling becomes a form of doing; and, in the context of the action of the play itself, narrative begins to take the place of 'life'" (*Canters and Chronicles* [Chicago: Univ. of Chicago Press, 1983], 7). Morrison's interpretation is somewhat limited in that she shifts too quickly to the significance of narration itself rather than exploring the *act,* or effect in performance, of telling per se. Moreover, her emphasis on the narrated event rather than the event of narration creates a sometimes unwarranted focus on the "psychological" ramifications of the narratives rather than their theatrical centers, their status as narratives designed for the stage. But her notion of "telling" constituting "doing" is a valuable way of expressing the extent to which the words of a monologue can take over the physical space in a play.

16. Susan Sontag, "Film and Theatre," in *Film Theory and Criticism,* ed. Gerald Mast and Marshall Cohen, 2d ed. (New York and Oxford: Oxford Univ. Press, 1979), 366.

17. For a brief but lucid explanation of stream of consciousness, cf. M. H. Abrams, *A Glossary of Literary Terms,* 4th ed. (New York: Holt, Rinehart & Winston, 1981), 186–87. While a full description of stream-of-consciousness technique is beyond the parameters of this discussion, readers interested in its narrative functions might consult the following studies: Leon Edel, *The Modern Psychological Novel,* rev. ed. (New York: Grosset & Dunlap, 1964); Melvin J. Friedman, *Stream of Consciousness: A Study in Literary Method* (New Haven, Conn.: Yale Univ. Press, 1955); Kate Hamburger, *The Logic of Literature,* rev. ed., trans. Marilyn J. Rose (Bloomington: Indiana Univ. Press, 1973), esp. chap. 3.

18. Elam, *Semiotics of Theatre and Drama,* 85. Elam defines *transcodification* as the phenomenon of the translation of semantic information from one system to another, or as one whereby the information can be supplied simultaneously by different kinds of signals (84).

19. Goffman, *Frame Analysis,* 231.

20. Peter Handke, *Offending the Audience, Kaspar and Other Plays,* trans. Michael Roloff (New York: Farrar, Straus, & Giroux, 1969), 20–21.

21. Euripides, *The Medea,* trans. Rex Warner, in *Euripides I,* ed. David Grene and Richmond Lattimore (Chicago: Univ. of Chicago Press, 1955), 59–60.

22. In addition to the Chorus in *Henry V,* see the prologue/Chorus figures appearing in *Romeo and Juliet, Troilus and Cressida, Henry VIII,* and *The Two*

Noble Kinsmen, as well as Rumour (the "presenter") in *2 Henry IV* and Gower in *Pericles.*

23. See Falstaff's "honor" speech in *1 Henry IV.*

24. Frieden, *Genius and Monologue,* 133.

25. James W. McFarlane, "Introduction," in *The Oxford Ibsen,* vol. 4, ed. and trans. James Walter McFarlane and Graham Orton (New York: Oxford Univ. Press, 1963), 4.

26. Andrew K. Kennedy, *Dramatic Dialogue: The Duologue of Personal Encounter* (Cambridge: Cambridge Univ. Press, 1983), 169.

27. Henrik Ibsen, *John Gabriel Borkman,* in *The Oxford Ibsen,* vol. 8, ed. and trans. James Walter McFarlane (Oxford and London: Oxford Univ. Press, 1977), 231.

28. Kennedy, *Dramatic Dialogue,* 179.

29. Richard Gilman, *The Making of Modern Drama* (New York: Farrar, Straus, & Giroux, 1974), 79–80.

30. Even as early as his preface for *Miss Julie* (translated by Walter Johnson as *Lady Julie*), Strindberg called for innovations in monologue (as part of a trio of "art forms" including mime and ballet) that would make the "unnatural" natural:

> Our realists have banished the soliloquy or monologue as unbelievable, but if I motivate it, it becomes believable and can be used advantageously. It is natural that a speaker walks his floor alone rehearsing his speech aloud, that an actor runs through his role aloud, that a maid talks to her cat. . . . To give an actor the opportunity to do independent work, for once, free of the dramatist's pointer, it is best that the monologue should be not written out, but just indicated. (August Strindberg, author's preface to *Lady Julie,* in *Pre-Inferno Plays,* trans. Walter Johnson [Seattle and London: Univ. of Washington Press, 1970], 82)

We see at this point an impulse toward a justification of the monologue only in ways that do not disrupt a play's veneer of naturalism, since Strindberg's primary concern here seems to be that these art forms do not cause the audience to withdraw its belief in what it is seeing. Yet underlying this is Strindberg's inherent dissatisfaction with the limitations imposed by the adherence to naturalism, such that he eventually broke with it entirely and allowed the dream world, with its attendant fluidity of language, to take over.

31. August Strindberg, author's note to *A Dream Play,* in *A Dream Play and Four Chamber Plays,* trans. Walter Johnson (Seattle and London: Univ. of Washington Press, 1973), 19.

32. And, of course, since the dreamer is also the playwright who "dreams" the material of the play, it is not surprising that the "monologue" of *A Dream Play* is autobiographical in nature.

33. August Strindberg, *Ghost Sonata,* in *A Dream Play and Four Chamber Plays,* 215–16.

34. Kennedy says, "From Strindberg to Beckett this or that mode of distortion thrusts the once robust confessional duologue more and more towards a dialogue of solipsists, or the parallel monologues of a tangentially connected pair" (*Dramatic Dialogue*, 200).

35. Eugene O'Neill, "Working Notes and Extracts from a Fragmentary Work Diary," in *American Playwrights on Drama*, ed. Horst Frenz (New York: Hill & Wang, 1965), 11.

36. One of the more outspoken critics is Ruby Cohn, who takes O'Neill to task for the "sloppiness" and "poverty of his insights," especially as compared to what writers like Joyce and Woolf were able to achieve with the use of interior monologue in their novels. See Ruby Cohn, *Dialogue in American Drama* (Bloomington: Indiana Univ. Press, 1971), 32. Cohn may have a point when she characterizes O'Neill's "weakness" in the play as the tendency toward "the discussion rather than the dramatization of emotion" (28). But it is also perhaps unfair for her to expect O'Neill to achieve the same results *theatrically* through interior monologue that one might attain through the written text of a novel.

37. Travis Bogard, *Contour in Time: The Plays of Eugene O'Neill*, rev. ed. (New York: Oxford Univ. Press, 1988), 307.

38. In this play one character (the night clerk) is silent except for his unspoken interior monologues, which are designed, as Bogard says, to be played as if the actor were speaking them. See Travis Bogard, "Introduction," in Eugene O'Neill, *The Later Plays of Eugene O'Neill* (New York: Modern Library, 1967), xxvii n.

39. Ibid., xix.

40. Ibid., xx.

41. Tennessee Williams, "Preface," *Cat on a Hot Tin Roof* (New York: New American Library, 1955), vii.

42. See, for example, Esther Merle Jackson, *The Broken World of Tennessee Williams* (Madison: Univ. of Wisconsin Press, 1966), 48.

43. Bertolt Brecht, *Brecht on Theatre*, ed. and trans. John Willett (New York: Hill & Wang, 1964), 22.

44. Ibid., 137.

45. Ibid., 138.

46. Ibid., 139.

47. Morrison, *Canters and Chronicles*, 6.

48. Brecht, *The Threepenny Opera*, trans. Desmond Vesey and Eric Bentley (New York: Grove Press, 1964), 5.

49. Brecht, "Notes to the Threepenny Opera," in ibid., 106.

50. Bertolt Brecht, *The Good Person of Szechwan*, trans. Ralph Manheim, in *Collected Plays*, vol. 6, ed. Ralph Manheim and John Willett (New York: Vintage Books, 1976), 72.

51. Ibid., 6:54.

52. See Ruby Cohn, "Outward Bound Soliloquies," *Journal of Modern Literature* 6 (February 1977): 17–38; Andrew Kennedy, *Dramatic Dialogue*, 31, 213–14; Andrew Kennedy, *Six Dramatists in Search of a Language* (Cambridge: Cambridge Univ. Press, 1975), 130–64.

53. Samuel Beckett, *Endgame* (New York: Grove Press, 1958), 70.

54. Samuel Beckett, *Happy Days* (New York: Grove Press, 1961), 27.

55. Cohn, "Outward Bound Soliloquies," 29.

56. For a discussion of the status of *Krapp's Last Tape* as monologue, see Cohn, "Outward Bound Soliloquies," 23–25; Andrew Kennedy, "Krapp's Dialogue of Selves," in *Beckett at 80/ Beckett in Context*, ed. Enoch Brater (New York: Oxford Univ. Press, 1986), 102–9.

57. As Katharine Worth argues, the silent Auditor in *Not I* is a significant presence, yet the Auditor does nothing other than lift its arms in a repeated "gesture of helpless compassion" that "lessens with each recurrence till scarcely perceptible at third" (Katharine Worth, "Beckett's Auditors: *Not I* to *Ohio Impromptu*," in Brater, *Beckett at 80/ Beckett in Context*, 168–92, esp. 168–73; Samuel Beckett, *Not I*, in *Collected Shorter Plays* [New York: Grove Press, 1984], 215).

58. See Enoch Brater, "The 'I' in Beckett's *Not I*," *Twentieth Century Literature* 20 (July 1974): 189–200.

59. Samuel Beckett, *A Piece of Monologue*, in *Collected Shorter Plays*, 266.

60. Ibid., 269. See also the earlier *Embers*, in which Henry's monologue uses a similar device—"Glare, stump to door, turn, glare"—in Beckett, *Collected Shorter Plays*, 96; the "voicing" of stage directions is also discussed in Brater, "'I' in Beckett's *Not I*," 197.

Chapter 2

Chapter epigraph is from Ihab Hassan, *Paracriticisms: Seven Speculations of the Times* (Urbana: Univ. of Illinois Press, 1975), 83.

1. Georg Lukács, "The Sociology of Modern Drama," trans. Lee Baxandall, in *The Theory of the Modern Stage*, ed. Eric Bentley (Middlesex: Penguin, 1968), 443.

2. M. M. Bakhtin, *Speech Genres and Other Late Essays*, ed. Caryl Emerson and Michael Holquist, trans. Vern W. McGee (Austin: Univ. of Texas Press, 1986), 92, 95. For a discussion of *langue/parole* and competence/performance, see Jonathan Culler, *Structuralist Poetics: Structuralism, Linguistics, and the Study of Literature* (Ithaca, N.Y.: Cornell Univ. Press, 1975), 8–10.

3. Lukács, "Sociology of Modern Drama," 443.

4. Bernard Beckerman, *Dynamics of Drama* (New York: Drama Book Specialists, 1979), 248–49.

5. See, respectively, Jean-François Lyotard, *The Postmodern Condition: A Report On Knowledge*, trans. Geoff Bennington and Brian Massumi (Minneapolis: Univ. of Minnesota Press, 1984); and Andreas Huyssen, "Mapping the Postmodern," in *Feminism/Postmodernism*, ed. Linda J. Nicholson (New York and London: Routledge, 1990), 234–77. Huyssen's essay was published in a longer version in *New German Critique* 33 (Fall 1984): 5–52, and in Andreas Huyssen, *After the Great Divide: Modernism, Mass Culture, Postmodernism* (Bloomington: Indiana Univ. Press, 1986).

6. Fredric Jameson, "Postmodernism and Consumer Society," in *The Anti-Aesthetic: Essays on Postmodern Culture,* ed. Hal Foster (Port Townsend, Wash.: Bay Press, 1983), 113. Also see Fredric Jameson, *Postmodernism, or, The Cultural Logic of Late Capitalism* (Durham, N.C.: Duke Univ. Press, 1991), esp. 3, 5, 45–46.

7. Lyotard, *Postmodern Condition,* 79.

8. Huyssen, "Mapping the Postmodern," 237; Jonathan Arac, "Introduction," in *Postmodernism and Politics,* ed. Jonathan Arac (Minneapolis: Univ. of Minnesota Press, 1986), xii.

9. Hal Foster, "Postmodernism: A Preface," in Foster, *Anti-Aesthetic,* xv.

10. Jameson, *Postmodernism,* 63.

11. Huyssen, "Mapping the Postmodern," 240–41.

12. Linda Hutcheon, *The Politics of Postmodernism* (London and New York: Routledge, 1989), 15.

13. Jean Baudrillard, "The Ecstasy of Communication," trans. John Johnston, in Foster, *Anti-Aesthetic,* 127. Cf. the allegorical character of Chance in Jerzy Kosinski's novel *Being There,* who represents the total domination of humanity by TV technology; this is particularly striking in Hal Ashby's film version of the novel (for which Kosinski wrote the screenplay), in which Chance's inability to function without television is epitomized in his statement that he has (literally and figuratively) "lost [his] remote control."

14. Huyssen, "Mapping the Postmodern," 246.

15. Ibid., 270–71.

16. Linda Hutcheon, *A Poetics of Postmodernism* (New York and London: Routledge, 1988), 130.

17. Ibid., ix–x.

18. Ibid., 11.

19. Ibid., 22.

20. Lyotard, *Postmodern Condition,* 81.

21. Antonin Artaud, *The Theater and Its Double,* trans. Mary Caroline Richards (New York: Grove Press, 1958), 74.

22. Hutcheon, *Poetics of Postmodernism,* 80–82; Emile Benveniste, *Problems in General Linguistics,* trans. Mary Elizabeth Meek (Coral Gables, Fla.: Univ. of Miami Press, 1971), 223, 226.

23. Huyssen, "Mapping the Postmodern," 264.

24. Hutcheon, *Poetics of Postmodernism,* 220.

25. Bertolt Brecht, *Brecht on Theatre,* ed. and trans. John Willett (New York: Hill & Wang, 1964), 55.

26. Hassan, *Paracriticisms,* 54–58. Some of my quotations from this description are edited versions of Hassan's phrases.

27. Ihab Hassan, *The Dismemberment of Orpheus: Toward a Postmodern Literature,* 2d ed. (Madison: Univ. of Wisconsin Press, 1982), 267–68.

28. Huyssen, "Mapping the Postmodern," 242.

29. Ibid., 244–45.

30. For example, in an admiring statement about Piscator's production of *The Good Soldier Schweik,* Brecht writes, "The performer's self-observation, an

artful and artistic act of self-alienation, stopped the spectator from losing himself in the character completely, i.e. to the point of giving up his own identity, and lent a splendid remoteness to the events" (*Brecht on Theatre*, 92–93).

31. Joseph Chaikin, *The Presence of the Actor* (1972; reprint, New York: Atheneum, 1980), 11.

32. C. W. E. Bigsby, *Beyond Broadway*, vol. 3 of *A Critical Introduction to Twentieth-Century American Drama* (Cambridge: Cambridge Univ. Press, 1985), 129.

33. The Open Theater, *The Mutation Show*, in *Three Works by the Open Theater*, ed. Karen Malpede (New York: Drama Book Specialists, 1974), 99.

34. Bigsby, *Beyond Broadway*, 60.

35. Robert Pasolli, *A Book on the Open Theater* (Indianapolis: Bobbs-Merrill, 1970), 12.

36. See Brecht, *Brecht on Theatre*, 136.

37. Hutcheon, *Poetics of Postmodernism*, 156.

38. Herbert Blau, *The Audience* (Baltimore and London: Johns Hopkins Univ. Press, 1990), 309.

39. Artaud, *The Theater and Its Double*, 81.

40. Ibid., 96.

41. Jerzy Grotowski, *Towards a Poor Theatre* (New York: Simon & Schuster, 1968), 41–42.

42. Pasolli, *A Book on the Open Theater*, 81.

43. Pierre Biner, *The Living Theatre* (New York: Horizon Press, 1972), 101.

44. Jean Baudrillard calls this "proving theatre by anti-theatre" (*Simulations*, trans. Paul Foss, Paul Patton, and Philip Beitchman [New York: Semiotext(e), 1983], 36).

45. Richard Schechner, *Environmental Theater* (New York: Hawthorn Books, 1973), 49ff.

46. Ibid., 40.

47. Artaud, *Theater and Its Double*, 75.

48. Timothy Wiles, *The Theater Event: Modern Theories of Performance* (Chicago and London: Univ. of Chicago Press, 1980), 115.

49. Herbert Blau, *Blooded Thought: Occasions of Theatre* (New York: PAJ Publications, 1982), 91.

50. Joseph Chaikin, "Notes on Acting Time and Repetition," in Malpede, *Three Works by the Open Theater*, 34.

51. Jacques Derrida, *Writing and Difference*, trans. Alan Bass (Chicago: Univ. of Chicago Press, 1978), 248.

52. Hassan, *Dismemberment of Orpheus*, 267–68.

53. Lyotard, *Postmodern Condition*, xxiv.

54. Hassan, *Dismemberment of Orpheus*, 267–68. Sometimes these narrative and antinarrative impulses become, in competition, the focus of interest in the postmodernist creation; Hutcheon says that "there is an urge to foreground, by means of contradiction, the paradox of the desire for and the suspicion of narrative mastery—and master narratives" (*Politics of Postmodernism*, 64). In his reading of Artaud, Derrida argues that "master" narrative is embodied in the traditional,

or "theological," theater—that which is logocentric, author dominated, textual, with passive spectators (*Writing and Difference*, 235)—and that the antinarrative of the "nontheological" theater of cruelty (Artaud's aim) would thus involve a murder/parricide in its destruction of the logos/God/father of theological theater, its force "against the God of a stage subjugated to the power of speech and text" (239).

55. Theodore Shank, *American Alternative Theater* (New York: Grove Press, 1982), xi. For visual/pictorial renditions of some of these plays, see the Performance Group, *Dionysus in 69*, ed. Richard Schechner (New York: Farrar, Straus, & Giroux, 1970), and the Living Theatre, *The Living Book of the Living Theatre* (Greenwich, Conn.: New York Graphic Society, 1971).

56. Artaud, *Theater and Its Double*, 98.

57. Pasolli, *Book on the Open Theater*, 20–21.

58. Herbert Blau, *The Eye of Prey: Subversions of the Postmodern* (Bloomington: Indiana Univ. Press, 1987), 164.

59. Ibid., 165.

60. Blau, *Blooded Thought*, 91.

61. Cf. Derrida, "Structure, Sign and Play in the Discourse of the Human Sciences," in *Writing and Difference*, 278–93, esp. 289, 292. Also see "The Theater of Cruelty and the Closure of Representation":

> Closure is the circular limit within which the repetition of difference infinitely repeats itself. That is to say, closure is its *playing* space. This movement is the movement of the world as play. (250)

It is also worth pointing out that many of the performances of the experimental theater result from theater "play," or "games."

62. Jean-François Lyotard and Jean-Loup Thébaud, *Just Gaming*, trans. Wlad Godzich (Minneapolis: Univ. of Minnesota Press, 1985), 16.

63. Ibid., 61–62.

Chapter 3

1. Epigraph to this section is from Sam Shepard, *Operation Sidewinder*, in *The Unseen Hand and Other Plays* (New York: Bantam, 1986), 226.

2. See, for instance, Bonnie Marranca, "Alphabetical Shepard: The Play of Words," in *American Dreams: The Imagination of Sam Shepard*, ed. Bonnie Marranca (New York: PAJ Publications, 1981), 14; Florence Falk, "The Role of Performance in Sam Shepard's Plays," *Theatre Journal* 33 (May 1981): 182–98.

3. Michael Smith, director of the original production of *Icarus's Mother*, was one of the first to use this term; since then it has become a common way of referring to Shepard's monologues. See Michael Smith, "Notes on *Icarus's Mother*," in Sam Shepard, *Chicago and Other Plays* (New York: Urizen, 1981), 27 (originally published as *Five Plays* [1967]).

4. Quoted in Kenneth Chubb and the editors of *Theatre Quarterly*, "Meta-

phors, Mad Dogs and Old Time Cowboys" (interview with Sam Shepard), reprinted in Marranca, *American Dreams*, 205–6.

5. As Sheila Rabillard points out, though early directors of Shepard's plays often had a difficult time understanding how they were to be staged (because of the absence of traditional plot, character development, etc.), "what these directors found unproduceable in Shepard is precisely what . . . is most theatrical" ("Sam Shepard: Theatrical Power and American Dreams," *Modern Drama* 30 [March 1987]: 59).

6. Leonard Wilcox goes so far as to say that "for Shepard the Lyotardian breakdown of the *grands récits* or master narratives is a constant preoccupation" ("Modernism vs. Postmodernism: Shepard's *The Tooth of Crime* and the Discourses of Popular Culture," *Modern Drama* 30 [December 1987]: 561).

7. Shepard says in an interview with *Theatre Quarterly:* "I would have like a picture, and just start from there. A picture of a guy in a bathtub, or of two guys on stage with a sign blinking—you know, things like that" (Chubb et al., "Metaphors, Mad Dogs, and Old Time Cowboys," 191).

8. Steven D. Putzel and Suzanne R. Westfall, "The Back Side of Myth: Sam Shepard's Subversion of Mythic Codes in *Buried Child*," *Journal of Dramatic Theory and Criticism* 4 (Fall 1989): 109.

9. Ann Wilson, "Fool of Desire: The Spectator to the Plays of Sam Shepard," *Modern Drama* 30 (March 1987): 46.

10. Sam Shepard, *The Rock Garden*, in *The Unseen Hand and Other Plays*, 35. Future references will be indicated parenthetically.

11. Ron Mottram, *Inner Landscapes: The Theater of Sam Shepard* (Columbia: Univ. of Missouri Press, 1984), 17.

12. Sam Shepard, *Chicago*, in *The Unseen Hand and Other Plays*, 59. Future references will be indicated parenthetically.

13. One might think, for example, of performance artists such as Linda Montano, who make everyday acts (e.g., the brushing of one's teeth) into works of drama by "framing" them as such, or of some of the early works of Robert Wilson. Wilson created tableaux for the stage out of simple actions magnified in intensity by having them performed in slow motion, etc., but again relied on the knowledge that the actions are *transformed* by being designated as theatrical "events."

14. For a literalization of the funhouse mirror image, see Adrienne Kennedy's 1964 play *Funnyhouse of a Negro*, in *Adrienne Kennedy in One Act* (Minneapolis: Univ. of Minnesota Press, 1988), 1–23.

15. Toby Silverman Zinman, "Visual Histrionics: Shepard's Theatre of the First Wall," *Theatre Journal* 40 (December 1988): 511.

16. Wilcox, "Modernism vs. Postmodernism," 561.

17. See M. M. Bakhtin, *Problems of Dostoevsky's Poetics*, ed. and trans. Caryl Emerson (Minneapolis: Univ. of Minnesota Press, 1984).

18. Of the train speech Gerald Weales argues that "it begins very positively, almost joyfully, but the description becomes uglier, more tired as it goes on as though the speech itself were the train ride, and the imagined riders who started

out in high spirits unravel in the process" ("The Transformations of Sam Shepard," in Marranca, *American Dreams,* 40).

19. Michael Bloom, "Visions of the End: The Early Plays," in Marranca, *American Dreams,* 74.

20. Herbert Blau believes that the hunger metaphor in Shepard is connected to a larger (American) fear of identity ("The American Dream in American Gothic: The Plays of Sam Shepard and Adrienne Kennedy," *Modern Drama* 27 [December 1984]: 524).

21. Rabillard, taking a different approach to describe Shepard's metatheatricality, would emphasize the *phatic* function of such a moment; using Anne Ubersfeld's *Lire le théâtre,* she argues that Shepard's characters speak for the purpose of commanding an audience as discourse becomes an exercise in (theatrical) power ("Sam Shepard: Theatrical Power and American Dreams," 61–62).

22. As Rabillard suggests, "What the characters [in *Icarus's Mother*] say is what they do to each other" (ibid., 60).

23. Sam Shepard, *Icarus's Mother,* in *The Unseen Hand and Other Plays,* 79. Future references will be indicated parenthetically.

24. Michael Bloom argues that the characters are devastated by the pilot's death because he was "the one bit of reality they had been clinging to" ("Visions of the End," 75). But even this supposed "reality" is only (at least for the audience) another creation through words.

25. Smith, "Notes on *Icarus's Mother,*" 26–27.

26. Sam Shepard, *Red Cross,* in *The Unseen Hand and Other Plays,* 125. Future references will be indicated parenthetically.

27. Jacques Levy, "Notes on *Red Cross,*" in Shepard, *Chicago and Other Plays,* 97.

28. Ren Frutkin, "Paired Existence Meets the Monster," in Marranca, *American Dreams,* 112.

29. Levy, "Notes on *Red Cross,*" 97.

30. Sam Shepard, "Language, Visualization, and the Inner Library," in Marranca, *American Dreams,* 216.

31. Sam Shepard, *Fourteen Hundred Thousand,* in *The Unseen Hand and Other Plays,* 107. Future references will be indicated parenthetically.

32. Epigraphs to this section are taken from Sam Shepard, *Geography of a Horse Dreamer,* in *Fool for Love and Other Plays* (New York: Bantam, 1984), 305; and Shepard, "Hollywood," in *Hawk Moon* (New York: PAJ Publications, 1981), 40.

33. For a discussion of Pop Art and parody in Warhol and Lichtenstein, see Silvio Gaggi, *Modern/Postmodern: A Study in Twentieth-Century Arts and Ideas* (Philadelphia: Univ. of Pennsylvania Press, 1989), 57–68.

34. Hutcheon, *Poetics of Postmodernism,* 35.

35. See, for instance, Carol Rosen, "Sam Shepard's *Angel City:* A Movie for the Stage," *Modern Drama* 22 (March 1979): 39–46; Robert Coe, "Image Shots are Blown: The Rock Plays," in Marranca, *American Dreams,* 57–66; Bruce W. Powe, "*The Tooth of Crime:* Sam Shepard's Way with Music," *Modern Drama* 24 (March 1981): 13–25.

36. Lynda Hart, "Sam Shepard's Pornographic Visions," *Studies in the Literary Imagination* 21 (Fall 1988): 81. It is not fully clear to me why Hart sees such a desire as "modernist." Hart's point that Shepard's seemingly utopian vision of the American past has potentially disturbing elements of conservatism is well taken; the same accusations have been made of neoconservative appropriations of postmodernism in general. I would argue, however, that Shepard's nonnaturalistic theatrical technique, as well as his eagerness to satirize in his plays the very American "values" he seems to admire, prevent him from falling uncritically into the type of nostalgia that Hart seems to be delineating here.

37. George Stambolian, "A Trip through Popular Culture: *Mad Dog Blues*," in Marranca, *American Dreams*, 86.

38. Hutcheon observes that "the ironies produced by that distancing are what prevent the postmodern from being nostalgic: there is no desire to return to the past as a time of simpler or more worthy values" (*Poetics of Postmodernism*, 230).

39. Sam Shepard, *Melodrama Play*, in *Fool for Love and Other Plays*, 117. Future references will be indicated parenthetically.

40. Sam Shepard, *4-H Club*, in *The Unseen Hand and Other Plays*, 85.

41. Sam Shepard, *The Unseen Hand*, in *The Unseen Hand and Other Plays*, 9. Future references will be indicated parenthetically.

42. See Gaggi, *Modern/Postmodern*, 115–28.

43. Hutcheon points out that postmodernist artists are frequently drawn to the genre of the western (Thomas Berger, John Barth, E. L. Doctorow, to name only a few) because this genre allows for the opportunity to rewrite and ironize earlier myths about the American past and the creation of history (*Poetics of Postmodernism*, 133).

44. Sam Shepard, *The Tooth of Crime*, in *Seven Plays* (New York: Bantam, 1981), 227. Future references will be indicated parenthetically.

45. Shepard claimed at one point that Brecht was his favorite playwright and that he was especially drawn to *Jungle of Cities*, a play with obvious connections to *The Tooth of Crime* (Chubb, "Metaphors, Mad Dogs, and Old Time Cowboys," 202). Bonnie Marranca argues that Shepard creates his own version of Brecht's concepts of character and epic acting by "situating narration in the present, in the equation of character as narrator, and so eliminating gestus in favor of the tone of voice. He substitutes myth for history, experience for theory" ("Alphabetical Shepard," 13).

46. Powe, "*The Tooth of Crime*: Sam Shepard's Way with Music," 17.

47. Wilcox, "Modernism vs. Postmodernism," 565–66.

48. Ibid., 565–66.

49. Ibid., 570.

50. Ibid., 571.

51. Sam Shepard, preface to *Angel City*, in *Fool for Love and Other Plays*, 61–62. Future references will be indicated parenthetically.

52. Or perhaps, as Steven Putzel puts it, her changed tone "forces the spectator to receive the semantic content as part of a different semiological system from that of the play's story-line or plot" ("Expectation, Confutation,

Revelation: Audience Complicity in the Plays of Sam Shepard," *Modern Drama* 30 [June 1987]: 151).

53. Falk, "Role of Performance in Sam Shepard's Plays," 183.

54. Gilles Deleuze, "The Schizophrenic and Language: Surface and Depth in Lewis Carroll and Antonin Artaud," in *Textual Strategies,* ed. Josué V. Harari (Ithaca, N.Y.: Cornell Univ. Press, 1979), 286; Jean Baudrillard, "The Ecstasy of Communication," trans. John Johnston, in *The Anti-Aesthetic: Essays on Postmodern Culture,* ed. Hal Foster (Port Townsend, Wash.: Bay Press, 1983), 133.

55. Baudrillard, "Ecstasy of Communication," 132.

56. Herbert Blau, *Take Up the Bodies: Theater at the Vanishing Point* (Urbana: Univ. of Illinois Press, 1982), 83.

57. Bigsby, *Beyond Broadway,* 239.

58. Gaggi, *Modern/Postmodern,* 32–33.

59. Sam Shepard, *Action,* in *Fool for Love and Other Plays,* 176. Future references will be indicated parenthetically.

As David Savran points out, our inability to define the crisis reflects the nature of the crisis itself: its "origin has been misplaced (or, more properly, displaced) and the 'crisis' itself has been institutionalized so that it permeates everything in the playworld, appearing solely as a kind of deformed status quo" ("Sam Shepard's Conceptual Prison: *Action* and the Unseen Hand," *Theatre Journal* 36 [March 1984]: 59).

60. Wilcox points out that "the master narratives no longer provide structure in the midst of linguistic fragmentation; they no longer 'shore up the ruins' in any modernist sense nor provide a grounding for social or individual identity" ("Modernism vs. Postmodernism," 561). Gerry McCarthy, in a significant essay on *Action,* expresses the characters' situation more theatrically, in terms of a kind of stopped motion: "Shepard imagines moments of perfect *stasis* in which the actor has nothing to do, and is left to contemplate his presence within a space exposed to a generalised threat" ("'Acting it out': Sam Shepard's *Action,*" *Modern Drama* 24 [March 1981]: 3).

61. Fredric Jameson, "Postmodernism and Consumer Society," in Foster, *Anti-Aesthetic,* 118–19.

62. Savran provides an insightful reading of this "inside/outside" distinction, arguing that Shooter sees the inside as more frightening because it has the terrifyingly "unlimited" qualities of the stage space: "language, sited inside in contrast to the silence outside, is revealed to be an obstacle which only perpetuates the breach between the self and others" ("Sam Shepard's Conceptual Prison," 65).

63. Unfortunately, as McCarthy indicates, Shepard cut out a significant amount of the material in this final monologue after its British publication (London: Faber & Faber, 1975); in the current published version Shepard omits Jeep's assertion that he would experience a moment of understanding that he was imprisoned in walls and space, with "no escape," and instead depends upon the actor to indicate, as McCarthy says, "the experience of empty time and space which he alone can and must fill with action" ("'Acting it out,'" 11).

64. See Christopher Norris, *Deconstruction: Theory and Practice* (London and New York: Methuen, 1982), 49.

65. Savran, "Sam Shepard's Conceptual Prison," 73.

66. Sam Shepard, *Suicide in B♭*, in *Fool for Love and Other Plays*, 194. Future references will be indicated parenthetically.

67. Mottram and Putzel argue that their search is actually an attempt to locate their own author (Mottram, *Inner Landscapes*, 123, 127; Putzel, "Expectation, Confutation, Revelation," 151).

68. As Wilcox says, "the desiring self may suddenly be transformed into the schizoid self, the language of self expansion into the language of self-destruction, where words function on an affective level, capable of doing bodily harm" ("Modernism vs. Postmodernism," 562).

69. Sam Shepard, "The Escapes of Buster Keaton," in *Hawk Moon*, 87.

70. Epigraphs to this section are taken from Sam Shepard, *Seduced*, in *Fool for Love and Other Plays*, 265; and Shepard, *Buried Child*, in *Seven Plays*, 78. Future references will be indicated parenthetically.

71. Sam Shepard, *The Holy Ghostly*, in *The Unseen Hand and Other Plays*, 196.

72. Sam Shepard, *True West*, in *Seven Plays*, 57. Future references will be indicated parenthetically.

73. See, for instance, Ruby Cohn, "Sam Shepard: Today's Passionate Shepard and His Loves," in *Essays on Contemporary American Drama*, ed. Hedwig Bock and Albert Wertheim (Munich: Max Hueber Verlag, 1981), 161. Susan Harris Smith modifies this label slightly by calling Shepard's style in the late plays one of "sur-Naturalism" ("Estrangement and Engagement: Sam Shepard's Dramaturgical Strategies," *Journal of Dramatic Theory and Criticism* 3 [Fall 1988]: 73). Lynda Hart argues that Shepard's movement toward "realism" implies his use of a "representational apparatus . . . that inevitably renders the feminine as a suppressed term" ("Sam Shepard's Pornographic Visions," 79–80). This realm has alternatively been described as the hyperreal or the superreal, as in the paintings of Edward Hopper and Ralph Goings; see Bigsby, *Beyond Broadway*, 150–58; and Toby Silverman Zinman, "Sam Shepard and Super-Realism," *Modern Drama* 29 (September 1986): 423–30.

74. See Teresa de Lauretis, *Alice Doesn't: Feminism, Semiotics, Cinema* (Bloomington: Indiana Univ. Press, 1984), 110. For a discussion of the narrative changes wrought by postmodernism, see Jean-François Lyotard, *The Postmodern Condition: A Report on Knowledge*, trans. Geoff Bennington and Brian Massumi (Minneapolis: Univ. of Minnesota Press, 1984), esp. xxiv; and Jean-François Lyotard and Jean-Loup Thébaud, *Just Gaming*, trans. Wlad Godzich (Minneapolis: Univ. of Minnesota Press, 1985), 42.

75. Cf. Ann Wilson's Lacanian reading of *Fool for Love*, in "Fool of Desire," 52–56.

76. Sam Shepard, *Curse of the Starving Class*, in *Seven Plays*, 167. Future references will be indicated parenthetically.

77. Perhaps the lamb meets Weston's need of an auditor yet allows him to retain the solace he finds in talking to himself. Rabillard argues that Weston's

delivery of the speech is primarily for himself, because "the speech suggests the nature of the hunger behind the need to be heard": "Even if the auditor is oneself, there is some satisfaction in speaking to a listening ear" ("Sam Shepard: Theatrical Power and American Dreams," 66).

78. Wesley even says, "I thought it was me bleeding" (195), a line that not only reinforces the castration image but also recalls the menstruation stories that Ella tells Emma.

79. Johan Callens, "Memories of the Sea in Shepard's Illinois," *Modern Drama* 29 (September 1986): 412.

80. Putzel and Westfall, "Back Side of Myth," 113.

81. Tilden says, "I had a son once but we buried him" (92); Dodge tells Shelly that Halie became pregnant after all of their sons were grown and "we hadn't been sleepin' in the same bed for about six years" (123); and he adds that Tilden knew about the baby's father "better than any of us" and used to walk around with the baby, talking to it and singing to it (124).

82. Wilson argues that the audience tends to place extra weight of "meaning" on this sight of the alleged corpse—we forget that it is only a prop "transformed by the spectator's imagination into a corpse"—because the theatrical experience prioritizes the visual. She adds that even the idea that the play contains secrets that must be uncovered by the end may be a result of the spectatorial thirst for "meaning": "We want to believe; we want the play to be meaningful because it sates our desire for theatrical action which signifies" ("Fool of Desire," 50). Bigsby places this need for meaning on the shoulders of the playwright rather than the spectator: "*Buried Child* taunts us with our capacity for concealing truth . . . [yet Shepard] continues to assume that at some level word and image carry a code and that the unlocking of that code, as much as the content of the message, is itself the source of meaning, but there is no denying the power of the absurd" *(Beyond Broadway,* 243).

83. Putzel and Westfall also point out that, since the unearthing of the buried child's corpse is not an actual rebirth, Shepard subverts the traditional mythic pattern in which the infant is rescued at a point of crisis (Oedipus, Moses, Jesus) and grows up to become the hero ("Back Side of Myth," 117–18).

84. Zinman suggests that the silhouette, which appears literally or figuratively in many of Shepard's plays, is "the perfect postmodernist visual image," with its paradoxical ability to "suggest both presence and absence simultaneously" ("Visual Histrionics," 513).

85. Sam Shepard, *Fool for Love,* in *Fool for Love and Other Plays,* 54. Future references will be indicated parenthetically.

86. Shepard apparently intended to use May in *Fool for Love* as an attempt to "take this leap into a female character," as he told Bernard Weiner of the *San Francisco Chronicle* (quoted in Don Shewey, *Sam Shepard* [New York: Dell, 1985], 150). But Wilson presents a persuasive argument that the "domination" of the Old Man, who represents the Father, "over the scene of representation" ultimately undercuts the credence given to May's perspective ("Fool of Desire," 51–56, esp. 56; also see Hart, "Sam Shepard's Pornographic Visions," 74–75).

87. Putzel sees the Old Man as a kind of "fifth wall," but Wilson also points out that, despite Shepard's indication that only May and Eddie see the Old Man, he is visible to the spectators as well, suggesting an immediate blurring of what in the play is to be considered "real" (Putzel, "Expectation, Confutation, Revelation," 155; Wilson, "Fool of Desire," 51).

88. The incorporation of actual persons into fictional worlds (and of fictional characters into renderings of "history") is a recurrent postmodernist technique that simultaneously makes the "real" appear fictional and the fictional appear real; in other words, it challenges the conventional boundaries of representation. For a discussion of this phenomenon as it appears in "historiographic metafiction," see Hutcheon, *Poetics of Postmodernism*, 5, 105–40.

89. Wilson argues that the Countess herself, because we never actually see her, is another example (like the corpse in *Buried Child*) of a fiction made real only through the audience's desire to believe that she exists ("Fool of Desire," 55).

90. Sam Shepard, *A Lie of the Mind* (New York: New American Library, 1986), 10. Future references will be indicated parenthetically.

91. Putzel, "Expectation, Confutation, Revelation," 157.

92. Beth's linguistic breakdown also resembles Deleuze's description of the schizophrenic's decomposition of language: "In this breakdown of the surface, all words lose their meaning. They may retain a certain power of designation, but one which is experienced as empty. . . . Yet as the pinned word loses its meaning, it bursts into fragments, decomposes into syllables, letters, and above all into consonants which act directly on the body, penetrating it and bruising it" ("Schizophrenic and Language," 287).

93. Hart, "Sam Shepard's Pornographic Visions," 78.

94. Again, consider the parallel to Deleuze's theory of schizophrenic language: "It is henceforth less a matter for the schizophrenic of recuperating meaning than of destroying words, of warding off affects, or of transforming the body's painful passion into a triumphant action" ("Schizophrenic and Language," 288).

Chapter 4

1. David Mamet, "Some Lessons from Television," in *Some Freaks* (New York: Viking, 1989), 62.

2. Bigsby, *Beyond Broadway*, 290.

3. Fredric Jameson, "Foreword," in Lyotard, *Postmodern Condition*, xi.

4. Epigraphs to this section are from David Mamet, *The Spanish Prisoner*, in *Goldberg Street: Short Plays and Monologues* (New York: Grove, 1985), 27; and Mamet, *Lakeboat* (New York: Grove, 1981), 105. Future references will be indicated parenthetically.

5. Pascale Hubert-Leibler, "Dominance and Anguish: The Teacher-Student Relationship in the Plays of David Mamet," *Modern Drama* 31 (December 1988): 557–70; see esp. 558.

6. Lyotard and Thébaud, *Just Gaming*, 94.

7. In the Piven Theater Workshop's 1985 production of the play (in Evanston, Illinois), the extent to which this "performance" was emphasized became almost Brechtian: the characters "constructed" the set at the beginning of the play and turned pages of a large book that announced the number and title of each "variation."

8. Dennis Carroll, *David Mamet* (New York: St. Martin's Press, 1987), 72.

9. David Mamet, *The Duck Variations*, in *Sexual Perversity in Chicago and The Duck Variations* (New York: Grove, 1978), 89. Future references will be indicated parenthetically.

10. Steven H. Gale, "David Mamet: The Plays, 1972–1980," in *Essays on Contemporary American Drama*, ed. Hedwig Bock and Albert Wertheim (Munich: Max Hueber Verlag, 1981), 208.

11. C. W. E. Bigsby, *David Mamet* (London and New York: Methuen, 1985), 31.

12. It is striking that Beckett is usually perceived, as chapter 1 mentioned, as a figure whose works span the movement between the modern and postmodern periods, with the early works (*Godot, Endgame*) characterized as "modern" and the later, minimalist works as "postmodern." Yet one might argue that the way Godot, the apparent protagonist, never appears or even has his existence validated is an example of the postmodern "decentering" technique being described here.

13. David Mamet, *A Life in the Theatre* (New York: Grove, 1977), 9. Future references will be indicated parenthetically.

14. Hubert-Leibler, "Dominance and Anguish," esp. 559–60, 563–66.

15. These include a scene from an "army" play (28–29), a "play in a lawyer's office" (46–49), an unspecified European period piece (52–54), a lifeboat scene (69–70), a doctor scene (85–87), and others.

16. Goffman's comments on this paradox, quoted in chapter 1, are fascinating to consider in light of the "double staging" of this play (*Frame Analysis*, 231).

17. See the discussion of soliloquy in chapter 1; also see Goffman, *Frame Analysis*, 233.

18. David Mamet, *Sexual Perversity in Chicago*, in *Sexual Perversity in Chicago and The Duck Variations*, 58. Future references will be indicated parenthetically.

19. Douglas Bruster, "David Mamet and Ben Jonson: City Comedy Past and Present," *Modern Drama* 33 (September 1990): 334–35.

20. John Ditsky, "'He Lets You See the Thought There': The Theatre of David Mamet," *Kansas Quarterly* 12 (Fall 1980): 27.

21. Robert Storey, "The Making of David Mamet," *Hollins Critic* 16 (October 1979): 4.

22. Bigsby, *Beyond Broadway*, 257–58.

23. Bigsby, *David Mamet*, 24.

24. Epigraphs to this section are from David Mamet, *American Buffalo* (New York: Grove, 1976), 83 (future references will be indicated parenthetically); and Mamet, *House of Games* (New York: Grove, 1985), 25.

25. Bigsby, *David Mamet*, 16.

26. See the section of chapter 1 entitled "(Pre)figuring Monologue" for further discussion.

27. Hubert-Leibler, "Dominance and Anguish," 568.

28. For a fascinating description of the details of staging the play, see Carroll, *David Mamet*, 134–36.

29. David Mamet, *The Water Engine*, in *The Water Engine and Mr. Happiness* (New York: Grove, 1978), note on production. Future references will be indicated parenthetically.

30. Hutcheon, *Poetics of Postmodernism*, 110.

31. Guido Almansi, "David Mamet, a Virtuoso of Invective," in *Critical Angles: European Views of Contemporary American Literature*, ed. Marc Chenétier (Carbondale and Edwardsville: Southern Illinois Univ. Press, 1986), 195–96.

32. David Mamet, "Concerning *The Water Engine*," in *Writing in Restaurants* (New York: Viking, 1986), 107–8.

33. David Mamet, *Glengarry Glen Ross* (New York: Grove, 1984), 46. Future references will be indicated parenthetically.

34. Bruster claims that Levene has been Roma's principal "teacher" and that, as he moves toward retirement, he "has already passed the subtleties of his verbal art to his younger apprentice, Richard Roma" ("David Mamet and Ben Jonson," 337). But there is little, if any, evidence in the play that Roma has actually learned his craft from Levene. Roma not only outstrips Levene but also seems to operate according to a completely different ethical (or anti-ethical) "system" than Levene does.

35. Bigsby, *David Mamet*, 118–19.

36. David Savran, *In Their Own Words: Contemporary American Playwrights* (New York: Theatre Communications Group, 1988), 137.

37. Epigraphs to this section are from David Mamet, *Film Crew*, in *Goldberg Street*, 95; and Mamet, "Black as the Ace of Spades," in *Some Freaks*, 174.

38. David Mamet, *Prairie du Chien*, in *The Shawl and Prairie du Chien* (New York: Grove, 1985), 57. Future references will be indicated parenthetically.

39. The Storyteller says that no one knew much about the jealous man who is the murderer in the tale, except that "there was talk he'd been a lawyer in the East" (62). This alleged former lawyer kills his wife and the hired hand because he suspects her of adultery, and the climactic point of the narrative consists of the Storyteller's insistence that he and the sheriff saw the apparition of the woman's burning red dress in the house after the sheriff had heard a voice telling them that the woman's and the hired man's bodies (which mysteriously join one another *after* the murder) are in the barn. The closing sequence of the narrative completes the emphasis on rumors and visions: the Storyteller says that afterward the sheriff was "never right" and slept constantly and that there "had been stories" (73), which culminated in a man finding the sheriff with his ten-year-old daughter. "This is what I'm told," says the Storyteller: when the man went to the sheriff's house, he discovered him "rocking in a chair" in a red dress, saying: "Please help him. They are in the barn . . ." (74–75).

40. Samuel Weber, "Afterword: Literature—Just Making It," trans. Brian Massumi, in Lyotard and Thébaud, *Just Gaming*, 110.

41. David Mamet, "A National Dream-Life," in *Writing in Restaurants*, 8.

42. David Mamet, *The Shawl*, in *The Shawl and Prairie du Chien*, 3. Future references will be indicated parenthetically.

43. Bigsby, *David Mamet*, 128.

44. David Mamet, *Speed-the-Plow* (New York: Grove, 1988), 21–22. Future references will be indicated parenthetically.

45. Jean-François Lyotard, "The Unconscious as Mise-en-Scène," trans. Joseph Maier, in *Performance in Postmodern Culture*, ed. Michel Benamou and Charles Caramello (Madison, Wisc.: Coda Press, 1977), 98.

Chapter 5

1. Hélène Cixous, "Aller à la mer," trans. Barbara Kerslake, *Modern Drama* 27 (December 1984): 547.

2. For a description of Schneeman's performance, see Lucy Lippard, *From the Center: Feminist Essays on Women's Art* (New York: Dutton, 1976), 126; and Moira Roth, ed., *The Amazing Decade: Women and Performance Art in America, 1970–1980* (Los Angeles: Astro Artz, 1983), 14–15. For a discussion of the implications of Schneeman's body/text, see Jeanie Forte, "Women's Performance Art: Feminism and Postmodernism," *Theatre Journal* 40 (May 1988): 221–23; and Sue-Ellen Case, *Feminism and Theatre* (New York: Methuen, 1988), 57–58.

3. Finley's work is discussed at greater length in chapter 7 of this study. Also see Jill Dolan, *The Feminist Spectator as Critic* (1988; reprint, Ann Arbor: Univ. of Michigan Press, 1991), 66; and Janelle Reinelt, "Feminist Theory and the Problem of Performance," *Modern Drama* 32 (March 1989): 55.

4. Dolan, *Feminist Spectator as Critic*, 63.

5. Julia Kristeva, "Oscillation du 'pouvoir' au 'refus,'" trans. Marilyn A. August, in *New French Feminisms*, ed. Elaine Marks and Isabelle de Courtivron (New York: Schocken, 1981), 165.

6. Reinelt, "Feminist Theory and the Problem of Performance," 51. Also see Sue-Ellen Case, "From Split Subject to Split Britches," in *Feminine Focus: The New Women Playwrights*, ed. Enoch Brater (Oxford: Oxford Univ. Press, 1989), 126–46.

7. Elin Diamond, "Brechtian Theory / Feminist Theory: Toward a Gestic Feminist Criticism," *TDR* 32 (Spring 1988): 91.

8. Patrice Pavis, "On Brecht's Notion of *Gestus*," trans. Susan Melrose, in *Languages of the Stage: Essays in the Semiology of Theatre* (New York: PAJ Publications, 1982), 45.

9. Hélène Cixous, "Le rire de la méduse," trans. Keith Cohen and Paula Cohen, in Marks and de Courtivron, *New French Feminisms*, 251; Ken Frieden, *Genius and Monologue* (Ithaca, N.Y.: Cornell Univ. Press, 1985), 20.

10. Scott Cummings, "Seeing with Clarity: The Visions of Maria Irene Fornes," *Theater* (Yale) 17 (Winter 1985): 52–53.

11. Maria Irene Fornes, *Promenade,* in *Promenade and Other Plays* (New York: PAJ Publications, 1987), 24.

12. Maria Irene Fornes, *The Successful Life of 3,* in *Promenade and Other Plays,* 49.

13. Maria Irene Fornes, *Dr. Kheal,* in *Promenade and Other Plays,* 130. Future references will be indicated parenthetically.

14. William Worthen raises the possibility that Fornes in these works is refusing to "assimilate" the various "enunciators" of the stage (character, plot, language, etc.) into a coherent whole the way the traditional theater would advocate, choosing instead to "suspend the identification between the drama and its staging." It is especially striking that Worthen goes on to characterize this process, in his discussion of *Tango Palace,* as "the dialectical tension between fiction and the flesh" (*"Still playing games:* Ideology and Performance in the Theater of Maria Irene Fornes," in Brater, *Feminine Focus,* 168, 171).

15. Maria Irene Fornes, *Tango Palace,* in *Promenade and Other Plays,* 78.

16. Cummings, "Seeing with Clarity," 53.

17. Maria Irene Fornes, *Fefu and Her Friends,* in *Wordplays [1]: An Anthology of New American Drama* (New York: PAJ Publications, 1980), 17. Future references will be indicated parenthetically.

18. Worthen, *"Still playing games,"* 176.

19. Beverley Byers Pevitts, "Fefu and Her Friends," in *Women in American Theatre,* ed. Helen Krich Chinoy and Linda Walsh Jenkins, rev. ed. (New York: Theater Communications Group, 1987), 316–17.

20. Maria Irene Fornes, *Mud,* in *Plays* (New York: PAJ Publications, 1986), 15. Future references will be indicated parenthetically.

21. Kathleen Betsko and Rachel Koenig, *Interviews with Contemporary Women Playwrights* (New York: Beech Tree Books/Quill, 1987), 161.

22. Dolan, *Feminist Spectator as Critic,* 109.

23. Betsko and Koenig, *Interviews with Contemporary Women Playwrights,* 161.

24. Bertolt Brecht, "On Rhymeless Verse with Irregular Rhythms," in *Brecht on Theatre,* ed. and trans. John Willett (New York: Hill & Wang, 1964), 115–16.

25. Dolan, *Feminist Spectator as Critic,* 109.

26. Betsko and Koenig, *Interviews with Contemporary Women Playwrights,* 166.

27. For a discussion of "centering," see Rudolf Arnheim, *The Power of the Center: A Study of Composition in the Visual Arts,* rev. ed. (Berkeley: Univ. of California Press, 1982), 72–3, 75.

28. Dolan, *Feminist Spectator as Critic,* 109.

29. Maria Irene Fornes, *The Conduct of Life,* in *Plays,* 68. Future references will be indicated parenthetically.

30. See Elaine Scarry: "The translation of pain into power is ultimately a transformation of body into voice, a transformation arising in part out of the dissonance of the two, in part out of the consonance of the two. . . . Power is in

its fraudulent as in its legitimate forms always based on distance from the body" (*The Body in Pain* [Oxford: Oxford University Press, 1985], 45–46).

31. See Catherine Belsey, *Critical Practice* (London and New York: Methuen, 1980), 59. Olimpia is also the only character who stands up to Orlando, as she turns his own vocabulary of torture back on him: "You are a bastard! One day I'm going to kill you when you're asleep! I'm going to open you up and cut your entrails and feed them to the snakes. (*She tries to strangle him.*) I'm going to tear your heart out and feed it to the dogs! I'm going to cut your head open and have the cats eat your brain! (*Reaching for his fly.*) I'm going to cut your peepee and hang it on a tree and feed it to the birds!" (Fornes, *Conduct of Life*, 80).

32. Leticia, perhaps as a response to her own marginalization, tries the alternate escape route of taking a lover. (Since she only admits the lover's existence under torture from Orlando, though, we never receive confirmation that he is more than a creation of Leticia's imagination.) As Leticia responds to Orlando's torture (which resembles his interrogation of his political prisoners) by shooting him, the play's ending is an inversion of *Mud*'s finale. Her final act of handing the gun to Nena, saying "Please . . . " (88), is left open for multiple interpretations, enacting the Brechtian legacy of avoiding catharsis and closure. Gayle Austin sees this final gesture as Leticia's request that Nena shoot her, thus "asking help of her double in ending her own torment" ("The Madwoman in the Spotlight: Plays of Maria Irene Fornes," in *Making a Spectacle: Feminist Essays on Contemporary Women's Theatre*, ed. Lynda Hart [Ann Arbor: Univ. of Michigan Press, 1989], 84). Dolan, though, argues that Leticia is forcing Nena to accept the blame for the shooting, and so the moment is part of a larger social *Gestus* of historicized violence (*Feminist Spectator as Critic*, 108).

33. Dolan, *Feminist Spectator as Critic*, 108.

34. See Elaine Scarry: "Intense pain is . . . language-destroying: as the content of one's world disintegrates, so the content of one's language disintegrates" (*Body in Pain*, 35).

35. Worthen, "*Still playing games*," 174.

36. Forte, "Women's Performance Art," 227.

37. See Elin Diamond, "(In)Visible Bodies in Churchill's Theatre," *Theatre Journal* 40 (May 1988): 188–204.

38. Maria Irene Fornes, *The Danube*, in *Plays*, 53.

39. Belsey, *Critical Practice*, 88.

40. Ibid., 65.

Chapter 6

Chapter epigraph is from Ntozake Shange, *for colored girls who have considered suicide / when the rainbow is enuf* (1977; reprint, New York: Bantam, 1980), 48. Future references will be indicated parenthetically. N.B.: Shange's spelling, punctuation, and diction make up her unique style and have been reproduced as printed in the texts of her works.

1. Donna Haraway suggests that "'women of color' might be understood as a cyborg identity, a potent subjectivity synthesized from fusions of outsider identities" ("A Manifesto for Cyborgs: Science, Technology, and Socialist Feminism in the 1980s," in *Feminism/Postmodernism*, ed. Linda J. Nicholson [New York and London: Routledge, 1990], 216).

2. Combahee River Collective, "A Black Feminist Statement," in *All the Women Are White, All the Blacks Are Men, But Some of Us Are Brave: Black Women's Studies,* ed. Gloria T. Hull, Patricia Bell Scott, and Barbara Smith (Old Westbury, N.Y.: The Feminist Press, 1982), 15.

3. See Alice Walker, "In Search of Our Mothers' Gardens," *In Search of Our Mothers' Gardens* (San Diego and New York: Harcourt Brace Jovanovich, 1983), 237.

4. Ntozake Shange, *nappy edges* (1978; reprint, New York: Bantam, 1980), 12.

5. John Timpane, "'The Poetry of a Moment': Politics and the Open Form in the Drama of Ntozake Shange," *Studies in American Drama, 1945–Present* 4 (1989): 96.

6. Geneviève Fabre, *Drumbeats Masks and Metaphor: Contemporary Afro-American Theatre,* trans. Melvin Dixon (Cambridge, Mass.: Harvard Univ. Press, 1983), 219.

7. Ntozake Shange, *boogie woogie landscapes,* in *Three Pieces* (New York: St. Martin's Press, 1981), 113.

8. Fabre, *Drumbeats Masks and Metaphor,* 226.

9. Claudia Tate, ed., *Black Women Writers at Work* (New York: Continuum, 1983), 153.

10. Helene Keyssar, *The Curtain and the Veil: Strategies in Black Drama* (New York: Burt Franklin, 1981), 213–15.

11. Tate, *Black Women Writers,* 156.

12. Janet Brown, *Feminist Drama: Definition and Critical Analysis* (Metuchen, N.J., and London: Scarecrow Press, 1979), 129. John Timpane adds that the women's chant at this moment "unites the subjective and the intersubjective" ("The Poetry of a Moment," 92).

13. Andrea Benton Rushing, "For Colored Girls, Suicide or Struggle," *Massachusetts Review* 22 (Autumn 1981): 544, 546, 550. Certainly, it would be difficult for Rushing to make the same accusations of *spell #7.*

14. Erskine Peters, "Some Tragic Propensities of Ourselves: The Occasion of Ntozake Shange's 'for colored girls who have considered suicide / when the rainbow is enuf,'" *Journal of Ethnic Studies* 6, no. 1 (Spring 1978): 82.

15. Augusto Boal, *Theater of the Oppressed,* trans. Charles A. McBride and Maria-Odilia Leal McBride (New York: Urizen, 1979), 25.

16. Michael W. Kaufman, "The Delicate World of Reprobation: A Note on the Black Revolutionary Theatre," in *The Theater of Black Americans,* ed. Erroll Hill (Englewood Cliffs, N.J.: Prentice-Hall, 1980), 1:206–207.

17. Kimberly W. Benston, "The Aesthetic of Modern Black Drama," in Hill, *Theater of Black Americans,* 62–63.

18. Ntozake Shange, *spell #7*, in *Three Pieces*, 7. Future references will be indicated parenthetically.

19. Hutcheon, *Poetics of Postmodernism*, 50. For instance, Hutcheon discusses Ishmael Reed's parodic use of black folk tradition (*Poetics of Postmodernism*, 134). Also see George C. Wolfe's play *The Colored Museum*, which parodies "black" drama forms, including Lorraine Hansberry's *Raisin in the Sun* and even Shange's *for colored girls*.

20. Tate, *Black Women Writers*, 173.

21. This technique of simultaneously asserting and pretending to lose authorial "control" is a favorite strategy among postmodernist novelists; see, for example, John Fowles's multiple endings for *The French Lieutenant's Woman* or John Barth's stories in *Lost in the Funhouse*.

22. Sigmund Freud, *Jokes and Their Relation to the Unconscious*, trans. James Strachey (New York and London: Norton, 1960), 220–21.

23. As Freud indicates, "precisely in cases where there is a release of affect one can observe a particularly strong difference in expenditure bring about the automatism of release. When Colonel Butler answers Octavio's warnings by exclaiming 'with a bitter laugh': '*Thanks* from the House of Austria!', his embitterment does not prevent his laughing. The laugh applies to his memory of the disappointment he believes he has suffered; and on the other hand the magnitude of the disappointment cannot be portrayed more impressively by the dramatist than by his showing it capable of forcing a laugh in the midst of the storm of feelings that have been released" (Freud, *Jokes*, 220–21).

24. Shange, "unrecovered losses / black theater traditions," in *Three Pieces*, xiii.

25. John Berger, *Ways of Seeing* (Middlesex: Penguin/BBC, 1972), 46–47.

26. Michelene Wandor, *Carry On, Understudies: Theatre and Sexual Politics*, rev. ed. (London and New York: Routledge & Kegan Paul, 1986), 128.

27. Shange, "unrecovered losses," ix.

28. Ibid., xiv.

Chapter 7

Chapter epigraph from Gray is quoted in David Savran, *Breaking the Rules: The Wooster Group* (New York: Theatre Communications Group, 1988), 63.

1. See Sue-Ellen Case, *Feminism and Theatre* (New York: Methuen, 1988), 59.

2. See Theodore Shank, *American Alternative Theater* (New York: Grove, 1982), 156. As Lynda Hart says, "performance art does not allow for the perception of distance between the performer and her language and gestures, which the actor has automatically through the historical use of 'character'" ("Motherhood According to Finley: The Theory of Total Blame," *TDR* 36 [Spring 1992]: 131).

3. Linda Frye Burnham, "Hands across Skid Row: John Malpede's Performance Workshop for the Homeless of L.A.," *TDR* 31 (Summer 1987): 130, 132.

4. Ibid., 134.

5. Ibid., 136–37.

6. Ibid., 136.

7. For a discussion of Ranson's work, see William Alexander, "Clearing Space: AIDS Theatre in Atlanta," *TDR* 34 (Fall 1990): 109–28.

8. Burnham, "Hands across Skid Row," 137.

9. Epigraph to this section is from Spalding Gray, excerpt from "Gray's Anatomy," *New York Times Magazine,* May 17, 1992, 48.

10. John S. Gentile, *Cast of One: One-Person Shows from the Chautauqua Platform to the Broadway Stage* (Urbana and Chicago: Univ. of Illinois Press, 1989), 151.

11. Spalding Gray, "About *Three Places in Rhode Island,*" *TDR* 23 (March 1979): 33–34.

12. Spalding Gray, "Preface," *Sex and Death to the Age* 14 (New York: Vintage, 1986), xi.

13. Savran, *Breaking the Rules,* 63.

14. Shank, *American Alternative Theater,* 177–78.

15. Savran, *Breaking the Rules,* 73. For an interesting discussion of *India and After,* see Savran, *Breaking the Rules,* 73–74.

16. Shank, *American Alternative Theater,* 178–79.

17. Savran, *Breaking the Rules,* 64.

18. Spalding Gray, *Terrors of Pleasure,* version filmed for Home Box Office (HBO) television, 1987. Rebroadcast on PBS (WLIW), September 22, 1991.

19. Alex Witchel, "Yes, Spalding Gray, This Is Your Life . . . ," *New York Times,* November 11, 1990, sec. 2, 8.

20. William W. Demastes, "Spalding Gray's *Swimming to Cambodia* and the Evolution of an Ironic Presence," *Theatre Journal* 41 (March 1989): 86–88.

21. See Bigsby, *Beyond Broadway,* 135.

22. Spalding Gray, "Perpetual Saturdays," *Performing Arts Journal* 6 (1981), 48; also quoted in Bigsby, *Beyond Broadway,* 135.

23. Spalding Gray, *Rivkala's Ring,* in *Orchards,* ed. Anne Cattaneo (New York: Knopf, 1986), 175.

24. For a discussion of *Route 1 & 9 (The Last Act),* see Savran, *Breaking the Rules,* 9–45.

25. Gray, *Terrors of Pleasure,* HBO version.

26. Epigraph to this section is from Karen Finley, *Modern Prayers,* in *Shock Treatment* (San Francisco: City Lights, 1990), 91–92.

27. Richard Schechner, "Karen Finley: A Constant State of Becoming" (interview), *TDR* 32 (Spring 1988): 152.

28. Karen Finley, *We Keep Our Victims Ready,* in *Shock Treatment,* 124.

29. Craig Owens, "The Discourse of Others: Feminists and Postmodernism," in *The Anti-Aesthetic: Essays on Postmodern Culture,* ed. Hal Foster (Port Townsend, Wash.: Bay Press, 1983), 59.

30. Hart, "Motherhood According to Finley," 128.

31. Karen Finley, *The Constant State of Desire, TDR* 32 (Spring 1988): 139–151; also printed in different forms in *Out from Under: Texts by Women Perfor-*

mance Artists, ed. Lenora Champagne (New York: Theatre Communications Group, 1990), 59–70; and in Finley, *States of Shock,* 1–26.

32. Finley, *The Constant State of Desire,* in Champagne, *Out from Under,* 60–61. Future references to this play are to this edition and will be indicated parenthetically.

33. Nancy Davidson, "Woman Writing Woman: Karen Finley's Performance as Autobiography" (unpub. essay), 15.

34. For a controversial example, see Elinor Fuchs, "Staging the Obscene Body," *TDR* 33 (Spring 1989): 47–49.

35. David Savran's quotation of Roland Barthes in reference to the Wooster Group has interesting resonances for Finley's work as well. Barthes writes, "The revolutionary task . . . is not to supplant but to transgress. Now, to transgress is both to recognize and to reverse; the object . . . must be presented and denied *at the same time.*" Savran underscores this peculiar quality of transgression: in order to exist as such, it "must operate as subversion from within; it must take place within the confines of the culture in question, 'within a play of structures and writings'" (*Breaking the Rules,* 92). Finley's work, too, draws its power for challenging culturally determined boundaries of sexuality, femininity, language, theatrical "behavior," and so forth from the transgressive positions her performances assert *inside of* a shared discourse, a communal articulation of ostensible "values." Linda Hutcheon sees the postmodern attraction to crossing over "previously accepted limits" as grounded—unlike in modernist art—in parody, a form that certainly characterizes Finley's work. As Hutcheon says, postmodern parody is "the intertextual mode that is paradoxically an authorized transgression, for its ironic difference is set at the very heart of similarity" (*Poetics of Postmodernism,* 9, 66). Similarly, Jon Erickson warns that transgressive acts risk a kind of self-subversion: "while transgression is used to undermine the power of hegemonic discourse through the appropriation and attempted devaluation of its images, that appropriation can then be reappropriated ironically into the hegemonic discourse once again" ("Appropriation and Transgression in Contemporary American Performance: The Wooster Group, Holly Hughes, and Karen Finley," *Theatre Journal* 42 [May 1990]: 235).

36. Herbert Blau, *The Audience* (Baltimore and London: Johns Hopkins Univ. Press, 1990), 231.

37. Cataloging some of Finley's more "outrageous" acts risks sensationalism and repeats previously well-documented accounts. For a good description of Finley's early performances, see C. Carr, "Unspeakable Practices, Unnatural Acts: The Taboo Art of Karen Finley," *Village Voice,* June 24, 1986, 17–19, 86.

38. This incident was reported to me by two of my students who saw Finley perform in the summer of 1991.

39. Jeanie Forte, "Women's Performance Art: Feminism and Postmodernism," *Theatre Journal* 40 (May 1988): 225.

40. Blau, *Audience,* 231. Jill Dolan, despite a perceptive assessment of Finley's subversion of the male gaze, ultimately seems critical of the failure of Finley's work to transcend "representational terms" that are male determined, as she "never takes flight into sexual and gender fantasies of liberation" (*Feminist*

Spectator as Critic, 67). I would argue, however, that it is precisely the refusal of fantasies of transcendence that allows Finley to conduct a radical critique of pornographic discourse through parodic forms that undermine—rather than simply reiterate—its conventions.

41. Schechner, "Karen Finley," 154.

42. See the discussion of Shange in chapter 6; also see Shange, *for colored girls,* 1–2.

43. Davidson, "Woman Writing Woman," 6.

44. Forte, "Women's Performance Art," 234.

45. See Schechner, "Karen Finley," 155, 158. In an interview with Andrea Juno, Finley says, "In my performance I wish I could relieve the audience of its suffering, but for women, that's really what relationships are about: somehow *feeling* the suffering and being the nurturer; somehow letting those feelings come through so they can be dealt with. I want to expose that private, secret process *in public*" (Andrea Juno and V. Vale, eds., *Angry Women* [*Re/Search* 13] [San Francisco: Re/Search Publications, 1991], 43).

46. Schechner, "Karen Finley," 157.

47. Karen Finley, *Quotes from a Hysterical Female,* in *Shock Treatment,* 54.

48. See Elin Diamond, "Brechtian Theory / Feminist Theory," 82–94.

49. Erickson, "Appropriation and Transgression," 231.

Afterword

1. For further discussion, see Leslie Savan, "Designing Democrats," *Village Voice,* July 21, 1992, 37.

2. See David Richards, "Picturesque May Be Pleasant, but Is It Drama?" *New York Times,* July 26, 1992, sec. 2, 5, 21.

3. See Gregory L. Ulmer, "The Object of Post-Criticism," in *The Anti-Aesthetic: Essays on Postmodern Culture,* ed. Hal Foster (Port Townsend, Wash.: Bay Press, 1983), 83–110.

4. David Harvey, *The Condition of Postmodernity: An Enquiry into the Origins of Cultural Change* (Oxford and Cambridge, Mass.: Basil Blackwell, 1989), 49–51.

5. Elinor Fuchs, "Presence and the Revenge of Writing: Re-Thinking Theatre after Derrida," *Performing Arts Journal* 9 (1985): 171–72.

6. Gilles Deleuze and Félix Guattari, *Anti-Oedipus: Capitalism and Schizophrenia,* trans. Robert Hurley, Mark Seem, and Helen R. Lane (New York: Viking, 1977), 42.

7. For further discussion, see Deborah Geis, "'Fighting to Get Down, Thinking It Was Up': A Narratological Reading of *The Basic Training of Pavlo Hummel,*" in *David Rabe: A Casebook,* ed. Toby Silverman Zinman (New York and London: Garland, 1991), 71–83.

8. For further discussion, see Nancy Backes, "Body Art: Hunger and Satiation in the Plays of Tina Howe," in *Making a Spectacle: Feminist Essays on Contemporary Women's Theatre,* ed. Lynda Hart (Ann Arbor: Univ. of Michigan Press, 1989), 41–60.

9. Adrienne Kennedy, *The Owl Answers,* in *Adrienne Kennedy in One Act* (Minneapolis: Univ. of Minnesota Press, 1988), 25. Also see Lois More Overbeck and Paul K. Bryant-Jackson, eds., *Intersecting Boundaries: The Theater of Adrienne Kennedy* (Minneapolis: Univ. of Minnesota Press, 1992).

10. See Irene Lacher, "In Monology, to Play It Right, Do It Yourself," *New York Times,* October 1, 1989, sec. 2, 5, 41.

11. John Fleck, *BLESSED Are All the Little FISHES, TDR* 35 (Fall 1991): 184.

12. Jean-François Lyotard, "Philosophy and Painting in the Age of Their Experimentation: Contribution to an Idea of Postmodernity," trans. Mária Minich Brewer and Daniel Brewer, in *The Lyotard Reader,* ed. Andrew Benjamin (Oxford and Cambridge, Mass.: Basil Blackwell, 1989), 190.

Index